Don Quixote in England

Don Quixote in England

THE AESTHETICS OF LAUGHTER

Ronald Paulson

The Johns Hopkins University Press
Baltimore and London

FRONTISPIECE:
William Hogarth, *Don Quixote Releases the Galley Slaves* (1726), etching and engraving. Reproduced by courtesy of the Trustees of the British Museum.

The Johns Hopkins University Press
2715 North Charles Street
Baltimore, Maryland 21218-4319
The Johns Hopkins Press Ltd., London

LIBRARY OF CONGRESS CATALOGING-IN-PUBLICATION DATA
Paulson, Ronald.
    Don Quixote in England : the aesthetics of laughter / Ronald
Paulson.
        p.   cm.
    Includes bibliographical references (p.   ) and index.
    ISBN 0-8018-5695-7 (alk. paper)
        1. Cervantes Saavedra, Miguel de, 1547–1616.   Don Quixote.
2. Cervantes Saavedra, Miguel de, 1547–1616—Appreciation—Great
Britain.   3. Cervantes Saavedra, Miguel de, 1547–1616—Influence.
4. English literature—18th century—History and criticism.
5. Comedy.   6. Empiricism.   7. Aesthetics, British—18th century.
8. Great Britain—Intellectual life—18th century.   I. Title.
PQ6349.E5P38   1998
863'.3—dc21   97-19114
                                                                   CIP

A catalog record for this book is available from the
British Library.

To Claudia and Harry Sieber

CONTENTS

Don Quixote was one of two books that profoundly shaped English writing of the eighteenth century. As Milton's *Paradise Lost* (1667) served as model for the sublime, Cervantes' *Don Quixote* (1605, 1615) served for the comic, an area in which English writers showed much the greater competence, occasionally equaling their model.

There were works of classical literature—Virgil's *Georgics*, Ovid's *Metamorphoses*, the satires of Horace and Juvenal, and above all Virgil's *Aeneid*—that dominated the generic considerations of the period. But it was *Don Quixote*, as well as the example of Shakespeare, that put in question these generic designations and classical authority itself. *Don Quixote* made it possible to read the *Aeneid* as another Quixotic fiction that says classical epic is as inappropriate to our "modern" times as chivalric romance was to Cervantes'. As Dryden and other writers noticed, Milton's Satan could be read as a Quixote whose grandiloquence has tragic consequences.

England took to *Don Quixote*, producing the first complete translation into another language (Shelton's in 1612), the first foreign reference to Quixote (George Wilkins, 1606), the first critical edition of the Spanish text (Lord Carteret's, 1738), the first published commentary (John Bowle's, 1781), and the first biography and "portrait" of Cervantes (in the Carteret edition).[1]

Henry Fielding called his play *Don Quixote in England* (written in 1729 when he was twenty-two), but in *Joseph Andrews* (1742), announced on its title page as "Written in Imitation of the Manner of

Cervantes," he created an "English Don Quixote." The Abbé Desfontaines, in a French review of 1743, called *Joseph Andrews* "the equal of *Don Quixote*, and . . . considerably superior to all of your French Novels"—and added: "The remarkable thing about this work is that just as *Don Quixote* is the picture of Spanish customs, the work at hand is the picture of English customs."[2]

To anglicize *Don Quixote* had been the tendency of the early English translations. When Peter Motteux called John Phillips's translation (1687) a travesty—Phillips has "changed the Sense, ridiculed the most serious and moving Passages"—one thing he meant was that Phillips had "remov'd all the scandalous places in London into the middle of Spain, and all the Language of Billingsgate into the mouths of Spanish Ladies and Noblemen. He has confounded the characters and the Countries."[3] Here for example is Phillips's translation of Sancho's description of the real Dulcinea del Tobozo, Aldonza Lorenzo:

> Cuds-bobs, cryed Sancho, and is Dulcinea del Toboso the Daughter of Dick Fogg of Stamwel, otherwise Nan Hogg? Uds fish, I know her as well as her Mother that bore her; she's a Strapper y' faith, and pitches the Bar with e're a young fellow i' the Village. The very same, quo Don Quixote, that's she, and she that deserves to be Mistress of the whole Earth. Is that she, quo Sancho! She's a Bouncer, Begar law; and one that will keep her Chin out O' the Mire, I warrant her, in despite of the best Knight Errant that wears a Head. Long Megg of Westminster was a Dwarf to her. One day I remember, she stood upon the top of our Steeple to call the Plough men home to dinner, that were at work above half a League off; yet they heard her as plain, as if they had been just under the Sun-dial. The best thing I know in her, is, that she is not Coy, but will bid he kiss the top of her Nock as briskly as e're a Coggshall Wench that goes to Market; there's ne're a Water-man upon the Thames can out-rally her.

Motteux's criticism, an example of the pot calling the kettle black, indicates the nationalizing effect of travesty—and one way that *Don Quixote* could be used to justify a disreputable mode. John Vanderbank's illustrations (first published in 1738) were criticized by a Dutch editor for representing "nothing but English attitudes and customs instead of Spanish ones."[4] But Vanderbank persisted, turning out painting after painting of Don Quixote and Sancho Panza in an English countryside. One of the chief attractions of *Don Quixote* in England, for writers as well as painters, was that the country gentleman Alonzo Quijano, calling himself Don Quixote and sallying forth on a knight-errant's quest in the contemporary Spanish world, permitted and encouraged a representation of the local and actual that could at the same time lay claim to the prestige of the ideal celebrated in the higher genres.

In England *Don Quixote* was read, interpreted, and utilized in a way it was not and could not have been in its native Spain or (where it was also immensely popular) in France, both centralized, absolutist Roman Catholic governments.[5] One reason was the rise, in England at the end of the seventeenth century, of empiricism, which accompanied the decentralizing of power in a wavering economy of Crown, Parliament, and the rights of the English people. As early as *The History of the Royal Society* (1667) Thomas Sprat cited empiricism as characteristic of "the general constitution of the minds of the *English*." England was "the Head of a *Philosophical league*, above all other Countries in *Europe*"—a "Country, a Land of *Experimental Knowledge*" (113–14).

Bracketing the intentions of Cervantes himself or the response of his Spanish readers in the seventeenth century, I examine the text of *Don Quixote* from the perspective of an eighteenth-century English reader—a reader of Locke, perhaps a critic of Hobbes, and a citizen of probably Whiggish inclination. I do not, however, wish to deviate from the Cervantean text: everything to which I draw attention is there. Perhaps characteristically, the English of the early eighteenth century demonized or aestheticized what Cervantes problematized.

By 1700 at least *Don Quixote* was an immensely popular work in England, one that we can be sure everyone we discuss in this book had read and probably reread. And this was a work that did not fit conventional categories, including critical categories laid down by continental (French and Italian) theorists. Above all, it put in question the conventional definition of comedy as satire, of laughter as ridicule, laid out by Thomas Hobbes in *Leviathan* (1651):

> Sudden glory is the passion which maketh those grimaces called laughter; and is caused either by some sudden act of their own, that pleaseth

them; or by the apprehension of some deformed thing in another, by comparison whereof they suddenly applaud themselves.[6]

Don Quixote is constructed on a basic contrast, formal and thematic, between Quixote's long, attenuated, spiritualized (desiccated) body and Sancho's plump, undignified, and plebeian body; between Quixote's elevated discourse of chivalry and Sancho's demotic, proverbial discourse; and between Quixote's idealistic actions and their contrary physical consequences. In one important regard, these contrasts center on Dulcinea del Toboso, to whose beauty there is not only Quixote's idealist but Sancho's realist response. Faced with the polarization of ideal and real, imagination and empiricism, the reader begins with the old satiric assumption that imagination is judged by an empirical norm and found wanting; but then one notices that empiricism is also judged by the norm of imagination—and after that, at length, there is nothing to do but balance imagination and empiricism, replacing satire with an incongruity that came to be the distinguishing feature of comedy.

Don Quixote served as a vehicle for both sides in the epistemological controversy known as the Battle of the Ancients and the Moderns. Swift, in *A Tale of a Tub* (1704) and other works, used Quixote's madness to sum up the Modern's quest to change the world. By using as his norm the common experience of the senses, he exposed the folly of the unfettered imagination, inspiration, and enthusiasm of the radical religious sects. Addison, on the other hand, in the *Spectator* (1711–12), took off from Quixote's madness to recover the imagination Swift regarded as transgressive. At the same time he utilized the Cervantean model to recover Swift's satire itself as comedy. *Don Quixote*, as he recognized, problematized both the imagination of Quixote and the ridicule directed at him by the outside world.[7]

Addison's creation, the aesthetics of laughter, is the recovery of a transgressive category (imagination, ridicule) by turning it into an aesthetic object—that is, taking it out of a moral discourse (though not necessarily out of a rhetorical discourse) and into an aesthetics of pleasurable response, sympathetic laughter, and comedy, an area which he designated as the Novel, New, or Uncommon.

This book is entitled *Don Quixote in England,* but it could also

have been called "Don Quixote and British Empiricism" or "Don Quixote and the Whigs" or "Don Quixote and the Aesthetics of Laughter."
I focus on this last strand, which I believe was the most important for
the creation of an "English Don Quixote" and an "English *Don Quixote*." By doing so I fill a lacuna in my argument in *The Beautiful,
Novel, and Strange: Aesthetics and Heterodoxy*, which mapped the terra
incognita of Addison's aesthetics of the Novel, New, Uncommon, and
Strange with which he filled the space in his "Pleasures of the Imagination" between the Beautiful and the Great.[8] The present book uses *Don
Quixote* to show how Addison began by aestheticizing satire and satiric
laughter before he could aestheticize the objects of satire.

In my use of the term *aesthetics* in relation to *Don Quixote* I owe
an obvious debt to Michael McKeon's chapter on *Don Quixote* in *The
Origins of the English Novel*: "One of the prescient implications of *Don
Quixote*," he writes, "is that the modern disenchantment of the world
entailed not the eradication of enchantment but its transformation, its
secularization." By this he means that "Madness, which is the naive
belief in the reality of romance, is the first and indispensable step in the
dialectical generation of extreme skepticism, which is the instrumental
and saving belief in romance." McKeon's dialectic of history moves
from the naive acceptance of romance (for which, in England around
1700, we can read religious belief) to skepticism and so to an "extreme
skepticism" that accepts romance *as a fiction*—which he defines as "that
species of belief-without-really-believing which would become, once
the mechanism itself proved unnecessary, the realm of the aesthetic."
By "aesthetic" he means "the autonomous realm of the aesthetic," the
formalism that designates pragmatic fictions of truth such as Humean
custom or belief.[9]

This is an alternative explanation to the one I explore, which is
based on specifics of the historical rise of aesthetics (that is, the philosophy of the perception of beauty, as opposed to religious or moral
"truth") at the beginning of the eighteenth century in England, particularly as Addison applied aesthetics to satire and comedy. I see the
effect of *Don Quixote* centered on four general areas of contested notions—the "madness" of imagination, the cruelty of the laughter of
ridicule, the problematizing of the beautiful (that is, what *is* beautiful
and what ugly or deformed), and, in many ways the most volatile issue,

the extension of the idea of "madness" in the face of empirical reason into the area of religious doctrine. I wish to distinguish aesthetics not only from the Marxian sense of formalism but also from other literary ways of dealing with recalcitrant "truth" (or trash or "dunghills") such as the models of the Virgilian georgic and the Ovidian metamorphosis.

What I examine in the aestheticizing of the Quixotic imagination and satire by Addison would fall under McKeon's general term "extreme skepticism"; but that is a term that includes the antithetical politics of Swift as well. Addison constructs a Whig aesthetics insofar as it designates the recovery through aesthetics of areas regarded as transgressive by both Tories and Whigs (the areas Tories call Whig and Whigs Tory).

The Whig party, originally a party of opposition, emerged from its first decade of power in the 1690s as the party of the Moderns. The three great issues of the Whigs were Stuart absolutism, France, and Roman Catholicism. Distrust of monarchy, church, and foreign influence produced on the positive side belief in liberty of the subject, including religious toleration (toleration for Dissenters, not for Catholics). It is the positive aspect that Addison emphasizes in his elevation of mirth over ridicule (an issue first raised a few years earlier by another Whig, the third earl of Shaftesbury). In *Spectator* essays of 1711–12, at a low point of Whig fortunes, the high point of Tory power in the Harley administration whose satiric spokesman was Jonathan Swift, Addison constructed a viable Whig ethos. This was the result of a campaign he inaugurated to counter the Tory propaganda of Swift's *Examiner* by aestheticizing Tory satire as Whig comedy, and Whig enthusiasm as the "pleasures" of the imagination.

Though the terms were established by Addison (with the probable influence of Shaftesbury's essays on enthusiasm and ridicule), two other phases of change followed, in each of which Whig ideas of politics were redefined. The first was the construction of an "opposition" position (drawing, of course, on the opposition politics of the first earl of Shaftesbury and the Whigs in the 1670s and 1680s) to the hegemonic rule of Sir Robert Walpole in December 1726, led by Nicholas Amhurst but more radically, because in graphic terms, by William Hogarth, and indeed implicating Swift through the common element, shared by all of these artists, of wit (another term that had been aestheticized under the Novel or Uncommon by Addison). The Opposition redefined the terms of satire and, at the same time, in the cases of Amhurst and Hogarth, directed it at "priestcraft" as the English equivalent of the chivalric romance.

So far these are mostly accommodations of the dark side of the Quixotic coin of imagination and satire, inspiration and wit; by the early 1740s when Walpole finally fell, the Opposition position was itself aestheticized and the satirized Walpole was recovered for comedy; and after the Forty-Five—the last attempt of the Jacobites to recover power—the emphasis shifted toward nostalgia and reflection; inspiration and chivalry were being revived, pointing toward the years when Quixote would be no longer a nexus of theories of laughter but a symbol of sublimity.

In an essay entitled "The Day Panurge No Longer Makes People Laugh" Milan Kundera cites Octavio Paz to the effect that "not until Cervantes does humor take shape"—and that humor "is an *invention* bound up with the birth of the novel. Thus humor is not laughter, not mockery, not satire, but a particular species of the comic, which, Paz says (and this is the key to understanding humor's essence), 'renders ambiguous everything it touches.' People who cannot take pleasure from the spectacle of Panurge letting the sheep merchants drown while he sings them the praises of the hereafter will never understand a thing about the art of the novel."[10] Addison aestheticizes satire in just this way. He has, therefore, laid the foundation for the particular disinterestedness of comic laughter in the novel—of Fielding, Sterne, and Austen. But while supporting in a general way my reading of Addison's reading of *Don Quixote*, Kundera's words also expose a problem.

Kundera defines the humorous as an "imaginary terrain where moral judgment is suspended"; this is not immorality but the "morality that stands against the ineradicable human habit of judging instantly, ceaselessly, and everyone; of judging before, and in the absence of, understanding" (7). This is to describe precisely Addison's transformation of satire into an aesthetics of the Novel, Uncommon, and Strange, with its epistemology of curiosity, wit, pursuit, and surprise in discovering and understanding the new. And this is the aesthetics that Hogarth defined in the comic works following his "progresses" of a *Harlot* and a *Rake* and in his aesthetic treatise, *The Analysis of Beauty*.

The humorous is also, as Kundera notes, an aspect of the "removal of gods from the world" in the modern era—a secularizing process. "The historical and psychological exploration of myths, of sacred texts, means: rendering them profane, profaning them" (that is, taking them outside the temple and into the *profanum*). We shall also see this operating in the aesthetics of Addison, Shaftesbury, and Hogarth.

Kundera seems to be defining exactly what I am tracing from Cervantes to Addison to Hogarth. But he prompts the question: *Is there such a thing as a disinterested "humor," an untendentious laughter?* Addison argued, against Hobbes, that there is. But was Addison's revaluation of satire as comedy in fact disinterested? *Is the novel, as Kundera has it, "a realm where moral judgment is suspended"?* Can this possibly be true of his own novels, or at least his earlier ones? It is, of course, to misunderstand Rabelais's intention: Panurge's drowning of Dindinault and his sheep is comic because it demonstrates a comedy of mechanization, a laughter of release. The effect is to laugh at the social order that reduces and mechanizes the human, or at the human being who cannot react in any other way than as a mechanism. Kundera is responding, as Rabelais was, to a rigidly "moralistic" system, which his refusal to judge is satirizing; and we can easily say the same about Addison against the judgmental satire of the Tories and Hogarth against the rules-aesthetic of the connoisseurs of art.

The Bergsonian theory of comedy is applicable: "Something mechanical encrusted on the living" is funny because, depending on the source of the mechanism, it leads one to laugh either at the deviation from the social order or the order itself.[11] Dindinault, responding to Panurge's proposition, fits Bergson's description of the human who slips on a banana peel—"through lack of elasticity, through absent-mindedness and a kind of physical obstinacy, *as a result, in fact, of rigidity or of momentum,* the muscles continued to perform the same movement when the circumstances of the case called for something else." "The attitudes, gestures and movements of the human body are laughable in exact proportion as that body reminds us of a mere machine" (66, 79). "This rigidity is the comic, and laughter is its corrective": these words could describe Kundera's satire on the totalitarian regimes of the Soviet bloc in the 1960s.

As the rigidity slips back and forth between the deviant person and the recalcitrant society it goes some way toward explaining the comic effect of *Don Quixote*. For Quixote's imitation of books of chivalry and his dogged repetition of that imitative pattern, we might refer again to Bergson's essay "Laughter": "To imitate any one is to bring out the element of automatism he has allowed to creep into his person. . . . The truth is that a really living life should never repeat itself. Wherever there is repetition or complete similarity, we always suspect some mechanism at work behind the living" (81, 82).

If this book began with the "Aesthetics of Laughter," it soon came to the conclusion that aesthetics, at least from Shaftesbury and Addison onward, was a handmaiden to politics. I saw that I was situating an aesthetics of laughter in relation to a politics of aesthetics. Aesthetics is always and in every case, at least in this period, a rhetoric, and a rhetoric is determined by politics and ideology.

The first English translation of *Don Quixote* was Thomas Shelton's version of part 1, published in London in 1612; part 2 followed in 1620, and in 1700 the whole was revised by Capt. John Stevens.[12] John Phillips's translation of 1687 ("truly a disgraceful performance") seems to have had little effect or currency.[13] The translation by Peter Motteux ("the odious Motteux translation"),[14] based not on the Spanish but on the English of Shelton and the French translation of Filleau de Saint-Martin, appeared in 1700. The fifth edition, of 1725, was revised by John Ozell. The effect of the Motteux translation, in Samuel Putnam's opinion, was to suggest to English readers "that *Don Quixote* was looked upon as being in essence a farcical production designed solely to provoke side-splitting laughter of the more ribald sort" (xiii).

At the beginning of the eighteenth century the best-known stage version of *Don Quixote* was Thomas D'Urfey's three-part *Comical History of Don Quixote* (first produced, 1694–95, still in repertory in the 1730s)—a work condemned for its immorality by Jeremy Collier along with *The Country Wife* and *Love for Love* in his *Short View of the Immorality and Profaneness of the English Stage* (1698). Aside from the distinction of having a musical score by Henry Purcell, D'Urfey's play dramatized what he took to be the highlights of Cervantes' novel, mixing the comic and romantic stories. The first part corresponds to part I of *Don Quixote*, with the adventures of the windmills, wine bags, the knighting of Quixote, Mambrino's helmet, the freeing of the galley slaves, the stories of Grisóstomo (or Christostom) and Marcela (or Marcella), Cardenio and Dorotea, and the attempt to return Quixote to his senses. The second part of D'Urfey's play, while retaining characters from these episodes (including the romance plot of Cardenio and Luscinda), starts with Sancho's attempt to convince Quixote that a "Country Wench" is Dulcinea and recreates the games the duke and duchess play with Quixote and Sancho, while enlarging the part of Marcela; and the third part dramatizes the adventure with the lions, Camacho's wedding, Sancho's whippings, and the episode of the puppet show, ending with Quixote's death.

As D'Urfey's choice of scenes suggests, *Don Quixote* meant at least two things to contemporaries: a madman who sees giants in ordinary contemporary reality and destroys a puppet show, but also the alternation of romance and comic plots. As John Oldfield put it in his instructions for illustrating *Don Quixote*, "the serious parts, in the novel inserted and interspersed," are "suited to relieve the eye from too constant an attention to the same persons, and the same kind of humorous and ludicrous actions."[15] D'Urfey's was the naive version of *Don Quixote* best known to the general public.

For the writers and artists with whom we are concerned, the sense of the *Quixote* was more profound. The primary and most basic topos— the one that underpins the empiricist position—is, of course, embodied in Quixote's attack on windmills and sheep, but there are also the episodes in which he mistakes an inn for a castle; Sancho laughs at Quixote over the fulling hammers and Mambrino's helmet; Quixote meets "Dulcinea"; Quixote attacks the puppet show; the canon, the curate, and Quixote discuss the theory of epic versus romance (and *comedia*); and Marcela speaks out on the subject of female beauty. Alongside these are the eighteenth-century commonplaces about Cervantes, that he "smiled Spain's chivalry away," was "father and unrivalled model of the true mock-heroic," and was the master of "grave irony"; and about Quixote, that he exhibits "madness in one point, and extraordinarily good sense in every other."

Swift had a copy of Shelton's translation in his library; Addison must have read *Quixote* in Shelton's translation before Motteux's translation (or Stevens's revision of Shelton) appeared in 1700. Hogarth, born in 1697, could have read either, but at a crucial point (the peasant maid's "flattened nose") he follows words that Shelton uses and that Motteux does not (see below, 216, n. 26). Fielding, born in 1707, could have read either the Shelton or Motteux translation. Charles Jarvis's more accurate and sober translation (1742) was, in fact, a response to the revaluation of Cervantes that took place in the 1700s, when the demotic anglicizing that culminated in Phillips and Motteux was replaced by the dignifying of style (by which Jarvis meant largely a more literal translation) that followed from the association of Cervantes with the mock-heroic and "sober irony." Tobias Smollett's translation (1755) came too late to influence any of the figures with whom this study is concerned.

As my base translation I have used Samuel Putnam's, because his clarity provides an accuracy and a normative sense of the text that, for me at least, bridges the English and Spanish. This may, of course, be because it is the one in which I have always read and loved Cervantes (Hispanists tend to prefer the John Ormsby translation of 1885). But I have compared the Spanish and the English versions where the meaning of certain terms is important. Unlike the Spanish text, the translations of Shelton, Motteux, Jarvis, and Smollett are divided into books and chapters.[16] This was the procedure followed by Fielding in *Joseph Andrews*, largely so that he could write introductory chapters, separating the essay from the narrative. Smollett returned in his novels (though not his translation of *Don Quixote*) to the single sequence of chapters, undivided into books. In my references I have followed Putnam and the Spanish chapter divisions.

The gestation of this book began when Harry Sieber invited me to open an exhibition of the Peabody Library's Cervantes collection with a lecture in September 1995. I am grateful for his advice, his careful reading of the manuscript, and his correcting of my Spanish. But then he and Claudia Sieber and I began talking about the picaresque thirty years ago and on my trips to Spain they have always guided my steps.

My thanks are also due for various assists, large and small, to Brian Allen, Scott Black, Jackson Cope, DeAnn DeLuna, Charles Dempsey, Robert Folkenflik, Jenifer Karyshyn, Bernd Krysmanski, Richard Macksey, Michael T. Newman, Willis Regier, Ann Stiller, and Diane Williams; for copyediting to Dennis Marshall and for indexing to Therese Boyd.

Don Quixote in England

ONE

Imagination and Satire

Quixote Mistakes an Inn for a Castle

When Don Quixote visits his first inn, he imagines it to be a castle. "Now," writes Cervantes,

> everything that this adventurer of ours thought, saw, or imagined seemed to him to be directly out of one of the storybooks he had read, and so, when he caught sight of the inn, it at once became a castle with its four turrets and its pinnacles of gleaming silver, not to speak of the drawbridge and moat and all the other things that are commonly supposed to go with a castle (1.2.32).[1]

Quixote identifies a swineherd's blast on his horn to summon his hogs as a dwarf "heralding his coming": "just what he wished it to be." The innkeeper he identifies as a castellan, the governor or warden of the castle, and two prostitutes loitering in the inn yard as beautiful damsels. His perception—or rather, imagination—is associated throughout with "lies" as opposed to the "truth," which is what the prostitutes and the innkeeper actually *see*.

A bit later, when Quixote insists that Dulcinea is the most beautiful woman in the world, the merchants ask him to "show her to us" (45). The conflict between Quixote's imagination and the world of the senses relies on a second perspective, in the long run furnished by Sancho Panza. But in this first episode, which predates the addition of

Quixote's squire, the two prostitutes respond first "with fright" at the sight of Quixote's armor, lance, and buckler. Then Quixote, to assuage their fears, raises his pasteboard visor and reveals "his withered, dust-covered face," and says ("imitating insofar as he was able the language . . . the books had taught him"), "Do not flee, your Ladyships," and refers to them as "highborn damsels": "Never having heard women of their profession called damsels before, they were unable to restrain their laughter, at which Don Quixote took offense." Their laughter is, of course, a response to Quixote's imagination—his madness. But it is, in this case, more precisely a response of surprise to the incongruity of Quixote's chivalric discourse and his "unprepossessing figure," by which is meant "this grotesque personage clad in bits of armor that were quite as oddly matched as were his bridle, lance, buckler, and corselet." It is also perhaps compensation for, or relief from, their initial response of fright.

This, the first example of the running game of Cervantes' novel—responses to Don Quixote—raises the question of the cause and the nature of laughter: Is it ridicule or surprise or pleasure at the discovery of incongruity? Or is it the laughter of relief following fright? Or is it release, as with a noise that breaks the silence of church and (as Shaftesbury will see it) disrupts its gravity? Other elements are introduced that will recur: Quixote's annoyance at being laughed at and the alternation or mingling of laughter and another response, that of "amazement" or "astonishment" or even "fear." Every scene of action in *Don Quixote* is one of response, both the responses of the senses—those senses Quixote himself is constantly denying (he *knows* that Dulcinea is beautiful, though this cannot be proved by the senses, and is in fact disproved by those unprejudiced by his "imagination")—and the comments, discussions, and arguments that follow. Each scene contributes to the theorization of laughter.

The laughter accompanying Quixote's arrival at this first inn (and at the second, where the innkeeper, his wife, and their servant Maritornes mix laughter and astonishment) is not unkindly. Quixote's own laughter—at his squire Sancho—is introduced in chapter 8 (64–65), and it is sympathetic, a response to Sancho's "simplicity" when he urges Quixote to admit to the pain he suffers as the result of his encounter with the windmills. And this vignette is followed by the response of the friars to Quixote, which is astonishment or wonder (67), also the response of the staff of the second inn (*admirábanse*, 16.117). Near the end of part 1, in chapter 49, we find again the mingled responses to Quixote of laughter *and* astonishment. The folk at the inn are the first to witness the phenomenon of Quixote; upon repeated viewing he comes to be known as a joke to be ridiculed and exploited.

The basic features of the Quixote figure were that he is mad; his madness is selective—he thinks he is a knight-errant but is otherwise sane; his madness is upward-aspiring, toward a heroic ideal well beyond his actual status and being; he puts his madness into action in the form of a quest; and, as a result, his actions are exposed as mad by contact with the real commonplace world.

Precedents for Cervantes' use of madness include the story of Ajax, who was driven mad by the gods to prevent him from killing Agamemnon, Menelaus, and Ulysses; maddened, he attacked sheep instead. Quixote's own model—for his love madness for Dulcinea—is Orlando Furioso. As these examples show, madness was an unstable metaphor, easily extended to test the sanity of the supposedly sane—indeed, to redefine insanity as a higher sanity. The most celebrated example was Erasmus's *Praise of Folly* (*Encomia Moriae*, 1509). It is possible to see Cervantes putting Erasmus's two-sided fiction of wise folly (folly as both satiric object and norm) into a narrative, naturalizing Erasmus's double irony. From Erasmus, Cervantes takes the idea that folly can be a higher wisdom; he follows Erasmus in contrasting simple Christian "folly" with scholastic reasoning, which seen from one direction is transcendence. Erasmus's Folly, like Quixote, is based on a refusal to face reality; but Folly, unlike Quixote, is spontaneous, has never read a book. Her reaction to the laborious definitions and divisions of the scholastic sermon is to "speak 'whatever pops into my head.' "[2]

As Michel Foucault, among others, has shown, "madness" carried from classical through medieval times a sense of superior truth, poetic *furor*, or, in Christian terms, divine or demonic possession; subsequently, in what Foucault called the "classical" period, it was "shut up" and reduced to "unreason," a purely negative attribute. Quixote's madness carries both senses. His act of freeing the galley slaves reflects the unreason of loosing dangerous criminals on the countryside, immediately realized in their criminal behavior, but also the generous instinct that transcends the law in order to alleviate suffering. The madman can become God's fool and an ideal of honor or simplicity against which the real world is measured and found wanting. He can become the anachronistic exemplar of an earlier and better age (Quixote invokes the Golden Age).

A survey of eighteenth-century citations in England would begin in 1700 with Motteux's generalizing of Quixote's madness:

> Every man has something of Don Quixote in his *Humour*, some darling Dulcinea of his Thoughts, that sets him very often upon mad Adventures. What Quixotes does not every Age produce in Politics and Religion, who fancying themselves to be in the right of something, which all the world tells 'em is wrong, make very good sport to the Public, and show that themselves need the chiefest amendment.[3]

Richard Steele in *Tatler* no. 178 (1710) plays upon the topos of the insanity of "sanity": "As much as the Case of this distempered Knight is received by all the Readers of his History as the most incurable and ridiculous of all Phrensies, it is very certain that we have Crowds among us far gone in as visible a Madness as his, tho' they are not observed to be in that Condition."[4] And Fielding, in 1729 in *Don Quixote in England*, compares the "mad" but virtuous Quixote with the "sane" but venal citizens—"All mankind is mad, 'tis plain." Says Quixote:

> Who would doubt the noisy boisterous squire [Badger], who was here just now, to be mad? Must not this noble knight [Sir Thomas Loveland] have been mad to think of marrying his daughter to such a wretch? You, doctor, are mad too, though not so mad as your patients. The lawyer here is mad, or he would not have gone into a scuffle, when it is the business of his profession to set other men by the ears, and keep clear themselves.[5]

By midcentury, Corbyn Morris in his *Essay towards Fixing the True Standards of Wit, Humour, Raillery, Satire, and Ridicule* (1744), sees Quixote's madness—his knight-errantry—as one foible in an otherwise virtuous, honorable, and amusing gentleman. And in 1750 Samuel Johnson (for whom *Don Quixote* was one of three favorite fictions, along with *Pilgrim's Progress* and *Robinson Crusoe*) reads "the knight of La Mancha" as Everyman. In his second *Rambler* essay, writing on his favorite subject of imagination and happiness, he acknowledges that "the mind of man is never satisfied with the objects immediately before it, but is always breaking away from the present moment, and losing itself in schemes of future felicity":

> [V]ery few readers, amidst their mirth or pity, can deny that they have admitted visions of the same kind [as Quixote]; though they have not, perhaps, expected events equally strange, or by means equally inadequate. When we pity him, we reflect on our own disappointments; and when we laugh, our hearts inform us that he is not more ridiculous than ourselves, except that he tells what we have only thought.[6]

One other source for Cervantes' sense of Quixote's madness" remains to be mentioned. In Horace's Satire 2.10, Damasippus argues that those people we think of as mad are not nearly so mad as the people we think of as sane. But Horace is being harangued by Damasippus, who is simply repeating the words of his teacher Stertinius, whose excesses implicate the speaker as well as his subject.

The specific satiric intention of *Don Quixote* is asserted in the prologue, though attributed by Cervantes to a "friend": "the entire work is an attack upon the books of chivalry" (15—*derribar la máquina mal fundada de los libros de caballerías*); and at the end of part 2, following the profoundly ambiguous denouement, Cervantes again distances himself by putting the words in the mouth of his "author" Cid Hamete Benengeli:

> I have had no other purpose than to arouse the abhorrence of mankind toward those false and nonsensical stories to be met with in the books of chivalry, which, thanks to this tale of the genuine Don Quixote, are already tottering and without a doubt are doomed to fall. (2.74.988)

Cervantes' satire is on books, on the source of the humor that Quixote has imbibed by reading them. Quixote, his author tells us, "string[s] together absurdities, all of a kind that his books had taught him, imitating insofar as he was able the language of their authors" (1.2.31).[7] "It must have been the devil himself who caused him to remember those tales that seemed to fit his own case"; thus Quixote answers the inquiries of his neighbor, the farmer, into his plight "with the very same words and phrases that the captive Abindarráez used in answering Rodrigo, just as he had read in the story *Diana* of Jorge de Montemayor, where it is all written down, applying them very aptly to the present circumstances as the farmer went along cursing his luck for having to listen to such a lot of nonsense" and realizing that "his neighbor was quite mad." In an attempt to cure Quixote, the curate burns the books themselves at what he calls "a public *auto de fe*," giving them the aura of religious heresy (1.5.49–50).

As Cervantes makes abundantly clear, Quixote's madness results from reading too many books and then imitating them—acting upon them or, in the terms of these particular romances, pursuing a quest. With Quixote it is "those cursed books of chivalry he is always reading that have turned his head" (1.50); and it is only a question of whether he "should imitate the monstrous things that Orlando did in his fits of madness or, rather, the melancholy actions of Amadis" (1.26.210).

The closest classical precedent is Aristophanes' *The Frogs*, in which Dionysus has been driven mad by reading Euripides' *Andromeda* (one of the earliest references to solitary reading of the sort epitomized by Quixote) and sets out for the underworld to recover and revivify the dead playwright. Because no one has descended to Hades before and returned, Dionysus dons the costume of Heracles (lion's skin and club), and in this equivalent of Quixote's armor he arouses various comic responses from, alternatively, the enemies and friends Heracles had made on his previous trip. Dionysus is also accompanied by his slave Xanthias, a distant ancestor of Sancho.

Sancho expresses the empirical position against which Quixote's quest is judged when he says, "the only thing that is real to us is what we have before our eyes." But even this is said in the context of his explanation to his wife Teresa: " 'I am not speaking for myself but am giving you the opinions of the reverend father who preached in this village during Lent, the last time. If I remember rightly, he said that all present things which our eyes behold make much more of an impression on us and remain better fixed in our memories than things that are past' " (2.5.542). In this chapter Sancho and Teresa have assumed, respectively, the positions of Quixote and Sancho, as Sancho has gradually internalized the assumptions of his master. Sancho has to justify his empiricism on the authority of a cleric, and produces his own version of Quixote's reading of chivalric romances.

Don Quixote's one fictional predecessor in Spain was *La vida de Lazarillo de Tormes* (1554). Cervantes defined his fiction against this earlier type of antiromance, one that offered a total contrast to chivalric romance, a contrary—therefore *real*—world: the narrative of a picaro, a boy appropriately named Lazaro (after the beggar in the parable of Lazarus and Dives), simply struggling to get by, as a servant, not in the coordinated world of romance but the *un*coordinated, unreliable world of cruel, self-absorbed masters instead of giants, whores instead of chaste maidens, and emptied chamber pots instead of knightly combat. Hunger and survival were the picaro's only motives; whereas Quixote, the opposite of the prudent, pragmatic picaro, aspires to the view that man *cannot* live on bread alone. Quixote is a man living by courtly manners that are anachronisms in his time and place; he is himself unlike the picaro in that he is a man of some substance, not immediately rejected by innkeepers until he behaves outrageously and according to standards that are no longer applicable to the society in which he finds himself.[8]

Sancho is the hero of *Lazarillo de Tormes*. But Quixote himself is faintly adumbrated in Lazaro's *hidalgo* master who postures above the reality of his situation. Cervantes refers to the *Lazarillo* in chapter 22 of part 1 in connection with the picaresque life of Ginés de Pasamonte. Most likely he read the censored edition published in 1573 (again in 1599), which omitted some of the episodes, leaving intact only the third chapter, on the relationship of Lazaro and the *hidalgo*.[9] The latter walks "slowly, holding his body straight and swaying gracefully, placing the tail of the cape over his shoulder or sometimes under his arm, and putting his right hand on his chest"; when he goes to church he waits until all the others have left before he leaves, so he will be seen; and he wears his sword as if it were a piece of jewelry, only for decoration. The *Lazarillo* was published in the 1573 and 1599 editions as an appendix to a courtesy book, which further focused attention on the master's parody of courtly manners.[10]

Imagination Demonized: Swift

The first imitators in mid-seventeenth century France turned Quixote's aping of chivalry into the aping of fine manners, treating him as an agent of social disruption. In 1660 the English court, returning from exile, brought back this version of Quixote, but while it obviously applied to the fops of Restoration comedy, the Stuart spokesmen applied it to the more urgent subject of disruptive figures who, in the wake of the Civil War, represented madness in religious terms as enthusiasm, in political terms as treason, and in practical terms as hypocrisy.

The English also applied to their reading of *Don Quixote* the new ("Modern") epistemology of Francis Bacon and his followers. For Don Quixote, Cervantes tells us, "continued to behold in his imagination what he did not see and what did not exist in reality" (1.18.132). Quixote's problem, when he believes an inn to be a castle, is his imagination. To many English readers of *Don Quixote* at the end of the seventeenth century the world against which Quixote knocks his head—and loses part of an ear and several grinders—began as the world of the senses posited by empiricism. "Imagination," Hobbes wrote in 1651, "is nothing but *decaying sense*": "there is no conception in a man's mind which hath not at first, totally or by parts, been begotten upon the organs of sense." Compounded or rearranged, he adds, sense impressions can result in images of the imagination:

> [W]hen a man compoundeth the image of his own person with the actions of another man, as when a man imagines himself a Hercules or an Alexander (which happeneth often to them that are *much taken with reading of romances*), it is a compound imagination and properly but a fiction of the mind. [emphasis added][11]

It is doubtful that Hobbes could have written this sentence without thinking of *Don Quixote*. "Reading of romances" leads to "a compound imagination"; that is, the creation of witty monsters, which are "but a fiction of the mind." So too with dreams, owing to a "distempered" brain that is unable "to distinguish exactly between sense and dreaming." "From this ignorance of how to distinguish dreams, and other strong fancies, from vision and sense, did arise the greatest part of the religion of the gentiles in time past, that worshipped satyrs, fawns, nymphs, and the like" (10–12). Closely connected with imagination was "inspiration" (which Hobbes opposed to "wit")[12] and ultimately "enthusiasm," which, Hobbes writes, "takes away both Reason and Revelation, and substitutes in the room of it, the ungrounded Fancies of a Man's own Brain, and assumes for them a Foundation both of Opinion and Conduct."[13] Enthusiasm, wrote Henry More in *Enthusiasmus Triumphatus* (1656), "disposes a man to listen to the Magisterial Dictates of an over-bearing *Phansy*, more than to the calm and cautious insinuations of free *Reason*."[14]

Enthusiasm, associated before the Restoration with Puritans and after with Nonconformists, has become Quixotic madness. The "English Quixote," Samuel Butler's Hudibras (1663 ff.), was a wily Presbyterian in Civil War England whose "enthusiasm" is a crazy knight-errantry that in reality masks a plan to marry a rich widow. Religious enthusiasm, in its Quixotic form of being learned from reading the wrong books, was the object to which Swift turned his attention in *A Tale of a Tub* (1704) and especially "A Digression concerning Madness."

Swift, following Butler, interpreted Quixote as a restless malcontent who reads not (as he should) the works of the Ancients, Phalaris and Aesop, but the fashionable au courant books of Richard Bentley and William Wotton with their doctrine of modern superiority. He shows his characters reading the books and internalizing the words of the Moderns, the projects of sharpers, the almanacs of quacks, and various modest proposals, all carrying the same taint of heresy. The "author" of the *Tale* is infatuated with "our Noble *Moderns*; whose most edifying Volumes I turn indefatigably over Night and Day, for the Improvement of my Mind, and the good of my Country."[15] This reading turns him into a madman convinced of his own self-sufficiency and sends him on a quest to change the world—to introduce new systems of philosophy, religion, and government. The folly and futility of the Modern's "quest" are demonstrated by his accidents and mishaps. However much he asserts the superiority of modern writings, he cannot make them survive for more than an hour or so after he posts them for the scrutiny of Prince Posterity.

The preeminently Modern sect of Aeolists (religious enthusiasts), whose inspiration and preaching depend on the ingesting and discharging of wind, naturally attack the "huge terrible Monster, called

Moulinavent, who with four strong Arms, waged eternal Battel with all their Divinities, dextrously turning to avoid their Blows, and repay them with Interest" (160). Swift is, of course, referring to the most famous of all the episodes in *Don Quixote*: "God help us!" exclaimed Sancho, "did I not tell your Grace to look well, that those were nothing but windmills, a fact which no one could fail to see unless he had other mills of the same sort in his head" (1.8.63).

Swift shows that the truth of inspiration, enthusiasm, or imagination is that it is merely imitated, secondhand knowledge, learned from books. When the discourse is learned from reading books, the delusion can be defined as a form of "aping." This began for readers of *Don Quixote* with the French interpretation of Quixote as a social climber. In England, Ben Jonson had extended the danger of theatrical imitation to social role-playing and the imitation of fashionable role models.[16] Swift makes the connection himself in the fashionable imitation of Peter, Martin, and Jack when they arrive in London society (*Tale*, sect. 2).

His particular insight, however, was that the Quixotic reader of a "romance" is not himself evil but *reflects* evil through his obtuseness—the knave being the romance-*writer*. In Swift's hands, he is a middleman, an embodiment of the banality of evil as distinct from absolute evil—and, from Swift's point of view, a more interesting object of satire. In terms of satire this insight suggests a further degeneration (the Grub Street Hack is not *even* evil, only a poor imitator of it), in mimetic terms pushing the satiric object in the direction of a subject, of a *character* (he is not as evil as his source).[17] In short, the Quixote fiction—shifting the emphasis from the author to the reader, from the agent to his accomplice—has the effect of both complicating and mitigating the satiric object by moving our attention to another, less culpable and more human source.

The words of the Moderns are all written down and published. Swift suggests the bookish or literary nature of imagination, which implicates the text Cervantes or Swift is writing as well as the romances of chivalry, or at least invites comparison and contrast. Following Cervantes, Swift's "author" of *A Tale of a Tub* acknowledges the fragility and destructibility of books, including his own; and like Cid Hamete Benengeli, a Moor known to be an untrustworthy purveyor of facts and perhaps envious of the protagonist whose history he is writing, he is an "unreliable narrator."

The *Quixote* introduced or at least authorized the subject of writing itself. Swift's parody and attack are on the *writings* of the Moderns, as Cervantes' was on chivalric romances. Following Dryden, Swift reflects the shift of the sense of chaos—the most feared phenomenon in post–Civil War England—from a political to a literary subject. Virgil's chaos in the *Georgics* and the *Aeneid* was summed up in an overturning of nature—in the *Georgics*, a storm, two male horses fighting over a mare, disease and ultimately plague, and the destruction, through civil war or blight, of a society and a political microcosm, a beehive; in the *Aeneid*, a storm, the blind grappling of soldiers within a falling Troy, a passionately self-destructive love (first Helen, in the midst of the fall of Troy, and then Dido in Carthage) sum up the fear of disorder that follows from antisocial emotions, primarily *eros*. Milton's *Paradise Lost* signaled a different sense of disorder in the geographical space of a realm called Chaos. Out of this space God has created the heavens and earth; and so chaos becomes everything that is not the order of creation, which at any moment may reclaim creation, but even in the process can become, as subsequently for Dryden and Pope, the kind of alternative order created only in poetry. For Addison this centralizing of the literary as a kind of synecdoche for political and religious issues led to the replacing of the satire of literary aberration with an aesthetics that contrasts nature and art as sources of pleasurable response.

Swift also shows that at bottom this imitation of inspiration, enthusiasm, or imagination is founded on nothing more than physical desire. This is the aspect of *Don Quixote* that René Girard has called mediated desire: Quixote loves Dulcinea only because other men have written books about her and he has read about her. "In most works of fiction, the characters have desires which are simpler than Don Quixote's. There is no mediator, there is only the subject and the object." But in the case of Quixote, his actions are always determined by the mediator. "The object changes with each adventure but the triangle remains": the barber's basin, the windmills, and, above all, Dulcinea herself are the objects determined by the common mediator, Amadis, or rather the book *Amadis of Gaul*, which Quixote has read.[18] And Sancho's character operates in the same way; he wants to be governor of an island because Don Quixote has put the idea in his head. "From the moment the mediator's influence is felt, the sense of reality is lost and judgment paralyzed," as Girard notes (4).

For Swift, at the (literal) bottom of imitation is the errant humor that always begins as "semen adust," a thwarted desire for a sexual object that finds its outlet in enthusiasm or some other form of madness.

Imagination Aestheticized: Addison

Part 1 of *Don Quixote* concludes with a long discussion of chivalric romance and its effects on its readers. The discussion is carried on by a canon of Toledo, the curate of Quixote's village, and Quixote himself, who during the early stages of the discussion is confined to a cage. Quixote is in the cage because, as he characteristically argues, he is enchanted "as a result of the envy and deceit of wicked magicians" (1.47.423). Quixote believes this, and the curate is exploiting his belief in order to return him to his village; Sancho remains skeptical. The canon's lengthy attack on romances is interrupted at the end of chapter 48 by Sancho's empirical test: for Quixote to answer the needs of nature, which force him to leave the cage to relieve himself, proves that he is not enchanted.

In this scene the canon sums up what will be Swift's position on "romance" in *A Tale of a Tub*. So disgusted was he with the romances he read that he threw them into the fire,

> for they are deserving of the same punishment as cheats and impostors, who are beyond the pale of human nature, or as the founders of new sects and new ways of life, for leading the ignorant public to believe and regard as the truth all the nonsense they contain. (1.49.437–38)

In "A Digression concerning Madness" we are told that

> if we take a Survey of the greatest Actions that have been performed in the World, under the influence of Single Men; which are, *The Establishment of New Empires by Conquest; The Advance and Progress of New Schemes in Philosophy; and the contriving, as well as the propagating of New Religions*: We shall find the Authors of them all [to have been madmen]. (162)

[margin handwritten note:] Canon's position on romance is Swift's

Swift agrees with both the canon's submerged hypothesis that the authors are heretics and should be burned at an auto-da-fé (the analogy used by the curate in 1.6 when he and the barber burned Quixote's books) and his conviction that, as he tells Quixote, "as is plainly to be seen from the things that you have done," they "have finally made it necessary to lock you up in a cage." This is what Swift does with the founders of new philosophies and religions, locking them up in the cells of Bedlam. Such consequences follow "when a Man's fancy gets *astride* on his Reason, when Imagination is at Cuffs with the Senses, and common Understanding, as well as common Sense, is Kickt out of Doors." And Swift's ironic persona adds:

> Those Entertainments and Pleasures we most value in Life, are such as *Dupe* and play the Wag with the Senses. For, if we take an Examination of what is generally understood by *Happiness*, as it has Respect, either to the Understanding or the Senses, we shall find all its Properties and Adjuncts will herd under this short Definition: That, *it is a perpetual Possession of being well Deceived.*

This is "because Imagination can build nobler Scenes, and produce more wonderful Revolutions than Fortune or Nature will be at Expence to furnish" (171–72).[19]

However, in Quixote's discussion with the canon of Toledo, Cervantes lays out both the Swiftean position on imagination and an alternative, which problematizes the term as it resides in the books of chivalric romance that are the object of his satire. As a *concessio*, the canon admits that "I can say that when I read such books without stopping to think how mendacious and frivolous they are they do give me a certain pleasure," and earlier he has introduced an aesthetic criterion for romance, based in his case on harmony and proportion (1.47.425). Quixote's reply is to invoke the aesthetic response of the reader, who (as he has himself so notably done) empathizes with the knight-errant. Defending chivalric romances against the canon's accusation that the stories are not true, he projects the adventure of the Knight of the Lake. He asks whether there could "be anything more fascinating than to see before us, right here and now, a lake of bubbling pitch" and then, not knowing where he is or what the outcome is to be, he suddenly finds himself amidst flowering meadows to which the Elysian fields cannot compare. It seems to him that the heavens there are more transparent, while the sun is brighter than he has ever known it to be. His eyes behold a charming grove composed of leafy trees whose greenery is a joy to the sight, while his ears are delighted by the sweet and untaught song of an infinite number of little brilliant-hued birds, flying in and out through the interweaving branches. Here he discovers a brook whose clear-running waters, which have the appearance of molten glass, glide along over a bed of fine sand and white pebbles. (1.50.442)[20]

And so he proceeds, testing one sense after the other ("His eyes behold . . . his ears are delighted by . . . he discovers a brook . . . there he sees . . .").

If Swift adapted the dark side of the Hobbesian (and Lockean) formulation, Addison revised it in another way in his essays in the *Spectator* on the "*Pleasures* of the Imagination" (1712). In no. 411 he turns Swift's satire on our "Power of retaining, altering and compounding those Images [of the senses], which we have once received, into all the varieties of Picture and Vision that are most agreeable to the Imagination" into praise. His version of the caged Quixote or the imprisoned madman of the "Digression concerning Madness" is "a Man in a Dungeon [who] is capable of entertaining himself with scenes and Landskips more beautiful than any that can be found in the whole Compass of Nature."[21]

In *Spectator* no. 413, Addison elaborates: "And what Reason can we assign," he asks, for the power of "ordinary objects" for "exciting in us many of those Ideas which are different from any thing that exists in the Objects themselves . . . were it not to add Supernumerary Ornaments to the Universe, and make it more agreeable to the Imagination?" At this point he echoes Quixote's description of the romance of chivalry (with "pleasing Shows and Apparitions," "imaginary Glories," and "Visionary Beauty") in his description of a Quixotic knight who wanders in an illusion of secondary qualities such as color but exists in a real black-and-white world of primary qualities such as extension and weight:

In short, our Souls are at present delightfully lost and bewildered in a pleasing Delusion, and we walk about like the Enchanted Hero of a

Romance, who sees beautiful Castles, Woods and Meadows; and at the same time hears the warbling of Birds, and the purling of Streams; but upon the finishing of some secret Spell, the fantastick Scene breaks up, and the disconsolate Knight finds himself on a barren Heath, or in a solitary Desart. (3:546–47)

But, Addison adds, "indeed the Ideas of Colours are so pleasing and beautiful in the Imagination, that it is possible the Soul *will not* be deprived of them, but perhaps find them excited by some other Occasional Cause"; that is, validated in some other way than either existential *or* religious knowledge permits.

In the "Pleasures of the Imagination" essays, Addison offers us that way. He goes a step beyond Hobbes and Locke, let alone Swift, and *accepts* the "fictions of the mind"—not denying that they are the source of conflict and error but recovering them as what he calls "pleasures" that can be enjoyed. In terms of the writings of the third earl of Shaftesbury, which laid the groundwork for the application of empiricism to the branch of philosophy that came to be known as aesthetics, Addison in effect "aestheticizes" the errant imagination and the dangers of enthusiasm. He has the "pleasures of the imagination" occupy a middle area between "sense" and "understanding," serving as a virtuous way to "Step out of Business" without stepping into "Vice or Folly" (no. 411, 3: 537, 539).[22] This can take the form of enjoyment of the Great or the Beautiful, but also of (his third, and privileged term) the Novel, New, and Uncommon; that is, the London of Mr. Spectator and spectatorship in 1712. But it can also reach into the countryside to the "Strange," the literary area of *faerie* ("the fairy way of writing"), folklore, and superstitions, which Hobbes had referred to as the worship of satyrs, fawns, and nymphs.

Satire: Sancho Laughs at Quixote

In chapter 20 of part 1, Don Quixote and Sancho Panza discover in the morning that the cause of their fright the night before at the terrible sounds in the dark was no more than the sound of fulling hammers: Quixote "was speechless and remained as if paralyzed from head to foot." This exposure of a shared case of overwrought imagination is followed by, in effect, an essay on the response to satire, and the relation between laughter and ridicule.

First, "Gazing at him, Sancho saw that his head was on his bosom, as if he were abashed. The knight then glanced at his squire and perceived that his cheeks were puffed with laughter as if about to explode." Then, "in spite of the melancholy that possessed him he in turn could not help laughing at the sight." And finally, "Thus encouraged, Sancho gave in to his mirth and laughed so hard that he had to hold his sides to keep from bursting." But

> Don Quixote was furious at this, especially when he heard his squire saying, as if to mock him, "Sancho, my friend, you may know that I was born by Heaven's will, in this our age of iron, to revive what is known as the Golden Age. I am he for whom are reserved the perils, the great exploits, the valiant deeds . . ." And he went on repeating all the other things that Don Quixote had said the first time they heard those frightening blows. (1.20.154)

Sancho laughs, the laugh becomes contagious—Quixote joins in the enjoyment of the joke on himself—but when he hears Sancho parody his discourse of chivalry, the mockery of conscious parody elicits the anger of Quixote the unconscious parodist.

Indeed, he is so angry that he "raised his lance and let Sancho have a couple of whacks. . . . The jest was becoming serious, and Sancho was afraid things might go further. . . . 'Calm yourself, your Grace,' he said. 'In God's name, I was only *joking*' "(154). When Quixote has calmed down, Sancho responds: "But tell me, your Grace, now that there is peace between us . . . tell me if it was not truly a laughing matter, and a good story as well, that great fright of ours?"[23]

> "I do not deny," said Don Quixote, "that what happened to us has its comical aspects; but it is best not to tell the story, for not everyone is wise enough to see the point of the thing."
>
> "Well, at any rate," said Sancho, "your Grace saw the point when you pointed your lance at my head—but it fell on my shoulders, thank God, and thanks also to my quickness in dodging it. But never mind, it will all come out in the wash." (155)

This dialogue on the relation between laughter and ridicule ends "in the wash" as comedy (Shelton: "all will away in the bucking").

[margin handwriting: he change has to do w/ when S. parodies chivalric discourse]

Cervantes' Spanish vocabulary is simple, based on two words, *risa* and *burla*. Literally, Sancho's "jaws were clenched and his mouth full of laughter" (*risa*); "he almost broke out in laughter" (*reirse*); and he "clenched his jaws with his fists in order not to explode laughing" (*riendo*). Cervantes uses only the one word for laughter. Shelton's seventeenth-century translation omits the word entirely for the physical effect: "And when *Sancho* saw that his Master had begun the Play, he let slip the prisoner, in such violent manner, to press his Sides hardly with both his Hands to save himself from bursting."[24] Putnam's "mirth," with its connotations of "cheerfulness and mirth," is part of the post-Cervantean vocabulary that Addison adapts to justify laughter. In the same way, "has its comical aspects" is literally in the Spanish "may not be worthy of laughter" (*risa*).

In the succeeding passage, however, "jest" or "joking" (Shelton's "jest") is the Spanish *burla* or "jest or trick, verbal or physical": *hacer burla de algo* or *de alguién*, or "making sport of—playing a trick on."[25] *Risa* is a response to *burla*. In Spanish one *laughs* at a practical joke, which in *Lazarillo de Tormes*, *Don Pablos*, and *Don Quixote* takes the form of punishment—or a phenomenon that later critics, probably thinking of Bergson's theory of comedy, have referred to as *cosificacion*, the thingifying of people, turning humans into objects.[26]

Quixote's conclusion to the problem of laughter and jest is that as servant and master he and Sancho talk too much, "a great fault, on your part and on mine: on your part because it shows that you have little respect for me; and on mine because I do not make myself more respected." As Quixote indicates, the social is one dimension determining the relative responses to satire of these two. Such punishments as blanket-tossing were usually (going back to Aristotle's formulation of comedy as engaging low types) relegated to servants; one of the innovations of Cervantes, piling similar or worse indignities upon his hero, is to confuse and question this distinction. The chapter ends with the response of Sancho the servant, who must retire into irony, proverbs, and coded response: "[Y]ou may be sure that from now on I will not open my mouth to make light of what concerns your Grace, but will speak only to honor you as my liege lord and master."

The next chapter, 21, opens with a reminder of Quixote's ire at "the offensive joke" (*pesada burla*) associated with the fulling ham-

[margin note: laughing at practical joke — cosificación — turning people into animals]

[margin note: idea that they talk too much together]

mers, and goes on to Sancho's prudent silence at Quixote's imagining a barber's basin to be a knight's helmet ("if I were free to talk as I used to," he remarks [157]): "Upon hearing the basin called a helmet, Sancho could not help laughing, but mindful of his master's ire, he stopped short" (159). Nevertheless, his inadvertence causes Quixote to respond, "What are you laughing at, Sancho?" With this the onus shifts from Quixote to Sancho, from master to servant, and how the latter responded to being tossed in a blanket by the servants of the inn back in chapter 17.

When Sancho complains of the treatment he received, Quixote tells him, "You are a bad Christian, Sancho, . . . for you never forget an injury that once has been done you. You should know that it is characteristic of noble and generous hearts to pay no attention to trifles" (1.21.160). By introducing the Christian context, Quixote has precisely set Sancho—and so ridicule as revenge—in the context of rewards and punishments versus Jesus' doctrine of forgiveness; and Sancho has already shown himself to be a follower of Jesus: He *remembers* the indignity but says he has no intention of acting upon it. And by introducing the words "noble and generous hearts," Quixote has, as happens repeatedly, made a social distinction between his own and Sancho's response. He continues, now assuming the Sancho position:

> You have no lame leg, no fractured rib, no broken head to show for it; so why can you not forget that bit of buffoonery? For when you look at it closely, that is all it was: a jest and a little pastime; for had I not regarded it in that light, I should have returned and, in avenging you, should have wrought more damage than those Greeks did who stole Helen of Troy." (160)

"Let it pass for a jest," says Sancho, "seeing that it cannot be avenged in earnest; but I know what jest and earnest mean, and I further know that this joke will never slip from my memory any more than it will from my shoulders" (160).

Sancho is part of the comic situation: "Who would not have had a good laugh over it all, at beholding the master's madness and his servant's simple-mindedness?" (1.30.260). By contrast with the tall, lean Quixote, there is Sancho "with a big belly, a short body, and long shanks."[27] From the "laughing sport" of tossing Sancho in a blanket, which is no laughing matter for the servant, follow the practical jokes on the master—ultimately at the end of part 1 Maritornes's jest that leaves Quixote hanging from the gate precariously balanced on the back of Rocinante (1.43.391–96) and finally caged and carted back home by the barber and curate; and these are followed by the jokes, violence, and pain, both physical and mental, of part 2.

The object of Cervantes' satire is the alleged Spanish penchant for living in a glorious, imaginary past. To ridicule this national delusion, Cervantes retains the picaresque "reality" defined by the word *burla*—by practical jokes and pratfalls, by purges, shattered teeth, and broken heads. The picaresque of *Lazarillo de Tormes* gives this physical reality a punitive form; punishment is a consequence that exposes, demonstrates, and defines the punished—in Quixote's case his chivalric folly. The blades of a windmill (a local Spanish windmill) send him sprawling as a physical reminder that here in Spain a windmill is not a giant, and the beatings and purgings he suffers along the road are tests of reality opposed to his delusion of knight-errantry.

In the *Lazarillo*, however, punishment of the innocent incriminated the punisher, satirizing the master's self-interest and cruelty; and so, in the *Quixote*, when it is meted out to an elderly gentleman, quite out of his wits, who has the best intentions behind his every act, the effect reflects on the punisher as well as the punished.[28] If Quixote is a dangerously deluded fool, the people he meets are as dangerously *un*-deluded; *his* impossibly high standards illuminate *their* crassly prudential ones.

Once Quixote is seen as an occasion for laughter, people humor him and set up situations in which they can "give him a further opportunity of displaying his absurdities" (1.13.93) and, sometimes, practical jokes that will expose or utilize his madness for the enjoyment—the laughter—of an audience. The usual response to Quixote is that of Vivaldo in chapter 13, which is laughter followed by the humoring of the knight-errant in order to give him the opportunity of "displaying his absurdities." Dorotea, another figure from the interpolated romances, "perceiving the mad character of Don Quixote's fancies and noting that all the others with the exception of Sancho were making sport of him, decided that she would have her share of the fun" (1.30.257).

[The jokers are not idealized.] Dorotea, for example, is herself a Quixote in relation to the egregious Fernando. In chapter 22 they are summed up in one of the prisoners freed by Quixote who has been condemned to the galleys for what he claims was essentially a joke: "I am here . . . for the reason that I carried a joke too far with a couple of cousins-german of mine and a couple of others who were not mine, and I ended by jesting [*burla*] with all of them to such an extent that the devil himself would never be able to straighten out the relationship" (1.21.171). This prankster, a Latin scholar, evidently jested once too often.

Response to Quixote, in short, covers a spectrum for the spectator from astonishment to laughter, and for the object from annoyance to pain, but with some registering of more complex affect along the way. We have seen two sorts of response to Quixote: what we might call an initial and disinterested response, and a subsequent and interested one. The first—the laughter of the prostitutes at Quixote in his armor—is at a breach of the usual order of things. Something has been imported into one situation that belongs to another, representing quite simply a laughter of incongruity; laughter at what Addison calls new and strange. At the other extreme is the jesting of the prisoner and of the duke and duchess and their cohorts, which ends in pain for the subject or object or both.

Satire Aestheticized: Addison's Creation of a Whig Ethos

The subject matter of comedy, as Aristotle explained in his *Poetics*, was the socially low and physically ugly: the "imitation of characters of a lower type [men worse than average],—not, however, in the full sense of the word bad [as regards any and every sort of fault], the ludicrous [usually translated as the *ridiculous*] being merely a subdivision of the ugly. It [the ludicrous] consists in some defect or ugliness [mistake or deformity] that is not painful [productive of pain] or destructive [of harm to others]."[29]

The only way to represent this "comic" material and remain within the limits of decorum was to ridicule it. The explanation of laughter as ridicule, against which all others in the eighteenth century were measured, was Hobbes's brutally empirical one. Hobbes, the

Stuart Royalist and proto-Tory, defined laughter as satire, as the result
of self-esteem (see preface, p. xi–xii); it is caused by the contemplation of the infirmities of others—a theory based on superiority of the
laugher and denigration of the object of laughter.

The *risus* that accompanied a *burla* was an extreme form of
Hobbes's superiority theory. In an early French *Quixote*, Paul Scarron's
Roman comique (1651), the Quixote figure is the lawyer Ragotin, who
aspires to the life of an actor and the love of a prima donna, and in
consequence is not only ridiculed but beaten, humiliated, tortured,
and finally drowned.[30] Whereas in *Don Quixote* the beatings point up
the supremacy of hard reality over the hero's dream, in the *Roman
comique* they externalize the essentially mean and unheroic being of
Ragotin, who, to top it all, happens to be a dwarf. Nature is simply
reasserting her sway over the small, proud man who would try to pass
himself off as something he is not. Ragotin lacks altogether the heroic
dimension of Quixote. While Quixote in his madness tries to change
the world, Ragotin presumes merely to change his own status. In
England this primitive strain of Quixotism was picked up in the 1740s
by Tobias Smollett, who merely moralized *Don Quixote*, developing in
all of his work an atavistic version of the punishments and practical
jokes visited upon Quixote.[31]

Don Quixote uniquely presented a story in which Quixote is mad
but the world that punishes him is bad. Quixote and the world are the
two elements of the comic situation—one the satiric object and the
other the norm by which it is judged (and punished). But in the *Quixote* the ideal was notoriously unstable, offering a model for comedy,
for which sheer incongruity—the balance of incompatibles, without
judgment—is the basic principle. They keep shifting back and forth
and the sense one gets is of both/and rather than either/or, of a double
irony rather than "a plague on both your houses." At the end Don
Quixote's recovery and renunciation seem to all around him, including
the reader, to involve a sense of loss, merely confirmed by his death.

But Cervantes moralizes the story, telling us at the beginning and
the end that *Don Quixote* is simply a satire on pernicious books of
chivalry (though he puts these words in the mouths of surrogates—a
"friend" and Cid Hamete Benengeli).

Before the eighteenth century, comedy (Aristotle's low and ugly) had at least to appear to be moral; that is, satire. When in the 1690s moralists attacked the comedies of Etherege, Wycherley, and Congreve as celebrating rakes and seducers, their defenders replied that the rakes and seducers were in fact being satirized. John Dennis's formulation, published as late as 1722, was typical: "How little do they know of the Nature of true Comedy who believe that its proper Business is to set us Patterns for Imitation. For all such Patterns are serious Things and Laughter is the Life, and the very Soul of Comedy. 'Tis its proper Business to expose Persons to our View, whose Views we may shun, and whose Follies we may despise; and by shewing us what is done upon the Comick Stage, to shew us what ought never to be done upon the Stage of the World."[32] It was difficult to find a literary precedent for comedy that was not satire (for example, the "comedies" of Ben Jonson); but there were two notable exceptions—Shakespeare and Cervantes, and primarily the characters of Sir John Falstaff and Don Quixote, both of whom exceeded the theory and called for explanation. Falstaff was a satiric butt who can laugh at himself, his own satirist. Quixote, seen one way, was a satiric object; seen the other way he was a wise man. Quixote served Steele and Addison, in their *Spectator* essays of the early 1700s, as the model for the third figure, Sir Roger de Coverley, and around him a club of comic, rather than ridiculous, figures.

Swift interpreted Don Quixote as a Modern, a "philosopher" who claimed his self-sufficiency while in fact parroting the words of other Moderns. As Addison was quite aware, in the context of the quarrel of the Ancients and Moderns, from which Swift's early satire emerged, one might more reasonably have expected to see Quixote as an Ancient, a vessel of outdated, outmoded "wisdom." This, in fact, is how Addison interprets him in Sir Roger, the elderly Tory gentleman whose "singularities" are "contradictions to the manners of the world." Sir Roger is defined by various Quixotic obsessions from the obsolescent past: He is a relic of the Restoration, an enemy of the Commonwealth (the last play he saw was *The Committee*, an attack on the Rump Parliament), a country gentleman given to hunting and obsessed with a widow (his Dulcinea) who rejected him years ago. Sir Roger is an old Tory, living on antiquated notions of the Cavalier past in a modern Whig world defined by the clear-thinking of the London merchant Sir Andrew Freeport. He imitates, does not initiate, and is slightly daft, therefore not wholly responsible; but there is also a sense in which his delusion casts a sharper light on the "sanity" of the world around him. In practice, he is loved by all, not least by Addison and Steele themselves, though in much the way Quixote is enjoyed by the duke and duchess, as a source of amusing diversion from the more serious business of governing. Sir Roger is an aestheticized, depoliticized version of Swift's mad, self-serving, and seditious Quixote.

Having created a modern Quixote, Addison then, in subsequent essays, redefined satire to correspond to this flawed but lovable character, a figure who elicits sympathetic laughter instead of ridicule—laughter *with* instead of laughter *at* an object. He begins by castigating ridicule, arguing the need to replace satire with comedy because satire is personal, cruel, and malicious. He implies that to satirize Sir Roger, as Swift would have done, is to distort our sense of empirical reality, creating a monster where we know a man.

One strand of the argument against satire was initiated by Steele in essays in the *Tatler*, which preceded the *Spectator*. In no. 242, published 10 October 1710, a few months after the Harley ministry assumed power and Harley's spokesman Swift began his attacks on the Whigs, Steele introduced the argument that there is a true and a false satire.[33] He considers "what true raillery and Satyr were in themselves":

> that Good-Nature was an essential Quality in a Satyrist, and that all the Sentiments which are beautiful in this Way of Writing must proceed from that Quality in the Author. Good-Nature produces a Disdain of all baseness, Vice, and Folly, which prompts them to express themselves with Smartness against the Errors of Men, without Bitterness towards their Persons." (*Tatler* 3: 241)

In another *Tatler* (no. 219, 3: 146) Steele implicates *Don Quixote* itself in the sin of satire: "It has been said," he writes, "the History of *Don Quixote* utterly destroyed the Spirit of Gallantry in the *Spanish* Nation; and I believe we may say much more truly, that the Humour of Ridicule has done as much Injury to the true Relish of Company in *England*."

The attack on personal satire is picked up by Addison in *Spectator* no. 23 (27 Mar. 1711): "Lampoons and Satyrs, that are written with Wit and Spirit, are like poison'd Darts, which not only inflict a Wound, but make it incurable" (1:97). In no. 249 he argues that false satire not only

fails to distinguish the personal from the general but blemishes from
the good qualities (perhaps in abundance) in the same man. It follows
that ultimately it ridicules "virtue": "If the talent of Ridicule were
employed to laugh Men out of Vice and Folly, it might be of some use
to the World; but instead of this, we find that it is generally made use
of *to laugh Men out of Virtue and Good Sense, by attacking every thing
that is Solemn and Serious, Decent and Praise-worthy in Human Life*"
(2:467). In no. 355, on invective, Addison writes that he has been "often
tempted to write Invectives upon those who have detracted from my
Works, or spoken in derogation of my Person . . . but found so many
Motions of Humanity rising in me towards the Persons whom I had
severely treated, that I threw it into the Fire without ever finishing
it (3:323)."[34]

The basis for Addison's reevaluation of satire was Aristotle's remark that personal invective was historically superseded by the greater
generality of comedy. (Similarly, Shaftesbury contrasted the buffoonery of burlesque and personal lampoon with the disinterestedness of
comedy.)[35] Although *Don Quixote* could be accused of ridicule and
burlesque, it was innocent of personal lampoon as well as invective.[36]

Addison develops one argument concerning the author and the
object of satire, replacing personal with general satire, spleen with good
nature. In no. 47 he undertakes a parallel argument concerning the
audience of satire/comedy and its response. These are the essays on
laughter, which begin by quoting in full Hobbes's definition of laughter as ridicule or "Sudden glory." In the central essay, no. 249, Addison
seeks to separate innocent laughter from the laughter of ridicule. Once
again he starts with Hobbes, with laughter regarded as "a Weakness in
the Composition of Human Nature," but then recovers it: "But if we
consider the frequent *Reliefs* we receive from it [laughter], and how
often it *breaks the Gloom* which is apt to depress the Mind, and damp
our Spirits with transient unexpected *gleams of Joy*, one would take care
not to grow too Wise for so great a *Pleasure of Life*" (2:466, emphasis
added). The assumption is that Hobbesian laughter inflates the self-
esteem of the satirist and those for whom he speaks. An indirect expression of satisfaction with the old-established order, this is implicitly
Addison's sense of the Tory satirist. In its place he proposes to redefine
Hobbesian laughter as a positive force, "both amiable and beautiful."

His examples are "the Laughter-loving Dame" Venus and Venus's offspring Mirth. His sources are literary: for Venus, Waller's "The Countess of Carlisle in Mourning" and Horace's *Odes* 2, 8, 12, and, for Mirth, Milton's "heart-easing Mirth, / Whom lovely Venus at a birth / With two Sister Graces more / To Ivy-crowned Bacchus bore" in "L'Allegro" (ll. 13ff.). With this female figure of Comedy, Addison begins to anticipate the connections with nature he will elaborate in the "Pleasures of the Imagination." The metaphor of laughing, he notes, is applied in most languages "to Fields and Meadows when they are in Flower, or to Trees when they are in Blossom" (the "enchanted wood" of no. 413). The laughter of ridicule, he concludes, should be complemented or replaced by another laughter, applied to (or merged with) beautiful natural objects—and with emotions of human love. "This shews that we naturally regard Laughter, as what is in itself both amiable and beautiful." For this reason Venus, the goddess of beauty, has been given the epithet "Laughter-loving" and is called "the Goddess who delights in Laughter." Thus Addison identifies Venus with the comic spirit, aestheticizing laughter in the same way he subsequently aestheticizes the disreputable imagination within the "Pleasures of the Imagination" essays.

Any discussion of comedy begins with the commonplace that it does not exist without laughter; most theories of comedy are affective, theories of the response of the subject, and concerned with the subject's "pleasure" (one of the most common adjectives found in such discussions).[37] Aesthetics is the philosophy of response to beauty (literally, *sense perception* of beauty), which is defined variously as admiration, appreciation, and enjoyment; but, as Addison realized as he formulated these concepts in his "Pleasures of the Imagination," one's response to the comic or ridiculous is analogous to one's response to the beautiful. There is, we have seen, a spectrum of response in *Don Quixote* to the deluded hero, not only *risus* but *admiratio*, from guffaws to Sancho's tight-lipped mirth; and this extends to the responses of Quixote and Sancho as well—for example, to the fulling hammers, when the range is extended to include fear and delight. All of these are aesthetic responses, including laughter, which Addison categorizes as "Pleasures of the Imagination" and subdivides into the Beautiful, the Great, and—the middle area—the Novel, New, Uncommon, and Strange.

One object of this redivision of the Beautiful and the Ugly into a triad was to recover from the Ugly areas not specifically Beautiful (that is, perfect); for example, enthusiasm as the Great and satire as the Novel. But satire comes first. Addison's argument proceeds from the aestheticization of satire to the more general "Pleasures of the Imagination," which subsume laughter as an aspect of the Novel, and the latter is clearly the privileged category in a journal called the *Spectator*. It is through laughter that he defines the surprise and delight of the Novel because, I submit, this was the way Cervantes showed him of doing it (essentially the "Modern" way of dealing with the Novel and Uncommon).

Swift and Addison are agreed that one source of laughter is novelty: we laugh at the new and strange, which can also be the incongruity of, in effect any breach of, the usual order of events—anything novel, uncommon, eccentric; in effect Quixotic. We laugh at the new versus the old, privileging one or the other, or we laugh at the new *and* the old when they are merely juxtaposed.

Swift's laughter is an expression of satisfaction with the old, established order of which he is a part—the order from which this novelty is a deviation and against which this incongruity is an indecorum. He causes us to laugh at the discovery of incongruity of a divisive sort: the importation into one situation of what belongs to another, universe-changing, disrupting, attitude-mixing, the reversal of values, or simply inappropriate behavior. One form this takes is masquerading as something one is not—mimicry, hypocrisy, and self-deception. The incongruity he attacks is the contrast between the rule and the breach of custom. The nonconformist is laughable. On the other hand, Addison's argument is that laughter does not have to be derisive: one can feel *pleasure* at the surprise, affection for the novelty.

Another reason satire/comedy comes first, anticipating the "Pleasures of the Imagination," is because Addison's first order of business was politics. Satire, the transgressive term, clearly refers to the work of the Tory satirists. In the margin of *Spectator* no. 23 attacking lampoons and satires, a contemporary wrote a comment: "The character of Dr. Swift" (1:97n.). Swift's contributions to the *Examiner* had been appearing since November 1710 (satiric attacks on the earl of Wharton were in no. 14, on the duke of Marlborough in nos. 16, 17), and the first *Spectator* appeared on 1 March 1710/11. It was not until late spring 1711 that Addison and Steele acknowledged that they knew Swift was the author, but as early as December 1710 they, and their Whig friends, responded to the *Examiner* attacks on their party leaders, in particular on Marlborough and Wharton, in the Whig journal the *Medley* (referring to the *Examiner* as "the falsest Paper that ever was printed").[38]

The gist of Swift's satire on Marlborough was that he was a skillful general but with glaring defects—his love of money, his desire to be captain-general of the army for life, and his building mania at Blenheim, the huge palace he was erecting at state expense as a monument to his fame. In *Examiner* no. 27 (8 February 1710), Swift acknowledges that Crassus (Marlborough) is "a most successful General, of long experience, great Conduct, and much Personal Courage," but he is "deeply stained with that odious and ignoble Vice of *Covetousness*." Swift calls upon him therefore to abandon this vice and become a "truly Great Man."

In the case of the earl of Wharton, the glaring defect was rakish vice concealed beneath hypocritical piety. Referring to his religious pretensions, Swift coolly notes that "He goeth constantly to Prayers in the Forms of his Place, and will talk Bawdy and Blasphemy at the Chapel Door. He is a Presbyterian in Politics, and an Atheist in Religion; but he chuseth at present to whore with a Papist."[39]

From the point of view of Addison, "such foibles could be exaggerated and distorted" by the Tory party satirists "into the image required for public consumption."[40] Don Quixote was a character of perfect wisdom with one glaring foible, his obsession with chivalry. The obvious response is therefore to create a Tory country gentleman whose foibles make him a humorous character but do not prevent Mr. Spectator and the members of his club from loving him and absorbing him into their society. In the same way, while they continue to praise Swift as "one of the greatest geniuses this age has produced," they attack the idea of vicious personal satire, which is *his* less lovable foible.

In the first *Spectator*, Addison is at pains to describe Mr. Spectator as a disinterested onlooker. While setting out an aesthetic position that distinguishes the satirist from the comic observer, this also implies a political disinterestedness: "I never espoused any Party *with Violence*, and am resolved to observe *an exact Neutrality* between the Whigs and Tories, unless I shall be forc'd to declare my self by *the Hostilities* of either side. In short, I have acted in all the parts of my Life as *a Looker-on*, which is the Character I intend to preserve in this Paper" (1:5, emphasis added). While the word "hostilities" designates Tory satire, "acted," "parts," and "character" introduce the metaphor of theater in which Mr. Spectator has chosen the role of audience rather than actor—a scene of provisional identities and extramural pleasures.[41] Disinterestedness, of course, is precisely what for Addison distinguishes comedy from satire.

disinterestedness distinguishes Comedy from satire

The spectacle, consisting of all London, focuses on Mr. Spectator's club and in particular on Sir Roger de Coverley, Addison's Quixote. Although he is the locus of the argument for comedy over satire, Sir Roger is, of course, thereby satirized more effectively perhaps than Swift had satirized his Whig contemporaries. The disinterested Mr. Spectator introduces Sir Roger in *Spectator* no. 2, in a passage that takes back with one hand what he has just given with the other:[42]

> He is a Gentleman that is [a] very singular in his Behaviour, but [b] his Singularities proceed from his good Sense [i.e., as opposed to Quixote's, from his madness], and are Contradictions to the Manners of the World [i.e., Quixote as idealist, superior to crass actuality], [a] only as he thinks the World is in the wrong [Sir Roger, the bigoted Tory country gentleman]. [b] However, this Humour [i.e., foible] creates him no Enemies, for he does nothing with Sowrness or Obstinacy; and [a] his being unconfined to Modes and Forms, [b] makes him but the readier and more capable to please and oblige all who know him.

This example of *Spectator* comedy, read by a Tory, could have served as a gloss on Pope's character of Addison ("Epistle to Dr. Arbuthnot" [1734]) as one who is accustomed to

> Damn with faint praise, assent with civil leer,
> And without sneering, teach the rest to sneer;
> Willing to wound, and yet afraid to strike,
> Just hint a fault, and hesitate dislike;
> Alike reserv'd to blame, or to commend,
> A tim'rous foe, and a suspicious friend . . . (ll. 201–6)

The crucial, most damning detail in the portrait of Sir Roger is the last: "but [a] there is such a mirthful Cast in his Behaviour, that [b] he is rather beloved than esteemed . . . [and, as a Justice of the Peace] [a] he fills the Chair at a Quarter-Session with great abilities, and [b] three Months ago gain'd universal Applause by explaining a Passage in the game-Act" (7–9). In short, he is not the demonic Quixote of Swift's satire but a trivializer, "rather beloved than esteemed," who is contrasted with his friend Sir Andrew Freeport, the good Whig London merchant (esteemed rather than beloved). Or rather, since Swift's Quixotes are also, and above all, trivializers (even of evil), Addison simply replaces Swift's satiric with his own comic response.

Don Quixote itself, read by Swift as a Tory-Ancient satire on reading the wrong books (that is, modern books with Whig values), is transformed by Addison into a blueprint for Whig-Modern politics. *Key pt.* Cervantes recovered Quixote's madness as a higher insight, above the crude jests and ridicule of the people (noble as well as plebeian) he met on the road. Addison recovers both imagination and satire, for him transgressive terms, as aesthetics; freeing them from the contamination of Puritan-Dissenter-heterodox associations on the one hand, and from Tory-Jacobite-High Church associations on the other.

Both imagination and satire are based on response; and Addison therefore recovers the first as the beautiful, as appreciation and admiration, and the second as comic, disinterested laughter. He recuperates imagination-enthusiasm from the disrepute of the Puritan Left and satire (Swiftean) from the Tory Right as the pleasures of "imagination" and as comedy. In the "Laughter-loving Dame" Addison not only redefines satire but also recovers the demonized figure of the female from Whig satire in the Restoration. The myth involved not only the Stuart threat of a strong monarch and his rakish, libertine courtiers but also the beautiful woman who is the object of their seduction—Charles II's royal "whores," whom he confuses (in Marvell's "Last Instructions to a Painter") with Britannia. Addison redefines the satirized whore as a "Laughter-loving" Britannia.

In the process he produces a positive civil space—creating an aesthetics of the Novel and comedy as a viable genre in a polite society. Taste, manners, and politeness are the ostensible aim of the Novel and "spectatorship," as opposed to the power implicit in the Great (the absolute monarch). But power takes different forms. The *Spectator* is constantly recuperating terms that *seem* to be of power into innocent versions that, however, bring power back in through another door. In theory Addison is at work on a stratagem for discrediting excesses of both Right and Left. Both, however, turn out to be primarily the excesses of the Tories, embodied in their chief spokesman, Swift, in the "Digression concerning Madness" as well as the particularized political satire of the *Examiner*.

Addison *depoliticizes* imagination and satire as he depoliticized *Paradise Lost* in his *Spectator* essays on that subject by aestheticizing it, diverting attention from its antimonarchical and revolutionary (indeed, regicidal) politics to what he designates as its "beauties." He had himself attacked the politically transgressive Milton in his early poem, "An Account of the greatest English Poets" (1694):

> Oh had the Poet ne'er profan'd his pen,
> To varnish o'er the guilt of faithless men;
> His other works might have deserv'd applause!
> But now the language can't support the cause;
> While the clean current, tho' serene and bright,
> Betrays a bottom odious to the sight.[43]

Now he writes essays on each of the twelve books of *Paradise Lost*, describing the "beauties" of that book: "wonderfully poetical, and Instances of that Sublime genius so peculiar to the author."[44] But also, within the context of the political agenda of the *Spectator*, he is cleansing *Paradise Lost* in order to make it the great English national poem—and in this sense, he is repoliticizing it, recovering the crucial Protestant-Whig element, at the center of Milton's myth, which is the liberty of human choice.[45]

The *Spectator*'s aim of teaching the virtues of politeness is yet another aspect of Addison's strategy. Politeness is the recovery of incivility (as in Tory incivility); all of those uncivil aspects of society such as enthusiasm and satire are civilized, for which read Whigized. Addison makes *polite, aestheticized,* and *depoliticized* parallel terms, part of an extraordinarily astute and effective strategy for promulgating a Whig ideology.

Addison's strategy stands out in contrast to that of his collaborator Steele (largely outside the *Spectator*)—misguided because he responded in kind to Swift's Tory satire. No one could meet Swift on his own chosen ground, and it is clear that Addison worked out an ingenious and in the long run successful strategy to counter it, at the same time producing for the Whig party what he would have called an ethos, or the presentation of oneself to the audience in a favorable light, which in this case meant against a negative other. What began as the castigation of satire ends as a more refined but more potent satire.

Addison defines comedy in terms of disinterestedness. Aesthetics itself, from Shaftesbury and Francis Hutcheson onward, was defined in terms of disinterestedness. But as Addison shows, disinterestedness is a pose if it is not a self-delusion; he uses aesthetics for the purpose of politics.

TWO   *Chivalry and Burlesque*

Cervantes "smiled Spain's chivalry away"

The Rev. John Phillips wrote in the preface to his 1687 translation that
Don Quixote is "a pleasant Story, to shew how vainly Youth mispend
their hours in heightning their Amorous Fancies, by reading those
bewitching Legends of *Tom Thumb* and *Amadis de Gaul.*"[1] The more
common observation, however, left out the reading and stated that
Cervantes' satire simply discredited Spanish chivalry. As early as 1690
Sir William Temple cited an "Ingenious *Spaniard* at Brussels" who
"would needs have it that the History of *Don Quixot* had ruined the
Spanish Monarchy":

> After *Don Quixot* appeared, and with that inimitable Wit and Humour
> turned all this Romantick Honour and Love into Ridicule, the *Span-*
> *iards*, he said, began to grow ashamed of both, and to laugh at Fighting
> and Loving, or at least otherwise than to pursue their Fortune or satisfy
> their Lust; and the consequences of this, both upon their Bodies and
> their Minds, this *Spaniard* would needs have pass for a great Cause of
> the Ruin of *Spain*, or of its Greatness and Power.[2]

From Temple to Anthony Ashley Cooper, third earl of Shaftesbury
(Cervantes "destroyed the reigning taste of Gothic or Moorish chivalry"), to Steele ("utterly destroyed the Spirit of Gallantry in the *Span-*

ish Nation"), to Lord Byron ("smiled Spain's chivalry away"), the emphasis was on "the Humour of Knight-Errantry."[3]

The discrediting of Spanish chivalry offered a range for many interpretations. For *chivalric*, in the course of the seventeenth and eighteenth centuries, we read: the untrammeled imagination, usually religious; theatrical behavior or role-playing social pretension; behavior that is inappropriate, anachronistic, and eccentric; behavior so idealized as to show up the crassness of the everyday prudential behavior surrounding it; and the literally chivalric—in *Paradise Lost* (insofar as it reflected the Quixotic model) or in Steele's *Spectator*s and *The Conscious Lovers* (1722), where it signified militarism, a too rigid code of honor, and dueling. In the context of the English Civil War, the defeat of the Cavaliers, and their return in 1660 as wits and rakes (Milton's "Sons of Belial"), *Don Quixote* carried a national significance not unlike the one it was supposed to have had in Spain. The Cavalier mode was reapplied by the Whigs to the Tories as code for Jacobite.

Edwin P. Knowles thinks the story that Cervantes destroyed Spanish chivalry is of Spanish origin, but he believes it first reached England following the Restoration in Rapin's *Réflections sur la Poétique de ce Temps* (1672).[4] As a matter of fact, the popularity of *Don Quixote* in England before the end of the seventeenth century has been somewhat exaggerated, especially if we compare the number of editions published in France during the same period.[5] In the 1680s and 1690s, however, four abridgments appeared, as well as translations of other Cervantes works, leading up to the two new translations of 1700 (Motteux's and Captain Stevens's revision of Shelton's). The first upsurge of interest may have come at the Restoration with the return of the Cavaliers from France, where the *Quixote* was a lively topic of discussion. Only three years later the publication and popularity of *Hudibras*, which turned the *Quixote* into a satire on Puritan Roundheads, most likely drew readers back to the original. In 1711 Ned Ward, a Tory, published a travesty translation of the *Quixote* in hudibrastic couplets and wrote in his dedication that *Don Quixote* was the Spanish *Hudibras* (its fame is "not inferior to that which is so justly due to the flourishing memory of our own English Butler").[6]

Thus the travesty of chivalry begins with that Royalist poem

Hudibras, where it is transformed into religious enthusiasm.[7] But a Whig, the Rev. Mr. Phillips, Milton's nephew and a supporter of Titus Oates (and the author of *Moronides, or Virgil Travestie . . . in Burlesque* [Hudibrastic] *Verse* of 1672), translated *Don Quixote* in the travesty mode of Paul Scarron. It was "now made English according to the humour of our Modern Language," he wrote, noting that Cervantes satirized books of chivalry. Although written in imitation of *Hudibras*, these Whig texts are also answers to Butler's satire, returning Quixote's madness from enthusiasm to chivalry.

The travesty of *Don Quixote* went hand in hand with the English-ing of the Spanish setting—the substituting of English proverbs, lo-cales, and jests for the Spanish. And, though Phillips's performance was not widely read, this interpretation of the *Quixote*, first projected in Shelton's translation, was presumably the one to which Temple referred when he nationalized Cervantes in the 1690s.

One reason the *Quixote* had not caught on in England as rap-idly as in France was that its publication followed too closely upon the threat to England of the Spanish monarchy, the Roman Catholic Church, and the Inquisition in the wake of the attempted invasion by the Spanish Armada.[8] When Defoe suggests in the *Serious Reflec-tions . . . of Robinson Crusoe* that Don Quixote may have been based on the Duke of Medina-Sidonia, he is referring to the fact that Medina-Sidonia commanded the Armada and, therefore, in English eyes was a Quixote.[9]

By the 1670s the Spanish threat had been replaced by the French, with the same ingredients, and after 1688 added to these was the threat of James II's return with the support of the French army. It was during the 1690s that references to the *Quixote* increase and focus on the effect it was supposed to have had on Spanish chivalry; and we can assume that this was partly as a response to the popularity of the prepon-derantly Cavalier interpretation of *Quixote* in *Hudibras*. It was in the 1690s that the Whigs, having ascended to power, began to fashion a myth of nationalism, a vision of English genius. Sir William Temple, William Congreve, and the third earl of Shaftesbury, for example, connected Cervantes' destruction of chivalry by ridicule with English liberty (contra Stuart tyranny) and Quixote's character with the idea that humorous character is a uniquely English phenomenon.

In two senses Sir Roger de Coverley is an English Quixote. In the first he burlesques chivalry. He is associated with Restoration rakes (he "supped with My Lord *Rochester* and Sir *George Etherege*") and with dueling: he "fought a Duel upon his first coming to Town." He was "crossed in Love, by a perverse beautiful Widow" and as a consequence "was very serious for a Year and a half," transferring his sexual drive to beggar and gypsy women, and continuing to wear Restoration costume into the eighteenth century. As a Quixote, disappointed by his Dulcinea, Sir Roger finds his equivalent of knight-errantry in the stereotype of the country gentleman, which was the Whig caricature of the Tory, including the hint of libertinism. His troubles with the widow would have recalled Hudibras's troubles with *his* widow, whom he was courting for her fortune. His Quixotism was, however, humorous and not ridiculous, or at least not in the terms of Swiftean satire.

In a second sense, Sir Roger is a true Quixote *because* he is English. A part of the myth of English nationalism that followed the Glorious Revolution was the notion that the English, in Temple's words, have "excelled both the Modern and the Antient" writers "by Force of a Vein Natural perhaps to our Country, and which with us is called Humour, a Word peculiar to our Language too, and hard to be expressed in any other." Temple is claiming for the English precisely the virtues (for which he acknowledges only Shakespeare) that he had assigned to Cervantes one page earlier. He distinguishes from the "Wits" whose ridicule is "so Malicious, so Smutty, and so Prophane," the "Matchless Writer of *Don Quixot*"—"much more to be admired for having made up so excellent a Composition of Satyr or Ridicule without those Ingredients, and seems to be the best and highest Strain that ever was or will be reached by that Vein."[10]

In 1695 Congreve echoed Temple's words and added that "what appears to me to be the reason of [this national propensity for humor] is the greater Freedom, Privilege, and Liberty which the Common People of *England* enjoy." Congreve also picks up on Temple's "vein" and introduces a metaphor that will inform the discourse of comedy: "Any Man that has a Humour is under no restraint or fear of giving it Vent."[11] By "Humour" he means "A singular and unavoidable manner of doing or saying any thing, Peculiar and Natural to one Man only, by which his Speech and Actions are distinguish'd from those of other men" (3: 248)—words that the eighteenth-century English writers apply above all to two literary figures, Sir John Falstaff and Don Quixote.

The myth Temple and Congreve and other Whigs projected was of a Cavalier ethos brought low by the ridicule of Cervantes—a free expression of a laughter that is essentially English. Against this the Tory version of *Don Quixote* noted that many are "still of opinion that the wonderful Declension of the Spanish Bravery and greatness in this last Century may be attributed very much to [Cervantes'] carrying the Jest too far, by not only ridiculing their Romantic love and Errantry, but by laughing them also out of their Honour and Courage."[12] Ned Ward, in his Hudibrastic translation, returns Quixote to the Puritan Hudibras, noting that Cervantes' moral shows "the ridiculous Vanity of such fanatastical Bravadoes, who, for want of true Magnanimity, only mimick Greatness by a theatrical deportment" ("Epistle Dedicatory"). He is describing a *miles gloriosus*, satirized for his mimicry of a noble model (a military hero, a Cavalier).

Addison synthesizes these views of Don Quixote. Sir Roger, the imitator of the Cavalier ethos in its degenerate Restoration form, also epitomizes Addison's recovery of chivalry (as embodied in the lovable Sir Roger) as another form of English politeness, focused on Sir Roger's country estate—the longest encounter we have with the good knight. He lives, as we might expect, in a Gothic abbey and when Mr. Spectator visits him he finds his familiar spectatorship (the Novel or Uncommon) extended to the Strange. This is the area of Old English superstitions, tales of *faerie*, gypsies, rescues from drowning, and the like.

Comedia: The Canon, the Curate, and Quixote Discuss Romance

In the dialogue between the canon of Toledo, the curate, and Quixote that serves as the climax of part 1, the canon defends the classical Aristotelian theory of poetry against the *romanzi* (by which he means the very "mixed" romances of Ariosto and Boiardo, combinations of love, fantasy, and burlesque). He criticizes the *romanzi* on moral and then formal grounds: they only entertain; they violate the principles of unity and verisimilitude.[13] He is willing to accept the pleasure accrued by reading them, which is the pleasure of variety, but, since the *romanzi* are "solely to amuse and not to instruct," they ought at least to be beautiful: "that beauty which the soul conceives . . . must come from the beauty and harmony that are presented to [the soul] by sight or by the imagination, and nothing that is ugly or inharmonious can give us any pleasure whatsoever" (1.47.425). A romance that represents such beauty is only a hypothetical reality, as Quixote acknowledges in his projection of the beautiful valley in which an enchanted knight wanders, and as further projected in the canon's own futile attempt to write one. It will be as contradictory to reality as Quixote's projection of an ideal Dulcinea brought up against a real peasant maid (2.9–10).

In the following chapter the canon illustrates the deformities of the romance, with which he also associates its popularity, by invoking the even more egregious case of *comedia*. *Comedia*—"our now-a-day comedies" as Shelton translates the Spanish word into its English homonym—are "human comedies" as opposed to the "divine" of the canon's ideal romance. The canon calls them "the disgrace of our *Spanish* wits: For strangers, which do with much punctuality observe the method of comedies, hold us to be rude and ignorant, when they see such follies and absurdities escape us."[14] He gave up his own attempt to write a chivalric romance when he realized that the people who crowded to see the incongruities and improbabilities of *comedia* would surely ignore his "regular" romance, based on principles of harmony and proportion.

Quixote's discussion of life as theater in part 2, chapter 12, when he recalls that his first love was the stage and acting, invokes "the *comedia* that we call life" or the topos of life as a play. In Spanish, as in English, comedy meant simply a stage play with a happy ending.[15] Lopez Pinciano, in *Philosophia Antigua Poetica* (1596), uses *comedia* to translate Aristotle's *komoedia*, defined as the "imitation of characters of a lower type" as opposed to tragedy's characters of high rank; "not, however, in the full sense of the word bad, the ludicrous [*ridiculo*] being merely a subdivision of the ugly. It [*ridiculo*] consists in some defect or ugliness."[16] Thus Pinciano uses *comedia*, referring with Aristotle to the structure of a play, in opposition to tragedy—showing that in this sense *comedia* means both play and comedy.[17]

The curate's reply, defining these stage plays as violations of the "rules," in effect equates *comedia* with romance, and this with Cervantes' Quixotic romance: "What more out of place," says the curate, "than an old man parading his valor, a youth who plays the cringing coward, an eloquent lackey, a page wise in giving counsel, a king turned porter, or a princess serving as a kitchen wench" (48.429–30). At the least, the "old man parading his valor," the "eloquent lackey," and the "princess serving as a kitchen wench" are the defining figures of Cervantes' own *comedia*. In relation to the Aristotelian "rules" of comedy, Quixote is himself deformed—with half an ear, few teeth—and ugly, with cheeks that appear to be kissing each other on the inside; and he is also constantly subject to pratfalls.[18]

Lope de Vega produced hundreds and Cervantes several *comedias* (as well as interludes—*entremeses*—that were performed, as variety, between the acts of plays). To judge by the *comedia* of Lope and Cervantes, many of these plays were essentially Plautine comedies. The Plautine plot involved incongruities (young and old, lovers or parents, clever servant and dumb master) but it was basically a romance plot with characters who are young and highborn—lovers separated, threatened, and happily reunited at the end. The beatings and pratfalls took place on the lower level of the subplot about their servants, plebeian and often ugly or deformed.

Quixote himself has raised the class issue, which from time to time he stresses, noting that Sancho's back is more suitable to the blows they are receiving than his own, which is more accustomed to silks and satins.[19] in his Golden Age speech, Quixote justifies romance as a means of reestablishing the lost social hierarchy (1.11.81–82). He is a *hidalgo*, a country squire, who (as unsympathetic neighbors notice) tries to pass for a *caballero*, a knight: Alonso Quijano calls himself Don Quixote de la Mancha. But as he notices himself, he has taken on the role and punishments that are usually allotted to the servant, the Sanchos of the world of comedy. And his encounters are with these same lower orders, although he believes them to be castellans, knights, and princesses.[20]

Of *Don Quixote*, where the beatings and pratfalls befall the master as well as the servant, we might say that the upper and lower plots (Quixote and Sancho respectively) are joined in one plot, where, as the plot proceeds, the master and servant keep exchanging roles; and the result is both a merging of the traditional double plot (the romance plots are diverted to the digressions, the interpolated tales of young lovers) and the model of a theory of laughter based on incongruity, on the contrasts between servant and master, their appearances and their fates. The discussion of romance-*comedia* concludes with Quixote's evacuation, which can be taken as an ironic reflection of Cicero's definition of comedy as "mirror of Nature" (cited by the canon), applied both to bodily functions and the violation of conventional unities and proportions.

Burlesque and "Grave Irony": Addison, Swift, and Milton

The third earl of Shaftesbury, grandson of the founder of the Whig party, commented on *Don Quixote*: "Had I been a Spanish Cervantes, and with success equal to that comic author, had destroyed the reigning taste of Gothic or Moorish chivalry," he would not have minded that afterward, "when it had wrought its intended effect and destroyed those giants and monsters of the brain," his "burlesque work itself" was "despised and set aside," as he implies such a mode should be. Burlesque, he writes, can be useful in "whetting and sharpening" the reader's palate "for use and practice in the lower subjects," in order to prepare him for "subjects of a higher kind which," he adds, "relate to his chief happiness, his liberty and manhood."[21]

Addison shows why burlesque was one of "the lower subjects." Pursuing his critique of ridicule in *Spectator* no. 249, he distinguishes the "two great Branches of Ridicule in Writing" as "Comedy and Burlesque." "The first ridicules Persons by drawing them in their proper Characters, the other by drawing them quite unlike themselves"; that is, one "represents mean Persons in the Accoutrements of Heroes, the other describes great Persons acting and speaking, like the basest among the people." The first Addison associates with Cervantes, the second with Lucian. *Don Quixote* is identified as the high burlesque, Lucian's *Dialogues of the Gods* as the low—or as mock-heroic and travesty.

Burlesque, as Addison makes clear, was conventionally defined in terms of contrasting discourses: either Dido talks as if she were a fishwife or a fishwife talks as if she were Dido.[22] This was the way burlesque operated in Quixote's employment of chivalric discourse. In the context of his critique of satire in no. 249 Addison sees the burlesque phenomenon as "when an Hero is to be pulled down and degraded"; that is, satirized. But in a larger sense, he disapproves of burlesque and (while retaining the term "ridicule") prefers "comedy" because of the indecorum of persons speaking "quite unlike themselves" *as if* they held a higher social status. For an author to depict a fishwife talking like Dido, or vice versa, changes a person's character— Addison would say, "drawing them quite unlike themselves." It is a kind of playacting, and he reflects something of the Puritan distrust of theatricality—the alteration of one's true character, embodied most shockingly for Addison and Steele in the Italian operas and masquerades (associated with the Swiss impresario Heidegger) to which all levels of London society flocked, often for immoral purposes.

Addison replaces burlesque (as he does satire) with his version of "comedy," pruning the transgressive aspect of theatricality by replacing deformity with "Persons in their proper Characters." He recovers the theatrical situation itself by placing his central intelligence in a spectator who disinterestedly regards life as a theater—essentially a comic play. The danger to the spectator is that, like Quixote, Sir Roger, and later Partridge, he may mistake appearance for reality, involving himself in a burlesque.

But *Don Quixote*, Addison's example of high burlesque, also offered a unique way around the problem of burlesque deformation. Cervantes' most celebrated device, as he was read in eighteenth-century England, was his own voice, his "grave irony" that soberly recounts the contrast between Quixote's discourse of chivalry and his actions. The high burlesque, as Norman Knox has noted, was "a quite natural flowering of simpler methods of ironic praise," that is, blame-by-praise.[23] Cervantes' fame was based on his particularly decorous use of high burlesque as solemnity of style and tone—apparent disinterestedness— in treating a ridiculous situation. Addison, without mentioning Cervantes, supported this positive evaluation in *Spectator* no. 33 on true and false humor: "For as TRUE HUMOUR generally looks serious, whilst every Body laughs about him; FALSE HUMOUR is always laughing, whilst every Body about him looks serious" (1:147).

By the 1750s Richard Owen Cambridge could remark that the

mock-heroic poem "should, throughout, be serious, because the origi-nals are serious; therefore the author should never be seen to laugh, but constantly wear that grave irony which *Cervantes* only has inviolably preserv'd."[24] This, Cervantes' "native dignity," was referred to as "the *true Burlesque*"—"the solemn irony of Cervantes, who is the father and unrivalled model of the true mock-heroic."[25] By midcentury at any rate, high burlesque had been revalued as Cervantes' "solemn irony." This was noted by Charles Jarvis when he justified the style of his trans-lation (1742) by contrast with Motteux's: "nothing can be more foreign to the design of the author, whose principal and distinguishing charac-ter is, to preserve the face of gravity, generally consistent throughout his whole work, suited to the solemnity of a *Spaniard*, and wherein with-out doubt is placed the true spirit of its ridicule."[26]

Don Quixote shows what happens when irony—in its particular form of the mock-heroic—is applied consistently in a narrative, rather than for local effect. But Cervantes' "grave irony," as we have seen, is embodied both in his sober acceptance of Quixote's elevated senti-ments and in Quixote's own discourse. Cervantes' most influential contribution to the English satirists was his embodiment of blame-by-praise irony, or the mock-heroic, in a character who imitates heroic discourse—in words that are played against the gross reality of the world that tests his elevated discourse.

Pace Addison, however, Quixote uniquely represented *both* high and low burlesque, both mock-heroic and travesty: For the first, Qui-xote was an ordinary *hidalgo*, old and decrepit, who aspired to, talked in the diction of, the knight-errant who sees whores as princesses and an inn as a castle; for the second, he was a soi-disant knight-errant who was constantly being dragged down to the lowest body equivalents—broken bones and teeth, purges and vomits, jests and indignities. This doubleness contributed to the doubleness of response to Quixote, be-cause the first points to satire whereas the second might elicit sympathy. But it also offered two versions of Quixote: for the Tories a symbol of the unbridled imagination; for the Whigs a symbol of outmoded chi-valric assumptions. In the first the attack was on religious enthusiasm and the Saints of the Commonwealth years; in the second on Tory-Jacobite ideals traced back to the Stuarts and their Cavalier supporters.

To Swift, burlesque meant showing the physical desire under the elevated concepts of imagination, enthusiasm, and inspiration. But the form he gave burlesque was blame-by-praise irony. After Cervantes, Swift was the most celebrated practitioner of "grave irony" in the eighteenth century. As early as 1727 Hogarth's friend Nicholas Amhurst, in the *Craftsman*, saw *Gulliver's Travels* and *Don Quixote* as similar, not in their plots but in the irony of mock-gravity shared by their style (two years later Pope attributed to Swift "Cervantes' serious air" in *The Dunciad*).[27] Swift's employment of blame-by-praise irony was extended and consistent over many pages; but it was also often, and most characteristically, embodied in the discourse of a fool who believes what he has read.

In the "Apology" (added in 1710) to *A Tale of a Tub* Swift explains why this work was misunderstood and maligned by pointing out, first, that "There generally runs an Irony through the Thread of the whole Book" and, second, by linking irony to parody, "where the Author personates the Style and Manner of other Writers, whom he has a mind to expose" (7, 8). Besides showing that "the Author" merely fills the Cervantes position vis-à-vis Quixote—and both are "personating" the style of other writers—Swift focuses on reading and imitation as the crucial features. The Swiftean imitator naturalizes what Addison refers to as the monstrosity and deformity of the burlesque. At the same time, he shares one characteristic with Addison's Whig revision, and that is the distancing of him from the absolute evil and the qualifying, if not humanizing, of the emblematic figure of past satire.

Quixotic burlesque lived another life in the Country, or opposition, wing of the Whig party. The epic similes Milton attaches to Satan are burlesque—or travesty—comparisons and contrasts; in book 4, for example, they reduce Satan in Eden to a wolf entering the sheepfold and, even more droll, a second-story man climbing over a London rooftop to rob mankind of paradise. Milton operates on a larger scale as well. As the great mediator between Rome and eighteenth-century England, *Paradise Lost* rewrites *The Aeneid*: Satan is a burlesque of Aeneas who transfers empire from the ruins in hell to the new earth God has created, with God (ironically, hardly part of Satan's plan) presiding over his every action as Jove presided over Aeneas's. This is both a "satanic" and a Quixotic parody in the sense that it is Satan's feeble imitation of the divine actions of the Trinity—as, again, when Satan, Sin, and Death, a parodic Trinity, construct a bridge connecting hell and earth for the easy transmission of sin and death to the descendants of Adam, outrageously imitating on their low level God's Creation.[28]

The Turnus role, that of Aeneas's antagonist, is also parodied by Satan—a role called for in the Virgilian epic, recalling, in the seventeenth-century context, the Civil War. Like Dido, his female counterpart, Turnus represents the anachronistic sense of heroism as chivalry and knight-errantry as opposed to the *pietas* of Aeneas, the Roman ethos of duty and self-sacrifice. Milton's Satan embodies an outmoded attachment to a belief in chivalry: the "long and tedious havoc fabl'd Knights / In Battles feign'd,"

> Or tilting furniture, emblazon'd Shields,
> Impreses quaint, Caparisons and Steeds;
> Bases and tinsel Trappings, gorgeous Knights
> At Joust and Tournament

These Milton opposes to "the better fortitude / Of Patience and Heroic Martyrdom / Unsung" (9, ll. 30–37).

Paradise Lost, the *other* great model for eighteenth-century writers, could be read as a tragic version of *Don Quixote*. The similarities—the Quixotic nature of Satan—may have struck Milton, himself a satirist of no mean ability, and in *Paradise Lost* the author of a work that parodies and mixes one genre after another (pastoral, tragedy, mockepic) as occasion requires.[29] Satan and Quixote are sublime and comic versions of the same figure. In both cases, delusion is tested against the real (God's) world; but for Satan there is finally no ambiguity, and the progression is reversed. Satan appears heroic in the early books of *Paradise Lost*, degenerating through cormorant, sheep, mist, and toad to serpent; while Quixote grows increasingly sympathetic and his values more positive as the world seems coarser and crueler. Satan, the "Prince of Liars," is of course primarily a hypocrite, who can deceive even angelic presences, but over and above that he shares Quixote's conviction that his imagination corresponds to some reality that is not totally subordinated to God's.

Addison draws attention to the "mock-majesty" of Satan (*Spectator* no. 309; 3:114). But he criticizes the comic elements of *Paradise Lost*—the "Sentiments which raise Laughter, [which] can very seldom be admitted with any decency into an Heroic Poem, whose Business is to excite Passions of a much nobler Nature." He mentions cases when Homer and Virgil "lapsed into the Burlesque Character," but "The only Piece of Pleasantry in *Paradise Lost*," he writes, "is where the Evil Spirits are described as rallying the Angels upon the Success of their new invented Artillery," and this is "most exceptionable"—nothing but a string of puns (no. 279, 2:589–90). However, from such passages as the one on Satan's chivalry, and the comic aspects of the war in heaven (which Addison singles out as examples of wit in *Paradise Lost*), as well as Milton's association of chivalry with the Cavaliers in the Restoration court, and with the help of Cervantes, Addison and Steele construct their Sir Roger de Coverley.

Satan's helplessness—his inability even to lift his head off the fiery lake without the permission of God the Father—is part of the myth of recovery involved in the Son's redemption of man. In the particular version of Quixotism described by Milton, the witty "evil" of Satan is transformed by the Son—and, by analogy, by the "inspired" poet—into "goodness, grace and mercy"; which, in terms of the poet, is into art, the art of the epic poem *Paradise Lost* itself. This is not only the model Pope uses in *The Dunciad*, another work about the perversion of creation (literary creation), to show that a poet can recover even the trash of the dunces; it serves Addison, at least partly because of its Christian context, perhaps more for its Miltonic, as the model for his recoveries in the *Spectator*, and specifically of the reputation of the poet as regicide and the political dimension of the poem *Paradise Lost*.

Milton's burlesque destruction of Satan theologically represents a recovery, but politically (as Addison and his contemporaries realized) it was subversive of the Restoration government. A similarly reductive burlesque was applied more directly to the court, in the same years Milton was writing, by his friend Andrew Marvell in "Last Instructions to a Painter" and other satires. There is no better example of First Whig burlesque than Rochester's comparison of Charles II's scepter to his penis, with the resemblance residing in the fact that his mistresses, by way of Charles's lechery, can control the one with the other.[30]

Graphic Equivalents of Burlesque: Quixote and Hogarth's Hudibras

The earliest English illustrators of *Don Quixote* produced crude demotic representations of Quixote, Sancho, and the other comic characters. The first sophisticated illustrations were by the French artist Charles-Antoine Coypel, painted as cartoons for tapestries, engraved and published in a deluxe folio in Paris in 1724.[31] Coypel's solution for comic equivalents of the scenes without losing the gravity of Cervantes' style was to model them on Watteau's *fêtes champêtres,* including the cloudy allegorical representations that complement the realistic figures (as in Watteau's *Pelerinage à l'Isle de Cythère*).[32]

The English illustrations of Hogarth and John Vanderbank, made circa 1726, were very different. Though the artists would have read the translation of Shelton or Motteux, their illustrations reflect the Shaftesburian aesthetics of John, Viscount Carteret, who sponsored the edition and whose views also influenced Charles Jarvis's translation.[33] Vanderbank's illustrations were used in both editions—Carteret's, which was finally published in 1738, and the Jarvis translation of 1742.[34] Hogarth's illustrations were (with one exception) not used and only published, with captions added, after his death (probably after 1767).[35] Whether they were intended to compete with Vanderbank's or to supplement them, they adhered to Carteret's program. They consisted of seven scenes in part 1, beginning with "The First Adventure" and ending with the disguising of the curate and barber (figs. 1, 8). Only the last did not duplicate a scene illustrated by Vanderbank.

In the Vanderbank drawing for "The First Adventure," signed and dated 1726, Quixote wears a full suit of armor (fig. 2). In the engraving he wears only a breastplate, Quixote's one distinguishing piece of clothing in Hogarth's illustrations; whereas Vanderbank consistently clothes him in a full suit of armor. (The only exception, for both artists, is when Quixote appears in mufti.) The breastplate does appear in Vanderbank's portrait of Alonso Quijano, engraved by George Vertue and dated 1723 (fig. 3): it is hanging on the wall above Quijano's fireplace, and Quijano, seated and contemplative, is fixedly gazing at it. The armor is that of his great-grandfather, which (however, according to Cervantes) "for ages had lain in a corner, moldering and forgotten" (1.1.28). But this breastplate is the armor Hogarth gives him when, as Don Quixote, he sallies forth.[36]

Apparently Hogarth began the project employed by Tonson, the publisher of Carteret's edition, to engrave Vanderbank's drawings, either to supplement or supplant the engravings of Gerard Vandergucht. At some point he decided to undertake an alternative series of his own, introducing variations. (He had submitted illustrations for Tonson's 12mo edition of *Paradise Lost* in 1725—again unsuccessfully.) An alternative explanation, that he wanted to share the job with Vanderbank rather than replace him, does not stand up: his distinct version of Quixote could not have cohabited with Vanderbank's.

Hogarth not only replaced Vanderbank's armor but elongated his squat Quixote and altered the poses of the two women and the innkeeper and the structure of the house in the distance (whereas Vandergucht copied Vanderbank's drawings directly; if he modified details he did not change the proportions of the figures). This engraving presents a slender and handsome Quixote, a dapper innkeeper, and two prostitutes genteel enough to deceive a saner man than Quixote.

Hogarth

This is the first illustration in the volume (of both the 1738 and 1742 editions) following the portrait of Quixote by Vanderbank and engraved by George Vertue, dated 1723. We might suppose that Carteret's project was under way as early as 1723; that by 1726 Vanderbank had finished his drawings and Hogarth was approached to engrave them (he had studied at Vanderbank's academy from 1720): and that he undertook the first scene, turned in the finished copperplate to Tonson, and Vanderbank rejected it on the grounds that Hogarth had taken too great liberties with his drawings. At any rate, Tonson kept this copperplate, presumably paying for it, and it was not replaced by an engraving by Vandergucht. This would explain why it could not appear with Hogarth's six other illustrations for *Don Quixote*.[37]

Five of the six correspond to Vanderbank's drawings, but with ever greater variations.[38] For example, "The Funeral of Chrysostom" brings Marcela down from the hill on which Vanderbank places her to confront the mourners, Quixote, and Sancho on their own level. In "The Freeing of the Galley Slaves" Hogarth turns Vanderbank's static scene (the figures lined up like a row of cards) into a major confrontation on horseback between a prominent Quixote and the guards (frontispiece); and by this time he has produced a finished drawing of his own, which suggests that he was making a formal proposal to Tonson.[39] His last illustration is of a scene not included in Vanderbank's series, the masquerade of the curate and barber (fig. 8), for which he also made a preparatory drawing.[40]

Hogarth's intrusion fits with what we know of him. A few years later he acted in the same way after Jacopo Amigoni had secured the commission for the St. Bartholomew's Hospital paintings; he offered to paint them gratis, and in this case he secured the commission.[41] That the other six *Quixote* engravings were finished and (unlike the trial run of the first plate) signed *invenit et sculpsit* (whereas "The First Adventure" is unsigned) suggests that he contemplated an independent alternative set of illustrations.

Hogarth may have chosen his scenes—each still roughly based on Vanderbank's drawings, but with "improvements"—to show off the range of an artist best known for his burlesque style. The great comic scenes one would expect to see are not illustrated by either artist: Quixote's attack on the windmills, the sheep, and the puppet show.[42] Vanderbank, who made twenty-four plates for part I alone, illustrated far more scenes from the romance stories than from the comic, and the latter are merely descriptive. The explanation lies in the rationale for Carteret's edition. In his "Dedication" published with the text, Carteret explains that he admires Cervantes as "one of those inestimable figures who . . . by the fertility of his immortal genius, has produced (albeit through burlesque) the most serious, useful, and salutary effects that can be imagined."

Carteret's politics were Whig. Cervantes' "salutary effects" are the discrediting of Spanish chivalry—which was also the one feature of *Don Quixote* noticed by those other staunch Whigs, Temple, Shaftesbury, and Steele, who referred to the Cavalier ideal and its degeneration into the Restoration "rake."[43] The Whigs continued to associate *Don Quixote* and Quixote's madness of knight-errantry with the Jacobite-Tory nostalgia for the Cavaliers. There may be some significance in Carteret's undertaking his edition of the *Quixote* following the Jacobite uprising of 1715 and the Atterbury "plot" of 1722. Henry

Sacheverell, the High Church preacher whose sermon and subsequent trial (1710) had brought down the Whig ministry, was a Jacobite hero who was referred to by the Whigs as Don Quixote.[44]

Carteret's position is clarified in the "Advertisement concerning the Prints" written by Dr. John Oldfield, a friend of Carteret's who apparently instructed the artists.[45] Oldfield indicates how important the illustrations were to Carteret. The French illustrations of Coypel were rejected, he says, because of their "injudicious" choice of subject; that is, "gross and unlikely" incidents such as the attacks on the windmill and the flock of sheep.[46] These scenes, "by being set immediately before the eye, become too shocking for the belief." Rather than the "extravagance and improbability" of these scenes, the illustrator should focus instead on the scenes that give "occasion for some curious and entertaining expression," which are "the most desireable and amusing." "Entertaining expression" is the key phrase, evoking *l'expression des passions*, the central principle of history painting according to the theorists of the French Academy. Such illustrations, Oldfield says, are "capable of answering a higher purpose, by representing and illustrating many things, which cannot be so perfectly expressed by words" (1.xxvi). Citing Rembrandt and Raphael as models, he envisions English book illustration as a form of history painting. By stressing the dignity of the subject, he proposes to raise illustration from a supplementary status to the level of a high art form.[47]

Aesthetically Carteret was part of the Burlington circle, with a neoclassical program that followed the doctrine of Shaftesbury in aesthetic theory and Palladio, Inigo Jones, and Colen Campbell in practice. The fact is significant that the frontispiece portrait of Cervantes commissioned by Carteret (engraved by Vertue, dated 1723) is by Burlington's chief protégé William Kent.[48] But while Carteret regarded a respectful representation of Don Quixote as necessary if the artist was to follow decorum (as the architect follows the Vitruvian orders) and distinguish the noble knight from his plebeian and comic retainer, he may also have seen Cervantes in the context of his own political career. Engaged in an unsuccessful rivalry with Walpole for supreme power, he found himself outmaneuvered at every turn by his crafty opponent. "Exiled" in 1724 to Ireland as lord lieutenant, he was in the difficult situation of having to deal with the Irish, Wood's Halfpence, and his friend Swift. He has Vanderbank in his frontispiece represent Cervantes as a classicized figure of Hercules of the Twelve Labors, allegorically Heroic Virtue. He has Oldfield explicate the design, specifying that it is, in fact, Cervantes' own "chivalry" that overcomes the monsters: "our author's chivalry has, in a great measure, put an end to the pernicious effects of the conflicts with them." The allegory, which strangely echoes Swift's *Battle of the Books* (1704), has Hercules "driving away the monsters that had usurped the seat of the *Muses*, and reinstating them in their ancient possession of it." Clearly there is a problem here, since it is books of chivalry that Carteret claims Cervantes to be defeating in *Don Quixote*. Oldfield gets around this difficulty by adding that chivalry serves "to set forth the humorous nature of our author's performance" by permitting him to don the mask of raillery and satire (1.xxi–xxii). But at bottom he has turned *Don Quixote* into another battle of the Ancients and Moderns in which he associates his noble patron with Heroic Virtue battling the Walpolean vices (datable to the first year of the organized opposition to Walpole).

The evidence of both the Vanderbank and Hogarth illustrations supports the supposition that the object was to idealize, elevate, and dignify the Cervantean action. There is none of the "burlesque" that Carteret condemns. Disparaged by everyone from Shaftesbury to Arthur Murphy, partly because it was utilized by the most brilliant Tory-Jacobite satirists of the age, burlesque was to be avoided.[49] But to omit burlesque in illustrating *Don Quixote* was to avoid the essential contribution of the novel to English literature and art.

Shaftesbury and Carteret saw burlesque as satire, its object ridicule and the representation of deformity.[50] Carteret distinguished from burlesque Cervantes' inimitable art of irony ("inimable arte de Ironia," 1:iii). Carteret's *ironia* was simply a translation of the English irony: there was no discussion of this term in Spain, only of *burlesco*. By midcentury, Cervantes' grave irony was being referred to in England as "the *true Burlesque*."[51]

If we study the iconography of breastplate and armor we discover that Vanderbank's elaborate suit of armor is in fact copied (down to the leggings) from Van Dyck's *Charles I on Horseback* (fig. 4), which existed in many copies, painted and engraved, in the early eighteenth century.[52] Vanderbank, presumably at the insistence of Carteret (since he had already introduced the breastplate in Quijano's study), made Quixote into a Cavalier, specifically based on the Cavalier-of-Cavaliers, Charles I, and so associated him with the Pretender and the Cavaliers: an archaic anachronism.[53]

Hogarth's breastplate remains to be explained. Cervantes makes clear that Quixote wore a full suit of armor by the fact that the one missing piece was a closed helmet, a helmet with visor; there was "only a morion, or visorless headpiece, with turned-up brim of the kind foot soldiers wore" (1.1.28).[54] I am not aware of any representation of Quixote before or since Hogarth's that shows him in such simple attire, indeed of a common soldier.[55] This is the way Parliamentary soldiers were popularly supposed to have looked, as contrasted with Royalist soldiers. In *Memoirs of a Cavalier* (1720) Daniel Defoe identifies Cromwell as commander of "a regiment whom he armed *cap-à-pie à la cuirassier.*"[56] In fact, they were hardly distinguishable, their outfitting being at the expense of their commanding officer, who usually wore elaborate armor himself (or at least had himself painted in full armor).[57]

Putting Quixote in the breastplate of a common soldier Hogarth makes him a Whig rather than an armor-clad Tory. But what he has overlooked or ignored is the Whig view of Cervantes, as the destroyer of chivalry, and so Quixote as the object of satire, burlesqued by his lobster-like armorplate. It seems likely that the indecorum of portraying Quixote in a breastplate was enough to have his illustrations rejected by Carteret. It does not seem possible that a literal-minded Hogarth simply followed what he saw in the one extant Vanderbank illustration of 1723, which showed only the breastplate hanging on the wall. (The rest of the armor, Vanderbank must have assumed, "lay in a corner, moldering and forgotten.")

There is no question that Hogarth idealizes Quixote. He does not want the burlesque effect of Charles I's armor but rather the simplicity of an ordinary Roundhead soldier. Vanderbank's Quixote also carried over the long hair from Van Dyck's Charles I, whereas the locks of Hogarth's Quixote, like those of Milton's Adam (another anti-Cavalier), "hung . . . not beneath his shoulders broad" (*Paradise Lost*, 4.302–3). My guess is that he intends to project a plebeian Quixote with memories of the Model Army and the "Ironsides"—a term first applied to Cromwell by Prince Rupert after the battle of Marston Moor and then transferred to his troopers, significantly for Quixote a regiment of cavalry. He is redefining Quixotism in terms of a humble social order, egalitarian political theories, and spiritual values that are now out-dated—values that were heavily antipapist and anticlerical. The soldiers of the Model Army were particularly remembered for their acts of iconoclasm, which included baptizing a horse or pig in a font filled with urine, stabling horses in churches, and even relieving themselves inside churches (as Hogarth was to do on the door of a church in Kent in June 1732).[58] Quixote is, of course, by any definition an iconoclast. These qualities Hogarth associates with an idealism he identifies with the Old Whiggery of the Shaftesburians, now outmoded and discredited in the reign of Sir Robert Walpole. It was in the second half of 1726 that Hogarth joined the opposition forming against Walpole.

Hogarth follows Coypel, whose illustrations for *Don Quixote* were a comic equivalent of *l'expression des passions,* representing the reactions to a comic rather than heroic scene—though Quixote's armor and his heroic gestures remind the viewer of the analogy with history painting.[59] Coypel showed, for example, the spectrum of comic responses to Sancho's being tossed in the blanket and Quixote's plight when, at Maritornes's urging, he stands with his feet on his horse's back and his hand tied to the window. Most significant for Hogarth, he showed the responses to Quixote's attack on the puppet theater (fig. 9).[60]

In one scene (fig. 7) Hogarth places Sancho on a distant hillock, observing and responding with either laughter or astonishment (it is not clear which) to Quixote's mad attack on the barber over his basin, which Quixote believes is Mambrino's helmet. In the more elaborate scenes (Quixote freeing the galley slaves and encountering Cardenio and the goatherd) Hogarth follows Coypel, though perhaps more successfully invoking history because his forms are monumental, his figures tending to fill the picture space, whereas Coypel's invoked Watteau's more modest *fêtes champêtres.* Hogarth's contrasts between monumental and comic (baroque and demotic) forms, however, do not deflate Quixote but only isolate Sancho.

The most elaborate of the spectra of expressions is the scene in the inn with the responses of Maritornes, the innkeeper's daughter, and Sancho, heightened by chiaroscuro (fig. 5). In this scene Hogarth produces virtually a mirror image of Vanderbank's illustration (fig. 6). Vanderbank's came first and Hogarth attempted to outdo him. Indeed, Vanderbank's illustrations can also be said to follow the principle of *l'expression des passions*, though, compared with Hogarth's, the effect is less emphatic. Hogarth increases the chiaroscuro by centering the torch and thereby illuminating the faces where Vanderbank had illuminated only the backs of heads, and intensifying the contrasts between the comic and the idealized characters.

The exaggeration of feature and expression of the comic figures owes its authority to Cervantes' description of Maritornes in this scene, which Hogarth extends to the other servant as well: "[A] lass from Asturia, broad-faced, flat-headed, and with a snub nose; she was blind in one eye and could not see very well out of the other. To be sure, her bodily graces made up for her other defects: she measured not more than seven palms from head to foot, and, being slightly hunchbacked, she had to keep looking at the ground a good deal more than she liked" (1.16.115). In his depiction of comic characters Hogarth follows more closely Cervantes' description of Maritornes than does Vanderbank, who gives her a straight nose and no hump.

Most strikingly, in Vanderbank's and later Hayman's illustrations of Quixote's meeting with "Dulcinea," none of the peasant maids is shown with a blemish or a flattened nose. The illustrators merely contrast a beautiful Quixote with an ugly Sancho—a slender figure with Lines of Beauty and a round, plebeian, and ugly figure—and add three buxom country women. (Coypel had added one indecorous detail: "Dulcinea" is about to brain Quixote for his impertinence.)

The meeting with "Dulcinea" was a scene not illustrated by Hogarth, who never reached part 2. But in his rendition of the scene in the inn, the ugly servant woman who is rubbing ointment in Quixote's wound (the ointment jar is held by the innkeeper's beautiful daughter), is given a decidedly snub nose; Maritornes, who only holds the light, has a retroussé nose. This servant succors Quixote as the noseless servant will succor the Harlot. And in the illustration of the freeing of the galley slaves, while Quixote fights the guard, the ugly, dwarfish Sancho does the freeing of the prisoners. This is not the scene of mistaken identities Fielding would take up at the end of *Joseph Andrews* and Smollett and Hayman emphasize in the edition of 1755 but a pathetic scene in which an ugly servant woman succors Quixote by rubbing ointment into his wounds that anticipates Hogarth's *Good Samaritan* of 1736.[61] Violent action is not a component of comedy for Carteret—but then neither is it for Hogarth, as it will be for Fielding and Smollett.[62]

Hogarth's illustrations are comic in the specific sense that he plays with different forms, contrasting a dignified figure with an ugly one. Quixote and the innkeeper's daughter are contrasted with Maritornes, another servant woman, and Sancho—and Sancho seems to be recoiling from an amorous look from Maritornes, their figures balancing each other in the foreground (fig. 5). This would appear to be an incipiently aesthetic rather than comic effect (there is no satiric effect in these illustrations). We are shown the dignity of Quixote as opposed to the comedy of Sancho, or the beauty of Quixote and the ugliness-deformity of Sancho and Maritornes (as opposed to the farcical battling of the two by Smollett-Hayman). The episode of Mambrino's helmet is comic in the sense of Quixote's action being responded to by Sancho's laughter or astonishment—but the fact that Sancho is literally *at a distance* shifts the emphasis from comic contrast toward aesthetic disinterestedness. The result is an aesthetic fable, or the announcement of an aesthetics of comedy.

Drawing attention to the predominantly aesthetic effect of Hogarth's book illustrations for *Don Quixote* of course draws attention to this aspect of *Don Quixote* itself—to its variety of affect and its emphasis on affect.

The last scene of *Don Quixote* that Hogarth illustrated (not drawn by Vanderbank and thus presumably not stipulated by Oldfield) finds comedy in the masquerading of the curate and the barber (fig. 8). This, the contrast of two different characters or aspects of character, of conflicting and mixed roles, is Hogarth's central idea of a comic situation. Sancho observing Quixote from a distance as he attacks the barber is, of course, only another form of the same theatrical situation. Although Oldfield did not permit his artists to illustrate either the curate's masquerading (which was a kind of burlesque) or Quixote's attack on the puppet show, he did note that illustrations "in some measure, receive the advantage of a dramatick representation" (1.xxvi).

This was one of the opinions Hogarth also absorbed from Jonathan Richardson's art treatises and put into practice. But Richardson, the Shaftesburian disciple, faulted the stage because it "never represents things truly"—the spectator is always aware of the discrepancy between the actor and the Oedipus or Caesar he plays.[63] This was precisely the comic discrepancy Cervantes, followed by Addison and Hogarth, focused upon.

Hogarth's earliest and latest references to *Don Quixote* are to the quintessential scene of theatricality, Quixote's attack on the puppet show. The earliest was in December 1724 in *The Mystery of Masonry brought to Light by the Gormogons* (fig. 10), in which Hogarth introduces Sancho and Quixote into a scene of contemporary London folly *as if* it were the famous puppet show. He borrows his figures from Coypel's "Don Quixote Attacks the Puppet Show," which had been published earlier in the year in Paris (fig. 9); he copies Sancho and Quixote, showing their responses to the parade of Gormogons (his parody of a splinter of Freemasonry led by the Jacobite duke of Wharton) with which he has replaced the puppet show and its threatened princess.[64] Politics enters with the puppet show and continues two years later with the twelve large plates for Butler's *Hudibras* (1726).[65]

In the *Quixote* illustrations Hogarth goes well beyond Vanderbank's smooth and bland designs, evolving (especially in Quixote's encounters with the barber and the galley slaves) compositions that, relying on baroque conventions, are genuinely monumental. What he could have carried to the extreme of burlesque he does not; this is apparent because in his large plates for *Hudibras* he did produce burlesque illustrations.

It was in these plates (presumably on the model of Coypel's independent series of plates for *Don Quixote*) that Hogarth found a graphic equivalent of the irony and parody of Cervantes' text, and indeed the morality. Oldfield, we recall, objected to such scenes as Quixote's attack on the windmills and the sheep because, "by being set immediately before the eye, [they] become too shocking for the belief." This would apply to the scene of Quixote attacking the sheep or Sancho being tossed in the blanket. With the windmills, however, he objected to Coypel's solution to the problem of placing these "shocking" scenes "immediately before the eye," which was "by representing them with the heads and hands of giants, the better to reconcile you to the extravagance of the knight's mistaking them for such: as, for the same ingenious reason, he might have put the flock of sheep into armour, to countenance the like mistake in relation to them" (1.xxvi). Coypel does not actually show Quixote attacking the windmills; he only, in his first plate, includes a cloudy windmill with a giant's head. This introductory plate shows Quixote sallying forth into an allegorical landscape—and presumably is meant to suggest Quixote's imagination. The allegory is the landscape as he sees it. He is conducted by baroque figures of Folly and Love (a Cupid) to indicate the extravagance of his love of Dulcinea. The last plate, Quixote's death, is similarly allegorized by the departure of Folly and the arrival on a cloud of Wisdom. Coypel is, of course, seeking a graphic equivalent of Quixote's madness.

Hogarth eschews allegorical figures. He places Hudibras, a small, misshapen figure, in the midst of a group of rustics who, in his eyes, are carrying out the crowd ritual known as a Skimmington;[66] but he depicts the scene in the composition of the procession of heroic revelers in Annibale Carracci's celebrated *Marriage of Bacchus and Ariadne* (figs. 11, 12).[67] The echo is burlesque: what better heroic parallel for a Skimmington, in which the mock husband and wife are carried in procession, than a Bacchus and Ariadne? Ariadne, jilted by Theseus and rescued by Bacchus, is here realized in the scold berating her cuckolded husband. The important point is that the forms of the baroque serve as the graphic equivalent of Quixote's madness. And this model, allusive and parodic, served Hogarth for placing his own contemporaries, who are also Quixotes in their poses of heroic and biblical delusion.

He adapts Coypel's method of externalizing Quixote's imagination but, working as he did in the context of Swift, Pope, and Gay, he represents the style rather than the allegory of the baroque; he employs graphic parody the equivalent of Cervantes' conscious (i.e., Quixote's unconscious) verbal parody.[68] He exaggerates the baroque forms of his *Quixote* illustrations and adds specific echoes of well-known Italian paintings.

He advertised the twelve plates of *Hudibras* as "(the Don Quixot of this Nation) describing in a Plesant Manner the Humor and Hypocrisy of those Times."[69] The reference to "those Times" suggests a Tory project: there is no question that Hudibras and Ralpho are Presbyterian and Independent respectively. The frontispiece, allegorical like Vanderbank's for Carteret's *Quixote*, shows figures of Rebellion, Hypocrisy, and Ignorance following at the tail of a cart drawn by Hudibras and Ralpho.

On the other hand, it is Hogarth's ingenious strategy to associate by means of high burlesque (the mock-heroic) the imaginary world of Quixote-Hudibras with the idealizing of history painting; and history painting for him (again, a point of contact with Whig politics) was aimed primarily at glorifying the "chivalry" of kings, wars, and the church—an absolute monarch, the Roman Catholic Church, and painting of the Counter-Reformation Baroque. The apotheosis of the Stuarts was to be seen in the paintings of the Whitehall Banqueting House and in engraved copies. By the same token, the apotheosis of the Protestant Succession in Greenwich Hospital, by Hogarth's mentor Sir James Thornhill, was presumably from their point of view a modified, native English baroque. The baroque painting of Renaissance-Catholic Italy was incidentally the art collected by the Shaftesburian connoisseurs, but the baroque architecture (even of English architects like Wren and Hawksmoor) was condemned as "gothic" by Shaftesbury, Burlington, and their followers and replaced by Palladian neoclassicism.

When he was not referred to as the Shakespeare of painters, Hogarth was said to be "the *Cervantes* of his Art, as he has exhibited with such a masterly Hand the ridiculous Follies of human Nature. In many of his Pieces there is such a grave and couched Kind of Humour, that it requires a discerning Eye to perceive the several latent Beauties; and he may be said to be the first, who has wrote comedy with his pencil." These are the terms usually associated with Cervantes' "grave irony" in this period, and they are prefixed with the statement that "Hogarth, like a true Genius, has formed a new School of Painting for himself"; that is, comic, or Cervantian painting.[70]

Hudibras, as the graphic equivalent of Quixotism, reappears in Hogarth's first "modern moral subject," *A Harlot's Progress* (1732), which is the story of a young woman from the country who, presumably having read the romances of amorous intrigue that were then popular (and that a few years later served as the object of attack that helped to define the new genre of novel written by both Richardson and Fielding), becomes a "lady" by going into keeping and, on the side, taking a lover.[71]

Already, however, Hogarth continues the graphic artist's strategy, begun in the *Hudibras* illustrations, of replacing books with paintings. These are both the allusions to paintings of the sort that defined Hudibras's madness—Hudibras in the pose of a triumphal process, the Harlot in the pose of the Virgin in an Annunciation scene; and the copies of paintings with which the Harlot, imitating her keeper, decorates her walls.

Hogarth's most fully developed Quixote-Hudibras is Tom Rakewell in *A Rake's Progress* (1735), which ends with both Rakewell and his discarded wife Sarah in the pose of Christ and Mary in a *Pietà*. To underline the theatricality of the plot, Hogarth introduced the *Rake* with a subscription ticket and a pendant called *Southwark Fair*, both about audiences and playacting.[72] It is also probably significant that following his "progress" of a young woman whose images include a religious medal of a sort that probably labels her a Roman Catholic and even a Jacobite, Hogarth treats that Whig symbol of Cavalier decadence, the Restoration Rake. But Rakewell is, as in Steele's description of a rake in *Spectator* no. 27, not the rake himself but merely one of those who are the rake's "Mimicks and Imitators," "little Pretenders," who affect rakishness.[73] He is satirizing what he calls "second-hand Vice" and "the Fatality (under which most Men labour) of desiring to be what they are not," which "makes 'em go out of a Method in which they might be receiv'd with Applause, and would certainly excel, into one, wherein they will all their Life have the Air of Strangers to what they aim at."

In Hogarth's first plate (echoing in some ways "The Curate and the Barber") Rakewell exchanges his clothes for those of a rake. In the next, however, he has become a "connoisseur," and he chooses Venus over Minerva and Juno because he collects such Old Master paintings as this one of *The Judgment of Paris*, which have taught him to choose Venus. He implies that Rakewell, by collecting such false models (essentially a form of idolatry), will believe in the miracles they propagate and (again recalling Steele's "Mimicks and Imitators") model his life on their assumptions. Graphically, the mediated desire of Hogarth's Rakewell is indicated not by books but by the pictures he chooses to hang on his walls, as in the *Hudibras* plates Hudibras and Ralpho seemed to be stepping into a painting by Carracci.

Hogarth's strongly anti-Catholic and anticlerical consciousness equated these evils with the Old Master paintings that represented them: for Hogarth an example of Counter-Reformation baroque in art, popery in religion, and Jacobitism in politics.

all these evils associated for Hogarth.

"Affectation": Fielding

Fielding was called "the English Cervantes,"[74] and he affirms on the title page of *Joseph Andrews* (1742) that it is "Written in Imitation of The *Manner* of Cervantes, Author of *Don Quixote.*" In the preface—the foundational document of his, or the comic, branch of the English "novel"—he starts with a large generic designation for "this kind of Writing, which I do not remember to have seen hitherto attempted in our Language" (that is, versus Cervantes' Spanish). He is responding to the canon of Toledo's suggestion that "the epic may be written in prose as well as in verse" (1.47.428) with his own "comic Epic-Poem in Prose," which he defines by analogy with Hogarth's "comic History-Painting."

Fielding uses "Comedy" in the theatrical sense based on Aristotle's contrast of tragedy and epic; he proposes to replace a stage comedy (the genre on which his reputation was based in the 1730s) with a "comic Epic-Poem in Prose."[75] Since comedy, as opposed to tragedy or epic, represents "Persons of inferiour Rank, and consequently of inferiour Manners," Fielding says he will represent "the Ludicrous instead of the Sublime." This leads him to introduce the "Burlesque itself"—for Shaftesbury and Addison one form of the ugly and deformed—which, writes Fielding (himself, he acknowledges, a master of the burlesque mode in the theater), will be permitted only in the diction, not in the "Sentiments and Characters" of *Joseph Andrews*.

He follows *Spectator* no. 249, where Addison distinguished the "two great Branches of Ridicule in Writing" as "Comedy and Burlesque." The high burlesque (which Addison associated with Cervantes) "represents mean Persons in the Accoutrements of Heroes, the [low] describes great Persons acting and speaking, like the basest among the people." By burlesque Fielding means "appropriating the Manners of the highest to the lowest, or *e converso*"—as opposed to the "ridiculous," which is confined "strictly to Nature." He means that the author may do this, embellishing his descriptions of battles with mock-epic similes, as in Joseph's skirmish with the squire's hounds; but Joseph "is himself above the reach of any Simile" and the mockery will not ridicule or dehumanize him. To "discover the sot, the gamester, or the rake in the cardinal, the friar, or the judge"—or the fishwife in Dido—(as he wrote around the same time in his "Essay on the Knowledge of the Characters of Men")[76] was clearly disturbing, raising the problems Fielding addresses in the preface.

Officially, he sets burlesque and the monstrous against nature, character, and the "ridiculous." The latter (Addison's "ridicule," which he equates with "comedy") "only . . . falls within my Province in the present Work." It applies not to "the blackest Villainies" such as Nero "ripping up his Mother's Belly" (he again cites Aristotle), but only to "affectation," "the only Source of the true Ridiculous."[77]

What Fielding does not specify, but is implicit in his description of *Joseph Andrews* as written in "The Manner of Cervantes," is that the memory of the paradigm was expressed by the curate just before the comments on Quixote's single foible: "[I]s it not a strange thing to see how readily this unfortunate gentleman believes all these falsehoods and inventions, simply because they are in the style and manner of those absurd tales?" (1.30.264). Fielding sticks as close as he can to the Aristotelian formulation, but his original insight is to focus on the imitation of the book, or what he calls "affectation."

As in the case of Swift's analysis of imitation, "affectation" is also burlesque recovered, embodied, and naturalized in a Quixotic character who thinks he is a knight-errant (himself "appropriating the Manners of the highest to the lowest"), and specifically by having read and emulated the wrong books—as so many readers had done with Samuel Richardson's *Pamela* (1742), to which *Joseph Andrews* was a response. In the process Fielding also justifies ridicule of the low (of "Poverty and Distress") by means of affectation. Implicitly, Quixote's distresses are ridiculous because of his affectation of knight-errantry.

Don Quixote was on Fielding's mind long before he read *Pamela* and began to write a Cervantean narrative. There are four allusions in his first play, *Love in Several Masques* (1728), and Helena herself, the heroine, is presented as a comic Quixote in that she knows the City only through books she read in the country. A year later Fielding wrote *Don Quixote in England* (1729; performed, 1734), a ballad opera that transplanted Quixote to Fielding's home terrain, as if to say that he is in fact an Englishman. This early version of Quixote is a mixture of the Swiftean and the Addisonian; the early fools in Fielding's plays are Quixotic characters such as Politic, Sir Avarice Pedant, and Sir Simon Raffler. These easily modulate into the villain Justice Squeezum in *Rape upon Rape* (1730), and, above all, the protagonist of *Jonathan Wild* (1743).

"Affectation," which Fielding applies to the Quixotic situation, was a theatrical term associated with the plays of Congreve, Steele, and Gay.[78] Steele comments in *Spectator* no. 6 that the "unhappy Affectation of being Wise rather than Honest, Witty than Good-natur'd, is the Source of most of the ill Habits of Life." Invoking the Quixote situation by way of Swift's *Tale of a Tub*, Steele continues: "Such false Impressions are owing to the abandon'd Writings of Men of Wit, and the awkward Imitation of the rest of Mankind" (1:28). Steele's concern is double, with "the abandon'd Writings of Men of Wit" and with "the awkward Imitation" of them by "the rest of Mankind."[79]

In his plays Steele put into practice the *Spectator*'s transformation of satire, proving that affectation can be a principle of comedy. Perhaps the fact that the imitators are female characters validated the comedy. In *The Tender Husband* (1705) Biddy Tipkin imitates romance heroines, and Mrs. Clerimont imitates French fashions. The point of origin is Cervantes: Biddy is a "perfect Quixote in petticoats! . . . she governs herself wholly by romance; it has got into her very blood. She starts by rule and blushes by example." This is the comment of Captain Clerimont, her suitor, who adds that if he could "but have produced one instance of a lady's complying at first sight [in a romance]" she should have been his at once.[80] The thesis about affectation is summed up in both Addison's prologue and Steele's epilogue to the play.

At this point we need to formulate a scale of Quixotic affectation:

1. There is fashionable affectation—imitation of, immersion in a fashionable text; examples are Jonathan Wild and "histories of great

men," especially modern accounts (panegyrics) of Sir Robert Walpole. In Gay's *The Beggar's Opera* (1728) highwaymen affect the manners of gentlemen, fences and jailers of merchants; however, being only imitators of the respectable and more successful "great men" who die peacefully in their beds, the ridicule is softened and deflected from "gallows-bait" to the invulnerable "great men" they imitate.

2. While these figures by their imitation conform to the fashion, Quixote deviated, returning to an older and outmoded set of manners. In *The Beggar's Opera* Gay also includes this *un*fashionable imitation: Polly's reading of romances is more truly Quixotic in that her romances introduce "love," which in Polly's discourse stands in striking contrast to the mercenary discourse of everyone around her. Even Macheath's reading of Shakespeare and imitation of gentlemen recovers a code of honor that is at odds with the cupidity of everyone else. In *Joseph Andrews* Parson Adams's reading of the Scriptures or Joseph's of Adams's sermons is a genuinely Quixotic imitation, out of sync with his surroundings. It matters whether the Quixote reads ancient or modern works; Adams follows from Sir Roger de Coverley, while Jonathan Wild, following from the satiric villains of Swift and Gay, imitates the modern models of the living or recently living Walpole and Jonathan Wild.

3. Finally, there is the imitation of a text that, whatever its old-fashioned virtues, binds or restricts—dehumanizes—the person, and is contrasted with the living, human response. Even Wild is not in perfect sync; he suffers from the discrepancy between the authority he follows and his all-too fallible humanity, which Quixotic impracticality (in Fielding's humanist terms) is what makes him interesting—someone one might want to know. Justice Squeezum is merely a hypocrite; Wild is more complex, employing hypocrisy as a stratagem while he himself vainly pursues a chimera of "greatness" as Quixote pursued his chivalry, constantly colliding with a reality (most often associated with love, either its positive or negative aspect) that unseats him and finally hangs him. Wild's opposite, his victim and nemesis Heartfree, embodies the second possibility—to see Quixote as a representative of idealism and simplicity, of a dedication to outmoded, unfashionable, and inward ideals that makes him the opposite of all the conformists

or pretenders to conventional and fashionable immorality. Heartfree's idealism, by contrast, makes the crassness of Wild and of the Wildean world in which he lives stand out in strong satiric relief. But Heartfree is a polar opposite, not a Quixote.

Polly Peachum (with Biddy Tipkin) shows that it is the woman who is most likely at this time to have imitated a literary text—part of the convention of the woman reader that comes to a climax in *Pamela* and Fielding's response to it. As William B. Warner has shown, by the 1720s, novels (by which were meant short narratives of amorous intrigue) were regarded as the locus for the representation of social vices, dangerous because they were both sexy and immersive.[81] The danger of reading such novels was incorporated into the novels themselves. Delarivier Manley, in the second part of her *New Atlantis* (1709), attributes Delia's misconduct to the romances that are read to her and her sister by "an old out of fashion aunt, full of the heroic stiffness of her own times [who] would read books of chivalry and romances with her spectacles. This sort of conversation infected me," Delia explains, "and made me fancy every stranger that I saw, in what habit so ever, some disguised prince or lover."[82] In the novels of Aphra Behn, Manley, and Eliza Heywood, Don Quixote has become a woman who reads novels, is absorbed into their "world," and lives them; they carry forward the Cervantean plot "by aligning the delusions of novel reading with the proverbial madness of love."[83]

We may suspect that Fielding assumed that reading is the origin of Pamela's Quixotism. If he took Hogarth's hint in his popular print *Before* (1736), where the young lady being seduced hides "Novels" behind copies of "The Practice of Piety," Fielding might have suspected that Pamela retains copies of novels the existence of which she does not reveal. The young lady still primarily exists in Hogarth's graphic world, appropriately decorating her bedhead with a shell since she evidently wants to see herself as Venus. Her reading, "Novels" and "Rochesters Poems," concealed by "The Practice of Piety," supplement the shell on the bedhead.

Pamela, though not ostensibly a young woman who reads novels, is living within one. The novel *Pamela* shifts the focus of immersion to the reader of *Pamela* itself, a modern Quixote reading a modern, realis-

tic romance, "written to the moment," consisting of endless letters ~~Pamela~~
from which it is difficult to extract oneself and recover the real world.
Biblically phrased and subsequently quoted from pulpits, *Pamela* "converted" all who read it: as Pamela's letters converted Mr. B., Lady
Davers, and their neighbors, *Pamela* itself sent readers out into the
world to seduce rich husbands.

Fielding's categories are Addison's: people "in their proper Characters" as opposed to people who are "quite unlike themselves," by
which he means affected or hypocritical or merely Quixotic. Shamela is
laughing at Mr. Booby's folly and discomfort; *we* laugh at Shamela's hypocrisy. But the laughter in *Shamela* is also at the discrepancy between
Shamela's learned hypocrisy and her natural passion; this corresponds
to the comic incongruity of Quixote's romance and his rickety body,
his ideals and the real world, and in *Joseph Andrews* it corresponds to
the incongruity of Parson Adams's ideals and his own natural feelings.

There is satiric laughter *at* the fashionable aping of Lady Booby
and Slipslop; and laughter of a different sort in relation to the *un*-
fashionable Adams—what can only be described as the equivalent of
Sancho's laughter at Quixote, which is pure, undiverted release, therefore without satire.

Fielding defines affectation-as-vanity in the old Swiftean way
(rather than Cervantes' own) as "affecting false Characters, in order to
purchase Applause," something that was never true of Quixote and is
not true of Fielding's chief Quixote, Parson Adams. And the effect is
not limited to ridicule: "From the *Discovery* of this Affectation," Fielding concludes, "arises the Ridiculous—which always strikes the Reader
with Surprize and Pleasure" (8). Surprise and pleasure, of course, are
the terms used by the theorists of wit and by Addison as the aesthetics
of the Novel or Uncommon into which Fielding is implicitly fitting his
discourse.

Hypocrisy is a more problematic term. Fielding adds that the ridiculous is "more surprizing, and consequently more ridiculous" in hypocrisy than in vanity. As hypocrites we "avoid Censure by concealing
our Vices under an Appearance of their opposite Virtues." For example,
"the Affectation of Liberality in a vain Man differs from the same Affectation in the Avaricious"; that is, the hypocrite. "Hypocrisy" probably

carries such emphasis because of its prominence in *Pamela*, in Mr. B.'s frequent accusations that Pamela is a hypocrite—and Fielding's conclusion that she *is*;[84] and subsequently in Fielding's hypocrite-manquée *Shamela*. In *Joseph Andrews*, however, the hypocrites are marginal figures. "The Character of *Adams* . . . is the most glaring in the whole," Fielding writes, and Adams is wholly unhypocritical. It is difficult to apply hypocrisy to anyone in *Joseph Andrews* except Lady Booby, Slipslop, and one or two of the clergymen—"for whom," Fielding insists at the end of his preface, "*while they are worthy of their sacred Order*, no Man can possibly have a greater Respect" (10, emphasis added).

Hypocrisy is presumably an extreme of Lady Booby's vanity, which slips from vanity into hypocrisy when she turns from Joseph to the great world of society and defends her "reputation." With Joseph, alone in her boudoir, Lady Booby is a lustful woman who would pass for a woman with a great passion—she is literally (as Joseph notes in his report to his sister Pamela) playing a stage role such as Dido to Joseph's Aeneas. Slipslop is much the same on a lower social level; she is vain when Fielding, in mock-epic similes, compares her to a fierce tiger; she is also a hypocrite insofar as from time to time he applies to her the adjective "chaste." As in the case of Don Quixote, these ironies of the author appear to be an aspect of the character's self-regard: Slipslop is more comic as she *believes* (in the Quixotic sense) that she is chaste than as she merely protests her chastity. The affectation in both women is of being a Dulcinea when she is only a country wench or (in Slipslop's case) a Maritornes. And in both cases, on their different social levels, the character aspires to a higher status, whether literary or social, and by way of literacy—by seeing plays or by reading books half-comprehended.

Affectation, then, is the imitating of a literary discourse, as in Mrs. Slipslop's confusing *irony* with *ironing*, but also in her mistress Lady Booby's imitating, when she is rebuffed by Joseph, the speech of a stage Dido addressed to her Aeneas.[85] Lady Booby's mock-heroic utterances ("Whither doth this violent passion hurry us! What meanness do we submit to from its impulse!") not only set her lust in mock-heroic perspective but demonstrate her self-delusion, revealing the unhappy, misguided woman who sees her petty affair as a great Didoesque love.

Again Mrs. Slipslop "at last gave up Joseph and his cause, and with a triumph over her passion highly commendable" went off to get drunk. The author's ironic blame-by-praise, in context, says that *she felt* that she had triumphed and should be commended. Whether from the character's own lips or from those of the commentator, the irony tends to become an expression of the character's psychology.

THREE

Wit and Humor

"Don Quixote's madness in one point,
and extraordinary good sense in every other"

The curate remarks of Don Quixote that "unless the topic of chivalry is mentioned, no one would ever take him to be anything other than a man of very sound sense" (1.30.265). Quixote, as Motteux put it in 1700, suffers from the "humour of Knight-Errantry."[1] Sarah Fielding referred in *The Cry* (1754) to Quixote as "that strong and beautiful representation of human nature, exhibited in *Don Quixote*'s madness in one point, and extraordinary good sense in every other."[2] He is a good man with a single flaw.

The theory of humors was the most popular explanation in England for Quixote's character. He is a character who is "humorous" in the sense that one humor predominates, and at the end he is de-humored. In many of Quixote's English imitations the character's sanity is recovered at the end by a blow on the head or some other accident. Before *Don Quixote* reached England there existed a kind of stage comedy, developed by Ben Jonson and John Marston, in which a humor character, whose humor was excess of spleen (or envy), found an outlet in satire. This was based on the old derivation of satire from *satyra* or, as popularly thought, a satyr, but absorbed within the therapeutic theory of comedy: one's laughter at follies purges one of the spleen; in this case, by dehumoring the fools who have given those in the audience the spleen, the satirist recovers normality.[3]

Humor itself, from being an excess that should be purged, had been defined (in the formulations of Sir William Temple and William Congreve) as an amiable idiosyncrasy, a defining characteristic—indeed a national character, the result of the English climate and the habit of eating roast beef, emblematic of "minds not shackled by a slavish submission to any authority" and a Shakespearean "variety."[4] Such writers as Sprat had claimed England as "a Land of *Experimental Knowledge*" (above, xi), and other writers claimed it as the country par excellence of humor—the only nation that understands humor and has humorous characters.

The utilization of Don Quixote to justify a theory that exalted humor over wit began with the dichotomy of inspiration and wit, another set of terms analogous to imagination and empiricism. Inspiration carried connotations of a power both religious and poetic, and wit of a secular alternative. The Cavalier poet William Davenant, in the preface to his heroic poem *Gondibert* (1650), set out the argument for wit against divine *or* vatic inspiration. His new kind of epic avoids "extemporary fury, or rather inspiration, a dangerous word which many have of late successfully us'd." He refers, of course, to the events of the 1640s, the Civil War culminating in the execution of the monarch and the rule of the Saints:

> *[I]nspiration* is a spiritual Fitt, deriv'd from the ancient Ethnick Poets, who then, as they were Priests, were Statesmen too, and probably lov'd dominion; and as their well dissembling of inspiration begot them reverence then equal to that which was paid to Laws; so these who now professe the same fury, may perhaps by such authentick example pretend authority over the people.[5]

Hobbes, in a laudatory letter to Davenant that was included in the front matter of *Gondibert*, echoes this sentiment; and both writers set against "inspiration" the term "wit." "*Witte*," Davenant writes, "is the laborious and the lucky resultances of thought, having towards its excellence (as wee say of the strokes of Painting) as well a happinesse, as care." As opposed to inspiration,

> *Witte* is not only the luck and labour, but also the dexterity of thought; rounding the world, like the Sun, with unimaginable motion; and bringing swiftly home to the memory universall surveys. It is the Soules

Powder, which when supprest (as forbidden from flying upward) blowes up the restraint.[6]

Dexterity, motion, swiftly, and *flying upward*—these are the ideas that come to be associated with wit by its proponents as well as opponents. At the outset, wit is a privileged term for Cowley, Dryden, and other supporters of the Crown—an alternative to Dissenter inspiration and imagination as a mode of expression; humor becomes a sort of secular substitute for inspiration, for everything that is opposed to wit. In *MacFlecknoe* (1678) Dryden associates Thomas Shadwell's humor comedies with "true blue" Whiggery and shreds their humor with his wit. For Swift, Pope, and the writers of the next generation wit was a chief mode of discourse, though one that had constantly to be defended (in the same way that a satirist habitually wrote satiric *apologiae*). Its function and reception tended to differ depending on whether it was used as a defensive weapon or one supporting the regime; that is, whether it was Country or Court, for the government or in opposition.

For Milton, one of the surviving Saints of the Commonwealth, wit was the craft of Satan:

> for in the wily Snake,
> Whatever sleights none would suspicious mark,
> As from his wit and native subtlety
> Proceeding . . .[7]

Milton, the divinely inspired poet, plainly states his debt to inspiration. And yet, as we have seen, Milton, the poet of mimesis, constantly employs wit in parody and burlesque, so long as they are attached to Satan. Wit is Milton's ultimate trope of fallen language, the furthest remove from the unity of God the Father and his "divine Similitude," the Son.

Locke, a spokesman for the principles of the first earl of Shaftesbury, in his *Essay concerning Human Understanding*, following the Glorious Revolution, finds "imagination" (the empiricist's version of inspiration) and "wit" dangerously close relatives. Both involve the loose association of ideas and seek the discovery of "any resemblance or congruity, thereby to make up pleasant Pictures, and agreeable Visions in the Fancy." If the first carried for Locke (as it did for Hobbes) associations of religious enthusiasm, the mysticism of the Quakers, Ranters, and other extremities of the Protestant Left, the second carried associations of the Restoration court wits, the Cavaliers, and the religious Right. The stage comedy of Etherege, Wycherley, and Congreve, seen as celebrating rakes and seducers, was a comedy of wit; that is, representing, and seen to celebrate, the ethos of libertines, rakes, and seducers. (Dennis's argument was that, as writers of comedy, they should be seen as *satirizing* the libertines, rakes, and seducers.)

What continues to distinguish wit, Locke notes, is "the assemblage of *Ideas* [rather than their invention, as by the religious fanatics], and putting those together with quickness and variety," for "entertainment and pleasantry"; as opposed to judgment, which "lies quite on the other side, in separating carefully, one from another, *Ideas* wherein can be found the least difference, thereby to avoid being misled by Similitude, and by affinity to take one thing for another."[8] Wit can distort truth, as Locke suggests, and in that sense it was a category that subsumed burlesque and irony, which also relate two things that, however entertainingly brought together, are essentially different and, in Addison's opinion, create a monster.

But the ultimate danger of wit—when used by wits inside *or* outside a church, by preachers or freethinkers—was that it produced laughter, and so, applied to subjects such as religion or politics, could be subversive.

Quixote's madness works by wit (a windmill is a giant waving his arms), whereas the Sancho mind, until it becomes Quixoticized, operates by distinguishing differences between objects that Quixote sees as similar. All that is negative but also positive in wit is manifested here.

Wit Aestheticized: Addison

Addison refers to satire in *Spectator* no. 23 as the result of a "barbarous and inhuman Wit"; and his counterproposal draws upon Archbishop Tillotson's remark: "A little wit, and a great deal of ill nature will furnish a man for Satyr, but the greatest instance of wit is to commend well." Satire and ridicule were the "easiest kind of wit"; "*ill nature* passeth for *Wit*."[9] Addison's position, as early as *Tatler* no. 192, is that "A chearful Temper joined with Innocence, will make Beauty attractive, Knowledge delightful, and Wit good-natured" (3:146). The placement of wit in the sequence is significant.

In an early series of *Spectator* papers Addison begins the recuperation of wit by revising Locke. Where Locke distinguished wit from judgment, in no. 62 Addison distinguishes "true wit" (or even "mixed wit") from "false wit"; that is, wit based on only a verbal (punning) similarity: essentially the arbitrary associations that distinguish wit as creation from wit as discovery. He writes that only true wit

> gives Delight and Surprize to the Reader. These two properties seem essential to Wit, more particularly the last of them. In order that the Resemblance in the Ideas be Wit, it is necessary that the Ideas should not lie too near one another in the Nature of things; for where the Likeness is obvious, it gives no Surprize. (1:264)

In contrast, he refers to the "Heroic Poets, who endeavour rather to fill the mind with great Conceptions, than to divert it with such as are new and surprising, have seldom any thing in them that can be called Wit."

Addison carries the "wit" associated with the words "to divert it with such as are new and surprising" straight into the "Pleasures of the Imagination" essays, where he finds a way to recover it under the middle category, between Great and Beautiful, the privileged term of spectatorship itself. The Novel or Uncommon "fills the Soul with an agreeable Surprise, gratifies its Curiosity" (no. 412, 3:541). Wit is related to comedy in that it is a way of knowing rather than condemning.

Wit produces laughter based on the form of novelty embodied in wordplay; for example, in Pope's line in *The Rape of the Lock* (1714): "stain her honor or her new brocade." Pope (or Swift) privileges "honor" over "new brocade." But for Addison, wit draws attention to neglected, unnoticed elements in a situation. Wit produces the pure intellectual pleasure in finding that a form of words meant to convey one meaning can bear a totally different one—"honor" *and* "new brocade," one simply balanced against the other. And this can lead to a form of pure play—pleasure in the ingenuity, the sheer "love of pursuit." The form that wit takes for Addison is indirection, irony, surprise, aestheticized by him in the service of novelty.

By associating wit with the Novel, Addison updates its role for Davenant, Hobbes, and Dryden as the new principle of composition that replaces inspiration. (Even false wit, in the allegory of no. 63, with its "enchanted Wilderness" and "several Wonders," anticipates the "pleasure" of the enchanted knight and the wood of no. 413.) The Novel, as Addison maps it out, is essentially the area of flux and change in which creation is taking place, and the process is carried out by a "wit" that has not altogether lost its satanic aspect. In his essays on *Paradise Lost*, for example, Satan's "transforming himself into different Shapes . . . give[s] an agreeable Surprize to the Reader" (no. 321, 3:172), and in the "Pleasures of the Imagination" essays, the Novel is represented in *Paradise Lost*, says Addison, by "the Creation of the World, the several Metamorphoses of the fallen Angels, and the surprising Adventures their Leader meets with in his Search after Paradise" (no. 417; 3:566). The last would include the "surprising Adventures" of Don Quixote as well.

Humor: Corbyn Morris and the Fall of Walpole

In the 1740s Corbyn Morris synthesized the schools of wit and humor as "the quick Elucidation of *one Subject, by a* just *and* unexpected Arrangement *of it with another Subject*," the purpose of which is "to enlighten thereby the original subject."[10] In Addison's scheme the "original subject" would be the Novel; in Morris's it is the humorous character. In his *Essay towards Fixing the True Standards of Wit, Humour, Raillery, Satire, and Ridicule* (1744) Morris bases his argument on three "humourous" literary characters, Sir John Falstaff, Sir Roger de Coverley, and Don Quixote.

When Sarah Fielding spoke of Quixote's character as "madness in one point, and extraordinary good sense in every other," she was echoing the formulation of Morris, for whom humor depends on its being exemplified "in real life"—"any whimsical Oddity or Foible, appearing in the Temper or Conduct of a Person in real Life" (12). He repeats "Person in real Life" over and over, anchoring humor to the criterion that we would enjoy knowing this person: of Sir Roger de Coverley, "you would be fond of Sir *Roger*'s Acquaintance and Company in *real Life*" (32); and of Don Quixote, "you yourself, if he existed in real Life, would be fond of his Company at your own Table; which proves him, upon the whole, to be an amiable Character" (40).[11]

In the case of Quixote, according to Morris, "The *Humour* appears, in the Representation of a Person in real Life, fancying himself to be under the most solemn Obligations to attempt *hardy* Atchievements; and upon this Whimsy immediately pursuing the most romantic Adventures" (38). This is Quixote's "Humour" or "Foible" (the words are used interchangeably by Morris).

Shaftesbury's aesthetics, in which beauty equals virtue, was based on the harmonious organism ("a body and parts proportionable" [1:96]) that he utilized as his model; therefore any disharmony—any blemish—is ugly. In his theory of "affections" the excess of one is essentially "humorous"—the disharmony of the single humor or foible. He connects this with a kind of Quixotism in his *Letter Concerning Enthusiasm*, noting that " 'Tis only the excess of zeal which in this case is so transporting as to render the devout person more remiss in secular affairs, and less concerned for the inferior and temporal interest of mankind." But "an ill balance in the affection at large . . . must of course be the occasion of inequality in the conduct, and incline the party to a wrong moral practice" (1:287, 289).

It follows that a particular species, in order to have an appropriate "economy of the passions," must have an excess of, for example, "an extraordinary degree of fear, but little or no animosity, such as might cause them to make resistance, or incline them to delay their flight." If the idea of an "economy of a particular creature" is applied to men, and to individual men, we have something closer to Addison's interpretation in the *Spectator*. Shaftesbury is projecting the *Spectator* when he speculates: "It might be agreeable, one would think, to inquire thus into the different tunings of the passions, the various mixtures and allays by which men become so different from one another" (1: 289, 291). For Morris, then, a humorous character is made up of "mixtures and allays" that distinguish particular men from the ideal or norm.

The Whiggish foible can be traced all the way back to Swift's satire on Marlborough, a skillful general but with glaring defects. Not surprisingly, Morris's second, subordinate term is wit. If Quixote is a "humorous character," his presentation by Cervantes is "witty"; thus, he is a character "wherein *Humour* and *Ridicule* are finely interwoven" (38). First, Morris adds, he pursues these romantic adventures "with Gravity, Importance, and Self-sufficiency" and "[t]o heighten your

Mirth, the *hardy* Atchievements to be accomplish'd by this Hero, are wittily contrasted by his own meagre weak Figure, and the *desperate Unfierceness* of his Steed *Rozinante*;—. . . by his miserable Disasters, and the doleful Mortifications of all his Importance and Dignity" (39).

After calling the effect "ridicule," Morris immediately explains the term by a variety of other terms that complicate and aestheticize the effect he wishes to describe: "the strange Absurdity of the Attempts," the "Poignancy . . . and consequently the Pleasure" of the "miserable Disasters" and "doleful Mortifications," and the "diversion" in, following these falls, his rise again in "your Esteem, by his excellent Sense, Learning and Judgment, upon any Subjects which are not ally'd to his Errantry" (that is, his foible or "humor"). Finally, to these Morris adds "the perfect *good Breeding* and *Civility* of the Knight upon every Occasion" and "his Courage, his Honour, Generosity, and Humanity." For, he concludes, "The *Foibles* which he possesses, besides giving you exquisite Pleasure, are wholly inspir'd by these worthy Principles; Nor is there any thing base, or detestable, in all his Temper or Conduct" (39–40).

The interplay of humor and wit, Morris notes (and he could be referring to the illustrations by Vanderbank, just published with Jarvis's translation in 1742), continues in the witty contrast of the two "humorous characters," Quixote and Sancho Panza—of "the grave Solemnity and Dignity of *Quixote*, and the arch Ribaldry and Meanness of *Sancho*; And the Contrast can never be sufficiently admir'd, between the *excellent fine Sense* of the ONE, and the *dangerous common Sense* of the OTHER." The result is "In *Quixote, Humour* made poignant with *Ridicule*" (41).

It has always been a puzzle as to why Corbyn Morris makes no reference to Parson Abraham Adams, the fourth literary example of the humorous character, who had appeared only two years earlier. Aside from the possibility that Morris had finished his essay before he read *Joseph Andrews*, I think the reason is that Fielding, in the *Champion* and (just the year before, 1743) in *Jonathan Wild*, had ridiculed Sir Robert Walpole.[12] Morris's dedication of his *Essay* is to Walpole, and unfolds his adaptation of Addison's Whig ethos.

He spends thirty-four pages on his dedication, including a résumé of Walpole's career ending with Hamlet's words on his father: "He was a Man, take him all in all, / We ne'er shall look upon his like again."[13] He writes that he presents to Lord Orford (the title bestowed on Walpole at his retirement) "as a Testimony of the Affection I bear to your Person, and Virtues" a book written as "a Composition, independent of Politics, which might furnish an occasional Amusement to your Lordship; and not inelegantly entertain one vacant Hour of your Retirement" (iii–iv).[14]

"Affection" and "retirement" already connect Walpole with the humor character, and Morris notes the "Pleasure" it is "to approach your Lordship, and to view that friendly Humanity and chearful Benevolence, which are visible in your Look"—the more so the "more intimately known" he is (vi–vii). Walpole "has thus placed the *Character* of a *Minister* in a new Light," and hereafter "All haugty [sic] Pretensions to superior Deference, and every contemptuous Treatment of others" will be unacceptable in a minister to the king (viii, ix).

But Walpole is also, in Morris's terms, a wit: "Your Lordship's unequalled *Quickness*, and your Happiness in *illustrating* the Merit, or *exposing* the Fallacy of a Subject, by arranging and comparing 'it with other Subjects, are abundantly known to the World" (v). But not a satirist: Morris defends Walpole's censorship of the stage in the Licensing Act of 1737, at least partially aimed to silence Fielding the playwright: "For these profligate Attacks [on Walpole] made Impressions more deep and venomous than Writings; As they were not fairly addressed to the Judgment, but immediately to the Sight and Passions" (x).[15]

In the *Essay* Sir Roger de Coverley ("something of an Humourist; and . . . his Virtues, as well as Imperfections, are as it were tinged by a certain Extravagance"),[16] who had served as Addison's aestheticization of the Tory country gentleman, serves as a barely disguised recovery of the much-satirized Sir Robert, now fallen from power, a country gentleman living the life of retirement at Houghton:

> His *foibles* are all derived from some amiable Cause.—If he believes that *one Englishman* can conquer *two Frenchmen*, you laugh at his *foible*, and are fond of a *Weakness* in the Knight, which proceeds from his high Esteem of his own *Countrymen*.—If he chuses you should employ a

Waterman or *Porter* with *one* Leg, you readily excuse the Inconvenience
he puts you to, for his worthy regard to the Suffering of a brave *Soldier.*—In short, though he is guilty of continual Absurdities, and has
little Understanding or real Abilities, you cannot but *love* and *esteem*
him, for his *Humour, Hospitality,* and universal *Benevolence.*

The only *concessio,* carrying over from the source (the Addison-Steele
Sir Roger), is the lack of "Understanding" and "real Abilities." The rest
could have come from the *concessio* of Pope's satiric portrait of Walpole
in his *Epilogue to the Satires* I (1738): "For you would be fond of Sir
Roger's Acquaintance and Company in *real Life*" echoes Pope's

> Seen him I have, but in his happier hour
> Of Social Pleasure, ill-exchang'd for Pow'r;
> Seen him, uncumber'd with the Venal tribe,
> Smile without Art, and win without a Bribe. (ll. 29–32)

One wonders if Morris wittily picked up Pope's "Walpole" and turned
it to his own ends. This, however, was also the "Walpole" of his supporters, as in the *Gazzetteer*'s accusation (30 July 1740) that Fielding
had slandered "Mr. Friendly" (Walpole), despite the fact that he "has
been very kind to some of his Relations."

Morris concludes of Sir Roger: "It is indeed true, that his *Dignity,
Age,* and *Rank* in his Country, are of constant Service in *upholding* his
Character. These are a perpetual *Guard* to the Knight, and preserve
him from *Contempt* upon many Occasions" (31–32).

"Humour" Addison had embodied not in the Whig Sir Andrew
but in the Tory Sir Roger, precisely because of what the Tories would
have regarded as his transgressive flaw, as opposed to his opposite, the
humor*less* Whig paragon. Thus Morris turns Walpole into the humor*ous,* Whig, living, human character, by which stratagem he brings
the Whig ethos up to date in 1744, in the years following the fall of
Walpole and the redefining of his political principles. Sir Roger has
become a Whig, a "humorous character" to be loved and (specifically)
lived with. Morris, the follower of Addison, aestheticizes the satiric
figure into a humorous one. In the process he rehabilitates humor as
Addison rehabilitated imagination, bringing together in a comic and
contained, therefore acceptable, form the transgressive aspects of both

inspiration and imagination; wit, too, is included as a proper way of
displaying the humorous character.

main ✗
pt.

One other point should be made. Morris demonstrates that a
critic trying to understand the novel effect of *Don Quixote* will turn to
Aristotelian categories; and these will be the categories of tragedy, since
only a sketch of Aristotle's comic theory survived. Thus Sancho's out-
burst of laughter would suggest the comic version of tragic catharsis.
The comic version of *peripeteia*, the tragic reversal or fall, would be one
of Quixote's comic disasters; and Quixote's return to normal at the end
would be regarded as a recognition scene, or *anagnoreisis*. And the
comic version of *hamartia*, the tragic flaw, would be the comic foible
(the curate's words about his being, except for the foible of chivalry, a
man of perfectly good sense). "The change of fortune should be . . .
from good to bad. It should come about as the result not of vice, but of
some great error or frailty, in a character" (*Poetics*, 13.4.37).

However, Aristotle's distinction remains: "Comedy aims at representing men as worse, Tragedy as better than in actual life" (2.4.13).
The aspects that distinguished *Don Quixote* are anti-Aristotelian, start-
ing with the indecorum of its hero's status and actions. Behind the
analogy with tragedy was the understanding that small misfortunes (as
opposed to great ones) are laughable; as behind burlesque was the idea
of reducing a tragic to a trivial situation, a great or beautiful to a low or
deformed character. The Aristotelian paradigm for comedy only fits
oddly (or comically) the case of Don Quixote, in whom dignity and
delusion joined in so ambiguous a way. The fact that the tragic coun-
terparts *could* be applied to Quixote at all would have been suggestive,
but only to suggest the instability of generic terminology.

A "Character of perfect Simplicity": Parson Adams

Fielding refers to Adams, in the preface and in chapter 3 where he
is first introduced, as "a Character of perfect Simplicity"; "Simplicity,"
he adds, "was his Characteristic" (10). The word *simplicity* was picked
up by Fielding's friend Arthur Murphy and used as the basis for his
theory of "the ridiculous." In an essay in the *Gray's Inn Journal* published in 1754, and elaborated in his "Essay" introductory to his edition
of Fielding's *Works* (1762, with Hogarth's profile of Fielding as frontis-

piece), Murphy shows that he has read and synthesized both Fielding's preface and Morris's *Essay*. He offers as an example of the incongruity theory Adams's discovery that, having made a trip of many miles "with no other Business upon Earth, but to dispose of [his] Sermons, we hear the Parson not being able to find them, very gravely say, '*I protest I believe I left them behind me.*'" "In like manner, when *Don Quixote* very gravely says, that he has seen the Sea, and that it is much larger than the River at *La Mancha*, we cannot help laughing at a Man who has formed his Ideas of Things by what he has seen at his own native Place, and to find an insignificant River compared to the Sea, presents such a repugnant Conjunction of Images, as must necessarily operate upon our risible Faculties."[17] Murphy describes Adams in these same terms:

> [H]is excellent talents, his erudition, and his real acquirements of knowledge in classical antiquity, and the sacred writings, together with his honesty, command our esteem and respect; while his simplicity and innocence in the ways of men provoke our smiles by the contrast they bear to his real intellectual character, and conduce to make him in the highest manner the object of mirth, without degrading him in our estimation, by the many ridiculous embarrassments to which they every now and then make him liable; and to crown the whole, that habitual absence of mind, which is his predominant foible, and which never fails to give a tinge to whatever he is about, makes the honest clergyman almost a rival of the renowned *Don Quixote*. (421)

According to Murphy it is his "habitual absence of mind," an aspect of his "simplicity and innocence," that is his Quixotic "foible." In the "Essay" of 1762 Murphy uses the same Adams example, contrasting it with Quixote's mistaking the barber's basin for Mambrino's helmet.[18]

Murphy also notes that Fielding's model for Parson Adams was the "living" Rev. William Young: "Mr. Young was remarkable for his intimate acquaintance with the Greek authors, and had as passionate a veneration of *Aeschylus* as Parson Adams; the overflowings of his benevolence were as strong, and his fits of *reverie* were as frequent, and occurred too upon the most interesting occasions"; and he retells the story of Young, an army chaplain, with his Aeschylus wandering oblivious of his surroundings into the enemy camp. What he overlooks, and Fielding himself diverts our attention from, is the Quixote analogy:

The "intimate acquaintance with the Greek authors" is ridiculed by contrast with "the overflowings of his benevolence" and "his fits of *reverie.*" As in Murphy's example of the importance to Adams of his sermons contradicted by his forgetfulness of them, the incongruity of Adams, like that of Quixote, is based on the contrast of the authority of a text and the human disavowal of it.

The ridiculous, says Murphy, "consists in a Coalition of circumstances repugnant to each other in their own Natures, but yet whimsically blended together in any Object"—to draw "this Inconsistency to public View, and to shew the heterogeneous Assemblance" leads one to "laugh at it with Contempt." Adams and his sermons is an example of the ridiculous because it "produces an Emotion of Laughter attended in this Instance with a Contempt for *Adam*'s Want of Knowledge of the World" (377).

In all of his examples, though he says that the discernment of incongruity elicits "contempt," he has precisely omitted the element of "affectation," which makes it a Quixotic or more-than-satiric situation. According to Murphy, it is the character's "simplicity" that elicits laughter of contempt.[19] By "simplicity" he means the characteristic of a simpleton. By the same word Fielding means that Adams is a Quixote whose "affectation" of Aeschylean authority collapses to *reveal* the "perfect Simplicity" underneath.

The "perfectly Simple" Adams is comic because he is a pious parson and yet is hindered and jostled not just by external reality of respectable officialdom, but by his own passions. He is a lusty man, siring six children and outrunning horses, wielding a crabstick and (despite his dogmatic acceptance of Abraham's sacrifice of Isaac) inconsolable over the "death" of his own child. It is Fielding's Quixotic adaptation that makes him comic *and* sympathetic, a completely new combination and precisely what Fielding sought as a corrective to Richardson's Pamela, as well as his to own earlier burlesque mode, and attempted to describe in the preface to *Joseph Andrews.*

Murphy identified Parson Adams as based on the living Parson Young. Fielding, although deeply read, was influenced by living people, or personalities, more decisively than by ideas or issues; and he employed them accordingly as his truest examples. He preferred Plutarch's *Lives,* and even more the examples of living contemporaries, over discursive philosophical or religious tracts. He frequently invokes Hogarth, David Garrick, and George Lord Lyttelton, as living artist, actor, and politician, but also as close friends. The best of his characters have living referents—Sophia in Charlotte Cradock (specifically not Helen, the Venus de Medici, and other art works), Joseph and Tom in Fielding himself. The worst have literary referents and so are "paragons"—Shamela, Pamela, and Blifil. The two most significant for Fielding—Walpole and Cibber—were both; they were living men and the creations of their own (and their audiences') imaginations and in that particular sense aestheticized—Cibber's "Cibber," the *Gazzetteer's* "Walpole."[20]

Morality Aestheticized: Collins's "Ode: The Manners"

Collins's *Odes* (1747) were published three years after Corbyn Morris's *Essay*, and the one ode that extends his aesthetics from tragedy (the tragic buskin) to comedy (the comic sock), titled "The Manners" (that is, the portraiture of character, disposition, and temperament), draws directly on Morris. The poet abandons Contempt and Satire (spelled Satyr in order to include both *satire* and *satyr*) for the various ("ever varying") characters of the Graces.[21] Although these "white-robed Maids" have also been connected by commentators with the Virtues, the Graces are more probably what Collins has in mind, recalling Thomas Parnell's characterization of Pope's poetry: "The Graces stand in sight; a Satyr train / Peep o'er their heads, and laugh behind the scene."[22] Collins is preferring the Graces to Contempt-Satire (in the form of a mocking half-man, half-goat) in a passage that echoes Morris's elevation of humor over wit and satire, ending with wit serving to free ("loose") laughter at the "Side" of "Humour" in precisely the formulation proposed by Morris. Wit, Collins tells Humor, "In laughter loosed attends thy side!" (l. 58).

Like Morris's examples, Collins's are prose narratives, centered on *Don Quixote*, but they include Milesian tales (at the time understood as love stories, to which the canon of Toledo had likened romances). While referring to the *Decameron* and *Gil Blas* as well as *Don Quixote*, in all three cases he draws attention to their interpolated stories of tragic love. He permits the reader to interpret the earlier reference to

Fancy's "Robe of wild contending Hues" (l. 48) as either Morris's incongruity theory of comedy or as the complementary tales of comedy and tragedy that define the essentially comic works he cites.[23]

His two couplets on *Don Quixote*—

> By Him, whose *Knight*'s distinguish'd Name
> Refin'd a Nation's Lust of Fame;
> Whose Tales ev'n now, with Echos sweet,
> *Castilia*'s *Moorish* Hills repeat: (ll. 63–66)

—are divided evenly between the commonplace that *Don Quixote* had brought down Spain's chivalric delusions—that is, the message of the comic plot—and the "Echos sweet" of its contrasting stories of love, intrigue, and death. The lines on the folly of chivalric Spain extend the earlier lines, in the context of Morris's argument, "O *Humour*, Thou whose Name is known, / To *Britain*'s favor'd Isle alone" (ll. 51–52). Like Morris, Collins contrasts the humor, the humorous character, indeed the uniquely English word *humor*, with the Quixotic character of Spain.

The *Odes* begin and center on (in the odes to pity, fear, simplicity, mercy, liberty, and peace) the war and politics of the Forty-Five (specifically alluded to in odes 5 and 6). Thus Quixote, the literary equivalent of the doomed Stuart chivalry, and especially the interpolated romances of betrayed maidens, is at the heart of "The Manners," because this representative of Spanish knight-errantry is corrected by Collins's English hope that the murderous Forty-Five will not be repeated but that England will return to its traditional national character of humor guided by wit.[24] (Collins's association of Aeschylus with his part in the Battle of Marathon—which connects poetry and politics—presumably refers to the Greeks' victory for liberty over tyranny, as opposed to the Quixotic sense of chivalry that he associates with the fratricidal Forty-Five, associated also with the "chivalry" of the Cavaliers and the Stuart cause.)

The intermediate ode "On the Poetical Character," dividing the odes to pity, fear, and simplicity from the 1745–46 odes, and carrying the reader back to Spenser's *Faerie Queene*, lays the groundwork for the metamorphosis of war into poetry—and points toward the ultimate Collins ode "On the Superstitions of the Scottish Highlands," which turns the poet specifically toward Scotland. He expresses a desideratum that includes a native poetry, alluding to the problems of creating one in the eighteenth century and the advantage of a backward, defeated, ruined Scotland.

In 1746 Joseph Warton, followed in the next year by Collins, published books of odes with a programmatic intention of replacing the kind of poetry Pope had perfected beyond the point of profitable imitation. There are, of course, interesting overlaps with Pope's own program: For Pope the question addressed in his major works of the late 1720s and thereafter was how to write poetry in an age of debased standards—of Grub Street, Walpole, and George II—and his answer was to show, primarily in *The Dunciad*, how such trash can be utilized and metamorphosed into poetry without sacrificing a moral standard of judgment. For Warton and Collins the question was how to write poetry in an age dominated by Pope's poetry—in Warton's words, "didactic Poetry," "Essays on moral Subjects," summed up as "the fashion of moralizing in verse." This was to be replaced, in his *Odes*, by "Invention and Imagination, which he claimed to be the chief faculties of a Poet."[25] For fanciful and descriptive poetry Warton went to a picturesque or literary environment—to "The Solemn Silence of the Pyramids. The Dark gloomy Scenes in Mines. The Fall of the Nile. Distant Noises. Indian Brachmins wandering by their Rivers. Medea's nightly Spells. Meteors in the Night."—and so on, places or objects or experiences in which Fancy, as opposed to morality, can be found.[26]

Collins's program, systematically outlined in his *Odes*, is less optimistic than Warton's: he merely chronicles the limitations and obstacles, the high standards (of the Greek tragedians, Shakespeare, and Milton) that prevent him from reaching Fancy. In one sense, this inability to write is the only response available now to the poet; his solution, however, is to write poems that, while acknowledging this fact, replace a poetics with an aesthetics: the poet's position with the aesthetic one of the spectator or reader. This solution has the further advantage of replacing didacticism and morality with aesthetic affect.

Collins's radical solution to the problem of Pope's poetry is evident in the contrasting, almost exactly contemporary poems of Thomas Gray. Both are proclaiming a new kind of poetry, but Gray not only retains the clarity of the Popean syntax (Collins's object, by way of Milton, is what Burke would call "obscurity," the chief feature of the "terrible," and so of the sublime) but the morality. Every Gray poem ends with an *applicatio*, whether "all that glisters [is not] gold" or "where ignorance is bliss, / 'Tis folly to be wise." Gray's allegorical figures—the same "Passions" of Anger, Jealousy, Sorrow, and the rest used by Collins—all carry moral baggage; Collins's personifications only respond, as the poet mimics that response and offers the reader the opportunity to enjoy the same response.

Warton set the seal on the new view of poetry by writing a book on Pope's poetry, opening with a hierarchy of poets in which Pope is demoted from "the first class" of "sublime and pathetic poets" (Spenser, Shakespeare, and Milton) to "the second class," those poets like Dryden who "possessed the true poetical genius, in a more moderate degree, but had noble talents for moral and ethical poesy."[27]

Thus Collins's odes open with invocations to Pity and Fear, the Aristotelian attributes of tragedy, whose definition is not in terms of moral application but the purgation of emotions—an affective theory. "The Manners" is followed by "The Passions. An Ode for Music": humor is nursed by the passions.[28] This ode sums up the replacement of moral with aesthetic versions of the passions, and "The Manners" simply extends the aesthetics, by way of Corbyn Morris, to laughter— but a laughter that requires the softening supplement of pity and fear, jealousy and anger, melancholy and (tragic, as opposed to comic) madness, in the place of moral judgment.

FIG. 1. Hogarth, *The First Adventure*, etching and engraving, c. 1726, 9 1/16 ×
7 3/16 in. Courtesy of the Trustees of the British Museum, London.

FIG. 2. John Vanderbank, *The First Adventure*, drawing, 1726, 7¾ × 6 in.
British Museum, London. Photo courtesy of the Paul Mellon Collection, Yale
Center for British Art.

FIG. 3. John Vanderbank, *Alonso Quijano in His Study*. Etching and engraving by George Vertue, dated 1723. In *Don Quixote*, trans. Charles Jarvis, 1738, vol. 1, opp. p. 1. 9 ¼ × 7 ¼ in. Courtesy of the Trustees of the British Museum, London.

FIG. 4. Sir Anthony Van Dyck, *Charles I on Horseback*. c. 1637, painting. The Royal Collection (c) Her Majesty Queen Elizabeth II.

FIG. 5. Hogarth, *Don Quixote Being Cared for by the Innkeeper's Wife and Daughter*, etching and engraving, c. 1726, 9 1/16 × 6 7/8 in. Courtesy of the Trustees of the British Museum, London.

FIG. 6. John Vanderbank, *Don Quixote, Sancho, Maritornes, and The Innkeeper's Daughter*, etching and engraving by Gerard Vandergucht, c. 1726, 9½ × 7⅜ in. Courtesy of the Trustees of the British Museum, London.

FIG. 7. Hogarth, *The Adventure of Mambrino's Helmet*, etching and engraving, c. 1726, 8⅞ × 7¹⁄₁₆ in. Courtesy of the Trustees of the British Museum, London.

FIG. 8. Hogarth, *The Curate and Barber Disguising Themselves*, etching and engraving, c. 1726, 9 × 6⅝ in. Courtesy of the Trustees of the British Museum, London.

FIG. 9. Charles-Antoine Coypel, *Don Quixote Attacks the Puppet Show*, etching and engraving by François Poilly, 1724, 10½ × 11⅛ in. Courtesy of the Trustees of the British Museum, London.

FIG. 10. Hogarth, *The Mystery of Masonry Brought to Light by The Gormogons*, etching and engraving, 1724, 8½ × 13½ in. Courtesy of the Trustees of the British Museum, London.

FIG. 11. Hogarth, *Hudibras Encounters the Skimmington*, etching and engraving, 1726, 9¹¹⁄₁₆ × 19½ in. Courtesy of the Trustees of the British Museum, London.

FIG. 12. Annibale Carracci, *Marriage of Bacchus and Ariadne*, etching by Nicolas Mignard, 5⅝ × 7¾ in. Courtesy of the Trustees of the British Museum, London.

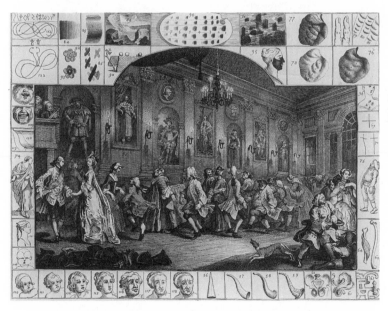

FIG. 13. Hogarth, *The Analysis of Beauty*, Plate 2, etching and engraving, 1752, 14⁹⁄₁₆ × 19⅝ in. Courtesy of the Trustees of the British Museum, London.

FIG. 14. Hogarth, *Columbus Breaking the Egg*, April 1752 (detail). Courtesy of the Trustees of the British Museum, London.

FIG. 15. Hogarth, *Sancho's Feast*, etching and engraving, c. 1730, 10⅞ × 11⁹⁄₁₆ in. Courtesy of the Trustees of the British Museum, London.

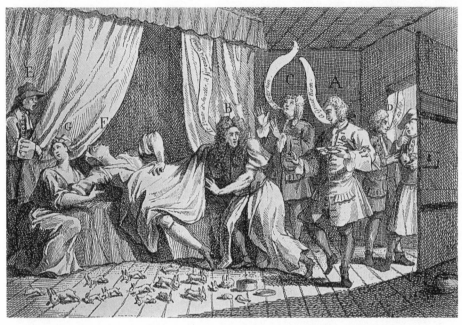

FIG. 16. Hogarth, *Cunicularii, or the Wise Men of Godliman in Consultation,* December 1726, 6⁵⁄₁₆ × 9⁷⁄₁₆ in. Courtesy of the Trustees of the British Museum, London.

FIG. 17. Hogarth, *The Funeral of Grisóstomo*, etching and engraving, c. 1726, 9¼ × 6¹⁵⁄₁₆ in. Courtesy of the Trustees of the British Museum, London.

FIG. 18. John Vanderbank, *Don Quixote, Marcela, and the Funeral of Grisóstomo*, etching and engraving by Gerard Vandergucht, c. 1726 (pub. 1738, 1742), 10 × 7½ in. Courtesy of the Trustees of the British Museum, London.

FOUR   *Aesthetics*

The Taste of Wine, the Sight of Dulcinea

Don Quixote, especially part 2, offered English aestheticians a paradigm and a problematics. The best-known case, of course, is the wine tasting in chapter 13. Sancho and another squire (the squire of the Knight of the Mirrors) carry on a conversation parallel to the one taking place between their masters. Thirst leads them to drink wine, and, once satisfied (now *disinterested*), they turn to a discussion of taste. Sancho claims that he can place any wine as to its precise vineyard and year. He inherited his "instinct" (*instinto*), he says, from his ancestors, whose senses were so acute that one kinsman was able to sample a wine vat merely by touching his tongue to the wine, another by smelling it. The first of these kinsmen said that it tasted of iron, the second that it smelled of leather. "The owner insisted that the vat was clean and that there could be nothing in the wine to give it a flavor of leather or of iron," but when the vat was eventually emptied a small key attached to a leather strap was found at the bottom of it, verifying the taste of Sancho's ancestors (2.13.589–90).

Addison starts off his "Pleasures of the Imagination" with a preliminary essay on taste (*Spectator* no. 409); and he begins with the example (appropriately, given the *Spectator*'s setting, the tea table) of the man who, "after having tasted ten different Kinds of Tea," can identify its source and "any two sorts of them that were mixt together in an equal Proportion" and "name the Parcels from whence the three several Ingredients were taken" (3:528). This he extends from the sense of taste to the metaphorical "Taste of Writing," but in the first "Pleasures of the Imagination" essay (no. 411) he returns to the senses and, first, to the sense of sight, "the most perfect and most delightful of all our Senses," and to the Beautiful, Great, and Novel.

The best-known utilization of the wine-tasting episode was by David Hume in his essay "On the Standard of Taste" (1757). Hume used the story to exemplify the problem of whether taste is relative or universal and argued that the "delicacy of taste" enjoyed by Sancho's differing kinsmen does not contradict the general opinion of either taster or of the "dull and languid" bystanders that the wine was good: "One of them tastes it; considers it; and after mature reflection pronounces the wine to be good, were it not for a small taste of leather. The other after using the same precautions, gives also his verdict in favour of the wine; but with the reserve of a taste of iron."[1] The qualities of good and bad exist at a different level from sweet and bitter or "iron" and "leather," and there are a few people, such as Sancho's kinsmen, who *have* a "delicacy of taste" and can demonstrate their superiority over other "pretended judges."

The Two Dulcineas

One wonders why Hume did not use, instead of the wine-tasting example, the immediately preceding example (chaps. 9–10) of the beauty of Dulcinea del Toboso—the beauty of a woman and the sense of sight. This episode is followed by the two chapters that parallel the disagreement of the wine tasters with the disagreement of Quixote and the Knight of the Mirrors over the beauty of Dulcinea. The latter ends in single combat and clearly suggests that wine tasting may be the proper standard by which to judge the beauty of Dulcinea—that the taste of wine is a small example that illuminates the more important sight of the beautiful. For, if Quixote's first mission as knight-errant is to right wrongs, his second is to defend the status of his lady's beauty: the first is moral, the second aesthetic.

Dulcinea's "peerless beauty" (*sin igual hermosura*)—her ideality—exists only in Quixote's chivalric imagination, which is tested when he makes a pilgrimage to El Toboso in order to see her in the flesh. Sancho, who earlier claimed to have delivered a letter from Quixote to Dulcinea, must now produce the woman. Obviously he cannot. To solve his dilemma, he simply identifies "three peasant lasses astride three ass-colts" as Dulcinea and her two serving women. Quixote complains that he *sees* only "these country maidens," "three farm girls on three jackasses": not a "queen and lady" but "a village wench, and not a very pretty one at that, for she was round-faced and snub-nosed" (569–70). Since Sancho insists that this is the beautiful Dulcinea, Quixote concludes that he is the victim of a spell by an enchanter who has "placed clouds and cataracts upon [his] eyes, and for them and them alone hath transformed [Dulcinea's] peerless beauty into the face of a lowly peasant maid" (571). After pretending, for the benefit of Quixote, to see the beautiful Dulcinea, Sancho adds as an aside:

> And yet, to tell the truth, I never noticed her ugliness but only her beauty, which was *set off to perfection* by a mole that she had on her right lip—it resembled a mustache, being surrounded by seven or eight red hairs of more than a palm in length. (572, emphasis added)

Although by the end of the sentence, the peasant maid is beginning to remind us of Maritornes, we sense that the last clause is added to humor his master: from the point of view of Sancho the peasant, "a figure as low and repulsive as that village girl" (572) *is* beautiful.[2]

Back in part 1 when Quixote encountered the ill-favored Maritornes, it was in the dark: "[H]e pictured her in his imagination as having the same appearance and manners as those other princesses. . . . So great was the poor gentleman's blindness that neither his sense of touch nor the girl's breath nor anything else about her could disillusion him, although they were enough to cause anyone to vomit who did not happen to be a mule driver" (1.16.119). To him it seemed that it was the "goddess of beauty [*diosa de la hermosura*]" whom he held in his arms." Foreshadowing Sancho's plebeian appreciation of the peasant maid, "a mule driver" (we are told) would not have vomited at Maritornes's touch or smell. Indeed, Quixote's failure of the senses was promptly corrected by the mule driver, who does appreciate her touch and smell: sensing a rival, he came down on Quixote "with so fearful a blow on the gaunt jaws of the enamored knight as to fill the poor man's mouth with blood. Not satisfied with this, the mule driver jumped on his ribs and at a pace somewhat faster than a trot gave them a thorough going-over from one end to the other"—and so on, the crudest of empirical evidence to correct Quixote's idealizing imagination. Thus Dulcinea's "pleasing scent," as opposed to the peasant maid's odor of garlic, prepares the reader with the sense of smell for the down-to-earth senses of taste and smell in the wine-tasting episode.

Sight, however, is the significant sense—the only sense—for correcting the errant imagination. Early on, in part 1, chapter 4, Quixote encountered four merchants and demanded that they "confess that there is not in all the world a more beauteous damsel than the Empress of La Mancha, the peerless Dulcinea del Toboso." Quite reasonably, the merchants ask him to "Show her to us," to which he replies: "If I were to show her to you, . . . what merit would there be in your confessing a truth so self-evident? The important thing is for you, without seeing her, to believe, confess, affirm, swear, and defend that truth" (45). They ask him to show them at least "a portrait of this lady" (46). Combat ensues.

Now, in part 2, confronted with the peasant maid, Quixote cannot give the lie to the sense of sight. But Dulcinea is also the one subject on which he cannot delude himself: she has always been at the center of his imagination; she was his first thought after donning his armor (1.1.29) and she has been the cause of his challenges, as she will be when he meets the Knight of the Mirrors. Dulcinea is the center of the knight-errant's world; she is the paragon of beauty. Quixote's delusion is essentially beauty-oriented and, hence, sight-oriented. Because she is the knight-errant's ideal, impossible and unreachable, when Quixote sees instead a living, accessible peasant maid, it must be Sancho, not Quixote, who takes note of the alternatives—the real and the ideal; and the ideal is definitively bracketed. From this point on Quixote's one mission is to have Dulcinea *dis*enchanted—returned to her ideal, imagined state, which significantly requires the physical punishment of Sancho with a thousand lashes (a disenchantment devised by the duke and duchess, who know that it was Sancho, not a magician, who "enchanted" the peasant maid).

In the Dulcinea scene, two senses of beauty are juxtaposed: Quixote's, which cannot be realized in anything but his idealizing imagination, and Sancho's, which exists in the real world and is, in a way, substantiated three chapters later by the story of the wine tasting, which shows the perfect taste that runs in his family. Further, we must remember that "Dulcinea" was based on Quixote's memory of a local girl. The real Dulcinea, the original of Dulcinea, Cervantes (or his source) tells us in the first chapter of part 1, was "a very good-looking farm girl who lived nearby, with whom he had once been smitten, although it is generally believed that she never knew or suspected it. Her name was Aldonza Lorenzo" (1.1.29; again, 1.25.204). This reality, only vaguely remembered (as *seen*) by Quixote, was recalled through Sancho's eyes, who, as he recounted in chapter 25, well remembered the living woman:

> [S]he can toss a bar as well as the lustiest lad in all the village . . . she's a sturdy wench, fit as a fiddle and *right in the middle of everything that's doing*. . . . Son of a whore, *what strength* she has and *what a voice!* [i.e., a loud voice] . . . And the best of it is, there's *nothing prudish about her*; she's *very friendly with everybody* and *always laughing and joking*. (1.25.204–5, emphasis added)[3]

And at this point Sancho turned to his master, adumbrating the episode of chapters 8 to 10 in part 2: "And so, I say to you now, sir Knight of the Mournful Countenance, that you not only may and ought to play mad for her sake, but you have good reason to despair and go off and hang yourself, and anyone who hears of it will say you did exactly the right thing, even though the devil takes you."[4] To Sancho she is real flesh and blood, calling for real action on his part. Against this woman, however, Quixote sets up his ideal Dulcinea—"I am content to imagine that what I say is so and that she is neither more nor less than I picture her and would have her be, in comeliness and in high estate. Neither Helen nor Lucretia nor any of the other women of bygone ages, Greek, Latin, or barbarian, can hold a candle to her" (206).

Quixote's and Sancho's different senses of beauty are also distinguished by differences in social status. Quixote's Dulcinea is distinguished by both "great beauty and a good name." His suspicion is aroused when he enters Toboso and sees only a stable yard and a "very small house" where there should have been palace of a "highborn princess." Sancho might have pointed out to Hume that when his kinsmen demonstrate the subtlety of their taste, they also indicate their class because they recognize only the plebeian objects with which they are most familiar.

The story of the two Dulcineas could have illustrated for Hume the radical relativism of taste, based on reading and social class, that he tried to circumvent in his "Standard of Taste" essay. Of course, the wine-tasting example he chose avoided the multiple problems connected with the beauty of the human body, which had been raised by Shaftesburian aesthetics. But the wine-tasting passage itself is misquoted by Hume for his own purposes.[5] What the passage actually says is that Sancho's kinsmen have extremely acute senses of taste and smell—but *not*, as Hume claims, that this permits them to judge the wine as good or bad.[6]

In the terms of Cervantes' novel, the story of the wine tasting says that Sancho may have inherited superior senses, for example, of taste and smell; and in fact, the inference to be drawn from the passage is that the wine is *not* good since it tastes of leather or of iron. Yet following upon Sancho's judgment of the peasant Dulcinea, the story of the wine tasting might suggest that the taste of leather and iron is, like the mole on Dulcinea's lip, a sign that wine should *not* have the perfect wine taste, and that impurity makes it from Sancho's point of view more beautiful.[7]

Hume's more famous and perhaps more convincing words on the relativity of responses to beauty were in his earlier essay, "The Skeptic" (1741):

> Euclid has fully explained all the qualities of the circle; but has not in any proposition said a word of its beauty. The reason is evident. The beauty is not a quality of the circle. . . . It is only the effect which that figure produces upon the mind. . . . In vain would you look for it in the circle, or seek it, either by your senses or by mathematical reasonings, in all the properties of that figure. . . . Till such a spectator appear, there is nothing but a figure of such particular dimensions and proportions; from his sentiments alone arise its elegance and beauty.[8]

What Hume says of relative responses to a beautiful object should be compared with the words of a modern theorist of laughter regarding a risible object:

It is well known, and indeed observable by all, that what makes one man laugh may even make another angry. Sugar is sweet, but it is sweet to everybody! You may not like it overmuch, but you cannot deny that it is sweet. . . . In this sense, a situation, if it is laughable, must be so to everyone, whether he is pleased to recognize it to be so or not. That this, however, is not so has been recognized by all. It is then fairly obvious that in assuming that persons laugh *at* a situation we are assuming more than the facts. We may assume only that in certain circumstances or situations people feel impelled to laugh.[9]

Theories of comedy ultimately arrive with aesthetics at the question of the relativity of response: Is the cause of laughter in the laugher or the laughable? Is it merely personal or a motor function? We saw, back in part 1, Quixote's and Sancho's responses to their respective cases as the objects of laughter. Like the wine cask, Don Quixote is an occasion for response, at its crudest for laughter; so people humor him and set up situations in which he can show his madness and, sometimes, practical jokes that will "give him a further opportunity of displaying his absurdities" for the enjoyment of an audience (1.13.93).

In "On the Standard of Taste" Hume is arguing for a certain kind of object—a perfect circle: "[I]t must be allowed, that there are certain qualities in objects, which are fitted by nature to produce those particular feelings," for example of beauty, though they are particularly discernible by those like Sancho's kinsmen with delicacy of taste. But, as Sancho shows, what will make Hume's circle beautiful—or, more precisely, humanly beautiful—is to mar its geometrical, its ideal circularity. In this sense, Sancho is the spokesman for the living—that is, the less-than-perfect woman; he sanctions the beautiful (Quixote's Dulcinea) while remaining skeptical of it, accepting instead the physical reality and reducing the issue of beauty to the level of sight, taste, and smell.

Three years before the "Standard of Taste" essay, in *The Analysis of Beauty* (1753), Hogarth focused his aesthetics on the woman, and specifically a woman's face he describes as *not* the perfect circle but an oval, and indeed an oval broken by an unruly lock of hair (perhaps recalling Sancho's reference to Dulcinea's hair, "loose over [her] shoulders" and "playing in the wind"). She is (Hogarth's words) a "living" woman: "Who but a bigot, even to the antiques, will say that he has not seen faces and necks, hands and arms in *living women*, that even the Grecian Venus doth but coarsely imitate?"[10] And the break in the oval makes her more "alluring." The reality of Aldonza Lorenzo, seen through Sancho's eyes (vigorous, unprudish, friendly, always laughing and joking) is a summation of Hogarth's laughing shrimp girl (or the singing milkmaid in *The Enraged Musician).*[11] The point of Hogarth's "beauty" is that it is found in a "living" woman and, to set it off from the ideal, is defined by a blemish of some sort (such as the mole on the peasant maid's face).

Hogarth also comments in the *Analysis* on the disproportion of the Apollo Belvedere, generally regarded as the acme of male beauty in antique sculpture: "[W]hat hath been hitherto thought so unaccountable *excellent* in its general appearance, hath been owing to what hath seem'd a *blemish* in a part of it" (72, Hogarth's emphasis). There is, therefore, the ideal, "beautiful" Dulcinea and there is the real, "living" Dulcinea, made so by her blemishes. They designate her not, in opposition to the Beautiful, as the Ugly, but rather, within the terms of the Beautiful and set against the Ugly, as what Addison called the Novel or Uncommon. In Hogarth's terms, the blemish is an allure beyond mere beauty, one form of "what the Italians call, Il poco piu (*the little more* that is expected from the hand of a master)" (59). In the case of the Apollo Belvedere the "blemish" that "strikes [the spectator] with surprise" (as opposed to "admiration only") produces "a superaddition of *greatness*," but in the case of "the living woman," it produces novelty, which, as Addison noted, "improves what is great or beautiful, and makes it afford the Mind a double Entertainment" (*Spectator* no. 412, 3: 541–42).

The scene of the two Dulcineas ends with the words: "It was all that the rogue of a Sancho could do to keep from laughing" (2.10.573). Hogarth's aesthetics of Sancho is, of course, based on an aesthetics of laughter. He developed his aesthetics out of Addison's "Pleasures of the Imagination" essays (the first of which began: "Our Sight is the most perfect and most delightful of all our Senses" [3:535]), but the figure who connects Aldonza Lorenzo with Hogarth's Shrimp Girl and ultimately the Venus in the *Analysis of Beauty* is Addison's Mirth, in *Spectator* no. 249, the central paper in his argument for replacing Swiftean satire with comedy. Addison's examples were "the Laughter-loving Dame" Venus and Venus's offspring Mirth; he cited Milton's "heart-easing Mirth, / Whom lovely Venus at a birth / With two Sister Graces more / To Ivy-Crowned Bacchus bore" ("L'Allegro," 13ff.). In this passage, with the female figure of Comedy, Addison began to anticipate the connections he elaborated in the "Pleasures of the Imagination." The metaphor of laughing, he notes, is applied in most languages "to Fields and Meadows when they are in Flower, or to Trees when they are in Blossom"—or, he adds, "applied to Love." The latter leads him to conclude: "This shews that we naturally regard Laughter, as what is in it self both amiable and beautiful." The laughter of ridicule, he argues, should be supplemented or replaced by another laughter, applied to (or merged with) beautiful objects and emotions of love.

Addison's equation of Mirth, Venus, and the Comic Spirit contributed to Hogarth's beautiful young woman and is summed up, following the *Analysis*, in the muse he shows himself painting in *Hogarth Painting the Comic Muse* (1758), the self-portrait he used thereafter as frontispiece to the folios of his engravings. In short, Addison's comedy together with Sancho's comic response provided Hogarth with the agency to write his particular version of an aesthetics.

Even Addison, discussing the relativity of response to the "Beautiful or Deformed," takes Sancho's position into account: "Thus we see that every different Species of sensible Creatures has its different Notions of Beauty, and that each of them is most affected with the Beauties of the same kind" (no. 412; 3.542). Basing his argument on the same metaphor of courtship, Hogarth proclaims a plebeian aesthetics based on the ordinary sense-perception of Sancho: in the *Analysis of Beauty* he urges us to use *our own* eyes, not the deluded vision of Quixotic connoisseurs, primed on books of theory.

Hogarth's key terms in his *Analysis* are also Addison's. The qualities Addison associates with novelty are "surprise," "the pursuit of knowledge," "curiosity," and "variety"—the last summed up by Hogarth as his "Beautiful," in which the largest variety is discovered within apparent unity. "Variety," writes Addison, is "where the Mind is every Instant called off to something new, and the Attention not suffered to dwell too long, and waste it self on any particular object" (no. 412, 3:541). It "gratifies" the soul's "Curiosity." The point is that all of these elements depend on laughter and the transformation of laughter into an epistemology of the discovery of novelty.

To Hogarth, aesthetics, an account of pleasures and sensations, explains why particular forms and objects are appreciated; whereas an account of taste (even Hume's skeptical one) seeks to define a "correct taste" and, equally, to discriminate against a "false [or bad] taste." It is not a question of defining what is true or accurate, as in the actual case of Sancho's kinsmen and wine tasting, but rather of defining what, in Hume's misreading of the story, is good or bad taste; that is, what is the "correct" thing to say, look for, or feel—most significantly, to own. The latter, as Hogarth realized and tirelessly demonstrated, was merely fashion.

Dulcinea and the Virgin

As they approach El Toboso to view the "true" Dulcinea, Quixote and Sancho talk of "fame" and compare knights-errant and Christian saints and their respective relics (recalling 1.13.93–95), preparing them for a confusion of devotion to the Virgin and to Dulcinea.[12] That confusion was foreshadowed at the end of part 1, in Quixote's mistaking "a covered image" of "the Immaculate Virgin" carried on a litter by penitents for "some highborn lady whom these scoundrelly and discourteous brigands were forcibly carrying off" (1.52.454–56). It is precisely the immaculateness that Dulcinea shares with the Virgin.[13]

"What evil spirit in your bosom spurs you on to go against our Catholic faith?" Sancho asked of Quixote, noting the dangerous proximity of religion, aesthetics, and (as Swift would have added) delusion (455). Earlier, Quixote's old books of chivalry were burned at "a public *auto de fe*," giving them the aura of religious heresy (1.5–6.50, 52). But even earlier the word *blasphemy* was attached by Quixote himself to the subject of Dulcinea: "You shall pay for the great blasphemy which you have uttered against such a beauty as is my lady," he said to the merchants who had simply asked, "Show her to us" (1.4.45–46). And in part 2 Quixote's chiding Sancho for "uttering blasphemies against that enchanted lady" leads them from the encounter with the peasant maid into the encounter with the troop of actors performing the Corpus Christi play *The Parliament of Death.* A few chapters later we have the story of Basilio's "miracle" or "trick" (*industria*) in which a priest, among others, has been "tricked and made sport of" by yet another theatrical performance, this one involving a prop sword (2.21.647).

In the discussion at the end of part 1, the canon of Toledo proceeded from the indecorum of chivalric romances and of *comedia* (the violation of the unities of time and place) to religious dramas (such as the *Parliament of Death*): "How many false miracles do their authors invent, how many apocryphal and erroneous incidents . . . "—followed by the curate's dismissal of the "harmless recreation" of this "kind of play," that is, *comedia* (1.48.430–31). Basing his argument as he does on the truth (on "true," historical figures), he and Quixote move into the shadowy area in which the "truth" or historicity of the deeds of Amadis of Gaul and knightly "relics" such as "Count Pierre's pin" are set against saints' lives and holy relics (49.440–41). The canon, arguing for verisimilitude, urges Quixote to substitute for his romances Holy Scripture and historical accounts of great men; and then Quixote, in his rebuttal, argues that many "historical" figures are no more or less dependent on our willingness to believe than romance heroes. As Alban Forcione notes, this passage "might have caused Cervantes trouble with the Inquisition if he had chosen to make the implication any more clear."[14]

Cervantes is reflecting many things in the Dulcinea-Virgin analogy: the historical fact of Maryolatry, illustrated in what C. S. Lewis referred to as the "allegory of love," which became one of the foci of the powerful counter-Reformation movement within the Roman Catholic Church.[15] An English reader might have inferred a dawning awareness that chivalry and Christian worship, insofar as they focused on a divine ideal of woman, offered not substantiation but alternatives; that the "miracles" of both were equally true or false, recuperable only on a level of aesthetic pleasure.

The purpose of Quixote's stop at the inn was to have himself dubbed a knight, for which he must spend a night's vigil in a chapel. As Quixote mistakes a swineherd for a dwarf, a prostitute for a damsel, and an innkeeper for a castellan who can knight him, he also mistakes the barnyard for a chapel, a horse trough for a baptismal font, and an account book for a Bible. These parallels are not so precise as they seem: There "was no chapel in this castle," but the barnyard tacitly served this purpose, and the innkeeper, when he came to knight Quixote, used his account book for a Bible and read "as if he had been saying a prayer" (1.3.40). Later Quixote makes a rosary of "a large strip from the tail of his shirt, which hung down over his buttocks" and in it he ties eleven knots (1.26.211) and proceeds to inscribe verses to Dulcinea in the bark of trees and in the sand. (Cervantes changed Quixote's shirttail to the galls of a cork tree in the second edition.)

Quixote's insistence that the "badly soaked and worse cooked codfish and a piece of bread as black and moldy as the suit of armor he wore" served him by the innkeeper is in fact a chivalric feast (the "fish was trout, the bread was of the finest") on some level parodies transubstantiation. The parody recurs in Quixote's transformation of a basin into a helmet, a packsaddle into a caparison (1.45.405). And the emblematic importance of *The Parliament of Death*, just following the failure of Quixote to see his Dulcinea, lies in the fact that it is a play of Corpus Christi, celebrating the Eucharist. This central miracle/sacrament of the church was, as Ruth El Saffar has noted, "one that Don Quixote was trying by his own will to reenact: to transform everyday objects into the image of the divine"; in particular, "from the base matter of Aldonza Lorenzo the exalted image of womanhood that his imagination has supplied" in Dulcinea.[16]

There would seem to be three elements: religious belief, romance imagination, and (in the next chapter) the "living" reality of the peasant maidens of Toboso. Although he maintains his piety, Quixote's imagination represents the secularization of belief into pure imagination and its object, the "peerless beauty of Dulcinea."

"Dulcinea's" Blemish

Quixote notices that the Dulcinea he is presented with by Sancho is not a "queen and lady" but "a village wench, and not a very pretty one at that, for she was round-faced and snub-nosed" (in Shelton's translation, "but a country wench, and not very well-favoured, for she was blub-fac'd, and flat-nos'd"). But Sancho remarks on "her beauty, which was set off to perfection by a mole that she had on her right lip" (Shelton: "her Beauty, which was infinitely increas'd by a Mole she had upon her Lip").[17]

The Shaftesburian Beautiful, with nothing opposed to it but the Ugly, is the ideal without blemish. Opposed to this idea, which is both Shaftesburian and Quixotic, is Sancho's idea of the Beautiful as the real, the living person, therefore with a blemish, and also therefore desirable. For Sancho at least, this must include bedding and a denial or redefinition of disinterestedness.

The issue was most provocatively set forth by Swift in his "Dressing Room" poems of the early 1730s. Among the possible models for these remarkable poems, one that so far as I know has never been proposed but in some ways fits best, is Don Quixote's encounter in El Toboso with the real Dulcinea.[18] Celia in "The Lady's Dressing Room" is a "Goddess"; and Chloe in "Strephon and Chloe" is also "of no mortal race," but here it is specified that this deification is "By every size of poet sung" (ll. 2, 8):[19]

> While she a goddess dyed in Grain
> Was unsusceptible of stain:
> And, Venus-like, her fragrant skin
> Exhaled ambrosia from within:
> Can such a deity endure
> A mortal human touch impure? (ll. 85–90)

Strephon thinks of Chloe as a "goddess," "And goddesses have now and then / Come down to visit mortal men." He has read of Thetis and Peleus and Jove and Semele, and as Chloe prepares for bed, "these reflections filled his head" (ll. 95–112). Swift's advice to Strephon would apply as well to Don Quixote, who never recovered from the experience in El Toboso:

> You think some Goddess from the sky
> Descended, ready cut and dry:
> But, e'er you sell yourself to Laughter,
> Consider well what may come after;
> For fine Ideas vanish fast,
> While all the gross and filthy last. (ll. 229–34)

Strephon's error is Quixotic imitation: He has read the poets who refer to their beloved as a goddess, and instead of accepting this as a poetic convention, acts upon it. Confronted with the empirical evidence of the lady's body, in "The Lady's Dressing Room" he spews. Quixote, faced with the real peasant maid, invents a fiction of enchantment and avoids the issue.[20] Sancho, however, confronted with the peasant maid, admires her "beauty." And in "Strephon and Chloe," Strephon, after actually bedding Chloe and suffering his disillusionment, follows Sancho's more plebeian response and "calls a spade a spade" and enjoys and shares with Chloe "society in stinking."

"Society in stinking" can be, like the initial discovery of Chloe's body, painful and nauseating, or, for Strephon in the sequel, sexually stimulating. Swift denies the latter; he cannot see bodily functions as arousing sexual desire, as, for example, James Joyce did with Nora or Havelock Ellis with his wife. According to Swift—or whoever in the poem expresses the view counter to Strephon's—only perfect beauty (given man's fiction of perfect beauty) can beget desire. And beauty must be supported by "decency," which "must fan the lover's fire," otherwise with the loss of decency beauty follows and then desire (l. 219 ff.). Decency, however, seems to signify never getting close to Chloe: in that case, Swift tells Strephon, "Your heart had been as whole as mine" (l. 250). Strephon would never have married or bedded Chloe in the first place; sexual desire would not have been his object. He would have replaced beauty with "sense and wit"—"decency" and "prudence."

Swift remarks that the wife, in order to retain her husband's desire, must "from the spouse each blemish hide / More than from all the world beside" (ll. 253–54). Sancho in fact focuses on the maid's blemish, finding the blemish itself, not the perfection, the confirmation of desire.

Swift, however, distinguishes his spokesman as a separate point of view, fussy and pedantic: "Authorities both old and recent / Direct that women must be decent," he writes, followed by the lines "And, from the spouse each blemish hide. . . . Now, ponder well, ye parents dear, / Forbid your daughters guzzling beer" (l. 115). The latter combines an echo of Polly Peachum's most famous aria in Gay's *Beggar's Opera*—a song defending her "husband" Macheath against her parents—and a comic admonition. These negations frame the sheer copia with which Swift represents the vigorous and irrepressible life of the physical world, denied in one way by the "poets" and in another by the Swiftean spokesman. His message is that mortals can never experience the height of satisfaction that they imagine, but that "society in stinking" is one solution, while "friendship" is another, the official one.

"Strephon and Chloe" is, of course, about morality and not aesthetics. Its message is illuminated by another poem of a few years later, "A Character, Panegyric, and Description of the Legion Club" (publ. 1736), in which Swift uses the madhouse (and the whips and other forms of "treatment" employed in madhouses) to contain the unruly members of the Irish Parliament. Though the solemnity of the Christian moralist is more obtrusive in "Strephon and Chloe" than in this political satire, the effect is the same: an attempt to contain an energetic and pervasive life that will not be contained.

There is, nevertheless, in the "Dressing Room" poems an implicit aesthetics of perfection and an ideal for which distance and disinterestedness are primary requirements. Strephon, climbing into bed with Chloe, whom he has idealized, "awefully his distance kept." The revelation of her bodily function collapses that aesthetic distance. Distancing according to Swift actually stimulates sexual desire. Once Strephon loses the distance and sinks into "society in stinking," without ideal beauty, sexual desire disappears.

In Shaftesbury's aesthetics, the statue, the body in its ideal state, aestheticizes the body, producing an aesthetic situation without desire (whether sexual or, since the aesthetician is wealthy, a collector's desire). However, in the theological version of Shaftesbury's aesthetics, according to Swift in "Strephon and Chloe," this *is* the condition of desire: the woman who wants to retain her husband's desire (implicitly this means keeping control of her husband) must conceal from this Platonist her blemish.

As an analysis of beauty, Swift substitutes the Christian for the potentially secularizing positions of both Quixote and Sancho. But another aesthetics is also implicit, that of the natural, blemished face, in accordance with the taste of Sancho's kinsmen for leather and iron. This is the unadorned face, without cosmetics or prostheses, that is characterized by mere decency: the face, for example, of Swift's own friend Stella. As part of his basic strategy, however, Swift juxtaposes incongruous responses to a beautiful and desirable object. The ostensible aim of the "poet" is to order the threat of the body, but the comedy acknowledges the incompleteness of any ordering process. The definition of beauty is ultimately, as with Sancho's reaction to the contrast of Quixote's ideal and the reality, as seen and appreciated by Sancho, comic ("it was all that the rogue of a Sancho could do to keep from laughing"). The comic as an aesthetics subsumes the Beautiful because it *requires* the real Dulcinea as well as the idealized Dulcinea.

The Blemish and the Foible

Aristotle defined the comic as the imitation of men worse than average and "a subdivision of the ugly. It consists in some defect or ugliness [or deformity] which is not painful or destructive."[21] On the other hand, the terms Ugly or Deformed of the classical tradition do not appear in the King James Bible—only the word translated as "blemish." In the Old Testament, it is announced that a sacrificial animal must be without blemish: the "lamb shall be without blemish." "But whatsoever hath a blemish, that shall ye not offer: for it shall not be acceptable for you. . . . [I]t shall be perfect to be accepted; there shall be no blemish therein." In short, nothing can be offered unto the Lord that is "blind, or broken, or maimed, or having a wen, or scurvy, or scabbed," "bruised, or crushed, or broken, or cut . . . because their corruption is in them, and blemishes be in them: they shall not be accepted for you" (Exod. 12.5, 29.1; Lev. 1.3, 3.1, 4.3, 22.19–25).

In the New Testament, however, Christ becomes the sacrificial lamb and Peter refers to "the precious blood of Christ, as of a lamb without blemish and without spot," referring to his heavenly origin, his virgin birth (1 Peter 1.19). Blemish by this time implies original sin and sexual transgression: "Spots they are and blemishes, sporting themselves with their deceivings while they feast with you," and "blemishes" are connected with the "lust of uncleanness" (2 Peter 2.13, 10).

There is a religious dimension to the mole on the real Dulcinea's lip—her ugliness (from Quixote's point of view) is focused on a blemish. Swift says that to be beautiful Chloe must be without blemish, and Shaftesbury writes in the same tradition, though his source is secular (Plato's idealism) rather than religious. In short, one who finds the blemish itself the attraction will be not only (with Sancho and Strephon) plebeian but heterodox as well, aestheticizing sin or what was theologically (at least in terms of the Old Testament) an "abomination."

As Hogarth showed in many of his prints, aesthetics must be based not on Platonic ideas but on contemporary social assumptions. The beauty spot, a minor blemish, was a way of designating beauty. But the beauty *patch*, a popular application, could be both the simulation of a blemish and the concealment of a real blemish (a venereal lesion).[22] In the *Analysis of Beauty*, as well as the references we have noted, Hogarth refers to a "blemish" covered by a patch. Too many beauty patches (too many blemishes), as in the case of Mother Needham in *A Harlot's Progress*, plate 1, turn beauty into ugliness and deformity, as it becomes evident that hers is a Swiftean cover-up for disease. At this point the beauty patch has become, as in Swift's series of poems about women and cosmetics, a prosthesis like the false teeth, eyes, and nose his "beautiful young nymphs" perforce wear.

Compared with Mother Needham's several beauty patches, M[ary] Hackabout's face is unblemished in plate 1; she has one beauty patch in plate 2, presumably indicating the added *allure* of a blemish; but in plate 3 there are two, and, to confirm that they now conceal lesions, medicine bottles appear near her bed; in plate 4 there are two additional bottles, small and near the first two as if to suggest the spread of the infection; and in plates 5 and 6 her face is barely visible, swathed in sweating blankets and, finally, enclosed in a coffin. Her blemish begins as an allure beyond ordinary beauty (as Hogarth puts it in the *Analysis*) but ends as the blemish that in London of the 1730s distinguishes her as the actual from the official, the unblemished sacrificial lamb. Hogarth ends the *Harlot's Progress* by showing his harlot to be a Sacrifice or Atonement for the men of London. In the final plate, in her coffin, in the composition of a Last Supper, surrounded by London whores, bawds, pimps, and a sexually engaged clergyman, she fills the position of the Host in a modern Eucharist.

The beauty mark is intended to stimulate and perpetuate desire. It is a necessary condition for desire; and as an aesthetic indicator it corrects a Quixotic desire for wholeness and perfection. It supplements the Shaftesburian sense of beauty, embodied not in the human body but in a statue that reproduces, idealizes, and perfects it, thus rendering it, among other things, nonhuman. But if Sancho and Hogarth practice an aesthetics of the blemish, Swift (or at least his official spokesman in "Strephon and Chloe") retains the religion of the blemish, the implicit theological assumption summed up in Hawthorne's story "The Birthmark," in which the attempt to remove the birthmark—and thus attain perfection—reveals that it extends all the way to the heart. For Swift, in his theological terms, the blemish designates evil; for Sancho and Hogarth—and Cervantes—it designates living humanity, and therefore a special form of beauty, and indeed goodness.[23]

Maritornes is described as "broad-faced, flat-headed, and with a snub nose" (Shelton: "flat-pated, saddle-nosed").[24] *Crooked Mary*, she is literally deformed, lame and a hunchback. But after everyone has laughed at the battered Quixote, "Maritornes felt sorry for him and, in order to refresh him, brought him a jug of water which she got from the well that it might be cooler." When Sancho, after his beatings and the consequences of Fierabras's balm, asks Maritornes for some wine, "She complied right willingly, paying for it out of her own money; for it is said of her that, although she occupied so lowly a station in life, there was something about her that remotely resembled a Christian woman" (1.27.128). The physical deformity of Maritornes is joined to a sweetness of temper, a charitableness (at least in Quixote's first encounter with her). Here the problematizing of the Ugly leads to the problematizing of the Platonic and Shaftesburian equation of beauty and virtue as well.

The blemish specified in *Exodus* designated unsuitable offerings; the blemish specified by Moses in *Leviticus* (in the laws he passed on to Aaron) was intended to define the priesthood. A man with a blemish cannot be a priest: "For whatsoever man he be that hath a blemish, he shall not approach: a blind man, or a lame, or he that hath a flat nose." Such a person "shall not go in unto the veil, nor come nigh unto the altar, because he hath a blemish; that he profane not my sanctuaries: for I the Lord do sanctify them" (21.18, 23). As Matthew Henry's commentary explained, "It was very likely that some or other in after-ages that were born to the priesthood would have natural blemishes and deformities: the honour of the priesthood would not secure them from many of those calamities which are common to men." They could be fed if blemished, but "they must not serve at the altar."[25]

The sacrificial lamb, we notice, is gendered female and aestheticized by Hogarth into the beauty of a blemish; the priest, gendered male, is moralized by Hogarth, though regendered once again female in order to keep in tension the issue of beauty and virtue. In *A Harlot's Progress* he takes the blemish of "a flat nose" singled out by Moses and gives it to the Harlot's servant woman, who has suffered from syphilis. This blemished woman is the only person in *A Harlot's Progress* who shows compassion for the Harlot.[26] The clergy (in plates 1 and 6), outwardly without a physical blemish but inwardly corrupt and self-serving, shun her. It is surely significant that the blemish is awarded to the one true "priest" who does serve, as it is to the sacrificial lamb.[27]

In the scriptural context of the unblemished priest, Maritornes is a model for the Harlot's servant; in *A Rake's Progress* she becomes Rakewell's faithful Sarah Young, whose blemish in plate 1 is her pregnancy. Sarah follows and succors Rakewell as the servant woman followed the Harlot, but this time out of eros as well as caritas, or out of the love of a woman as well as the duty of a servant. These English versions of Maritornes are, of course, based on Jesus' parable of the Good Samaritan (directly reflected in Hogarth's painting of the subject in St. Bartholomew's Hospital). Then twenty years later in Hogarth's Sanchoesque aesthetics, the blemish breaks the perfect oval, increasing its "allure," or rather giving it something more (*poco piu*), which is novelty. The blemish does not so much designate virtue or beauty as suggest that virtue or beauty may not be where one conventionally looks for it. The addition of allure is to seduce, to lead one into the Novel or Uncommon, and away from the strictly, or at least conventionally, beautiful *and* moral. The way into aesthetics is by way of the Harlot's beauty spots and her servant's nose, to the countess's lock of hair in *Marriage A-la-mode*, and in the *Analysis* to Eve's lock and the serpent's tempting shape. On a spectrum from the errant lock of hair to the concupiscence Hogarth associates in his *Analysis of Beauty* with Eve, Venus, and Cleopatra, the blemish primarily distinguishes the singular "living woman."

Addison accommodated intransigent remains of the Ugly and Deformed within the Novel by way of its epistemology of wit. The statement, "the Description of a Dung-hill is pleasing to the Imagination" was his version in the "Pleasures" essay (no. 418) of his earlier formulation that the georgic poet "breaks the Clods and tosses the Dung about with an air of gracefulness."[28] Both of these are examples of wit as well as of the georgic recovery of a transgressive object. One recovers a dunghill to the "Pleasures of the Imagination" by the wit of the juxtaposition of primary object and secondary description (by "the aptness of the Description to excite the Image"; 3:566–67).

Hogarth, who is aware also of the theological overtones of the blemish, uses the blemish (flaw, sin) wittily, to define human charity against the religious rules of sacrifice and priesthood. His version of Addison's georgic tossing dung "with an air of gracefulness" is, however, Xenophon's Socratic dialogue, translated for him by his friend Morell: Aristippus asks Socrates, "Is then a labourer's hod, or a dung basket a beautiful thing?"—to which Socrates answers: "Undoubtedly, . . . and a shield of Gold may be a vile thing, consider'd as a shield; the former being adapted to their proper use, and this not."[29] Fitness, or function, is not only the subject of Hogarth's first chapter of the *Analysis* but the crucial element added to make beauty in the climactic chapters on proportion and motion. If Socrates shows that the beauty of a dung basket is embodied in its suitability for holding dung, Hogarth shows that fitness includes moral utility as well—the everyday morality that replaces the golden but "vile thing" known as priestcraft.

Excrement, apparently a wholly ugly object, is in fact another blemish like the mole or flattened nose. In Swift's "Dressing Room" poems excrement is called a "blemish" on the beautiful human body, an exaggerated example of its fallenness.[30] In the same way Swift extends the touch of rouge used by Pope's Belinda to aestheticize her fallen blush to the extreme of false teeth, nose, and eyeballs. On the other hand, Pope, the Tory, starts with a classical ideal—in the past, in ancient Rome, in the society of Augustus, Maecenas, Virgil, and Horace—against which he judges the world of the 1720s–1730s (essentially the writings of Dissenter, Nonconformist, Enthusiast, and Whig) and finds it "trash" (often a metonymy for excrement). He satirizes the works and their creators but recovers them—aestheticizes them, perhaps; but the act includes the discrediting and destruction as well as the recovery, and the recovery is by the single isolated (last) poet, Pope himself.

Yet the way Pope makes "beauty out of a blunder" (as Swift put it) in such lines as "The fresh vomit run forever green" is by his wit—his bringing together the transgressive "vomit" and "forever green" in the formal beauty of his couplet; by absorbing it into his own (essentially demiurgic) poetry, he (as he never tires of telling us) contextualizes it properly and so immortalizes its ugliness. Pope invokes a religious discourse, equating the beautiful and the virtuous, and, like a surrogate redeemer, recovers the ugly-vicious, without forgiving it, as his own beautiful poetry.

For Hogarth as for Cervantes, excrement is part of the burlesque process for Quixote—not something to be recovered or aestheticized but to designate the human. Quixote and Sancho both vomit as a result of imbibing Quixote's version of Fierabras's miraculous oil. Quixote's need to relieve himself demonstrates to Sancho that the knight is not enchanted. These are equivalents of the broken teeth and cracked ribs, accidents that are not to be metamorphosed or concealed. They are of a piece with the mole or flattened nose that "set off to perfection" the real Dulcinea's beauty.

burlesque designates the human [marginal annotation]

Between the *Harlot's Progress* and *The Analysis of Beauty* the blemish became a staple of the description of beauty in the emergent novel. In *Joseph Andrews,* Fanny Goodwill is characterized by the "flaws" that prove her a living woman. The original object of Fielding's novel was to substitute for the paragon Dulcinea (Samuel Richardson's Pamela) the real-life peasant maid Fanny—her name itself referring to her lower parts—who has never even learned to read. Fielding urges his readers, if they are "of an amorous Hue," to avoid his description of her—"so plump, that she seemed bursting through her tight Stays, especially in the Part which confined her swelling Breasts." And he confirms her beauty by her blemishes: "Her teeth were white, but not exactly even. The Small-Pox had left one only Mark on her Chin. Her complexion was fair, a little injured by the Sun" (2.12.119).

In 1750 John Cleland's Fanny Hill describes her face as "a roundish oval, except where a pit in my chin had far from a disagreeable effect," and other "flaws" such as a smallpox scar (52). And a year later Fielding's Amelia has a scarred nose: "her Nose, as well proportioned as it is, hath a visible Scar on one Side" (1: 454). And earlier he adds the remark, which is significantly the author's and not Booth's: "I know not whether the little Scar on her Nose did not rather add to than diminish her Beauty" (IV.7.184). This will be precisely Hogarth's argument, concerning the contingencies without which Beauty cannot exist, in the *Analysis*.[31]

It should, however, be evident that in the context of the aestheticizing of Lockean truth Corbyn Morris produced a formulation in which his humorous character (invariably male) corresponds to the beautiful woman, as the amiable humor or foible corresponds to the blemish, and both are based on the reality of a living person. Indeed, the foible or blemish proves the reality of the person in nature, as opposed to in either the Quixotic imagination or the Platonic ideal. Morris's "Person in real Life" corresponds to Hogarth's "living woman."

Sancho's (and Hogarth's) beautiful woman is analogous to the "humorous character" who has a foible (in the old sense of "humor"), is living, and is sociable, clubbable, and lovable. And by humor the English meant a lovable foible. Thus the very English (or at least Hogarthian) analogy between the lovable foible in a character and the blemish in a beautiful woman.

Odd Mixtures

Nor does the aesthetic of the blemish end with the humorous character. If the Ugly begins with the blemish that disqualifies for either sacrifice or priesthood, it ends with the "abomination" of "odd mixtures" that must be avoided by all.

Cervantes related the concept of ugliness and deformity, with the same associations of contrasting good qualities found in Quixote (or Maritornes), to the author (himself) and his book. The book *Don Quixote* is acknowledged by Cervantes to be "a tale that is as dried as a rush"; he refers to Quixote as "withered" and "with little flesh on his bones and a face that was lean and gaunt," and asks what can be "expected of a sterile and uncultivated wit such as that which I possess if not an offspring that was dried up, shriveled, and eccentric?" (1. Prol. 11–12; 1.1.25). *Don Quixote* is the epitome of the "odd mixture": when we first see Quixote himself, he is described as "this grotesque [*contra heche*] personage clad in bits of armor that were quite as oddly matched [*desiguales*] as were his bridle, lance, buckler, and corselet" (1.2.32). He equates the author, his book, and his protagonist all as something completely different, equally deformed, and yet the more interesting for all of that. And as written by Cid Hamete Benengeli, *Don Quixote* is, instead of (as Quixote would wish) a noble and inspiring history, composed "haphazardly and without any method" (*a tiento y sin algún discurso* [2.3.530]).

In the biblical context, with the "blemish," Leviticus also censured the "abomination" of ritual impurities; that is, "thou shalt not sow thy field with mingled seed: neither shall a garment mingled of linen and woolen come upon thee," and so on toward the "abomination" of a man's lying "with mankind, as he lieth with a woman" (Lev. 19.19; 20.13). In Deuteronomy the list proceeds from "The woman shall not wear that which pertaineth unto a man, neither shall a man put on a woman's garment" to "Thou shalt not sow thy vineyard with divers seeds: lest the fruit of thy seed which thou hast sown, and the fruit of thy vineyard, be defiled. Thou shalt not plow with an ox and an ass together. Thou shalt not wear a garment of divers sorts, as of woolen and linen together" (Deut. 22.5, 9–11). Matthew Henry's commentary on the "garment" of "diverse sorts" was that "Odd mixtures are here forbidden" as "[t]hat which is contrary to the plainness and purity of an Israelite. They must not gratify their own vanity and curiosity by putting those things together which the creator in infinite wisdom had made asunder. . . . Nor must their profession and appearance in the world be motley, or party-coloured, but all of a piece, all of a kind."[32]

In the Old Testament the garment shall not be mingled of linen and wool; in the New Testament, when the soldiers take Jesus' "garments" and divide them, including his coat, we are told: "[N]ow the coat was without seam, woven from the top throughout" (*John* 19.23). Jesus is taken down from the cross and wrapped in a "linen cloth" (Matt. 27.59; Mark 14.51; Luke 24.12; John 20.5). In Revelation "seven Angels" appear "clothed in pure and white linen" (Rev. 15.6). This image of purity and unity was extended by the church fathers to the church itself and a religio-aesthetics that shared with Shaftesbury elements of Platonism.

Thus Swift used the seamless garment in the "tale" of the three brothers in *A Tale of a Tub*—"of very good Cloth, and besides, so neatly sown, you would swear they were all of a Piece"—and so the brothers, to be with the fashion, add shoulder knots, gold lace, and flame-colored satin linings until their attire is a very odd mixture.[33] He also used Cervantes' equation of the author and his book, turned to satire. *A Tale of a Tub* itself is a corrupt, deformed, and illegible text that reflects a grotesquely deformed "author," though defined in contrast to a Virgil, Homer, or Swift. And in its allegorical postscript, *The Battle of the Books*, Virgil and Homer are literally the volumes of the *Aeneid* and *Iliad*, Bentley and Wotton shoddy modern productions.

Shaftesbury exclaimed at "what wonder it is, if the *monstrous* product of . . . a *jumbled* brain be *ridiculous* to the world?" (1:48). The mixed or jumbled *is* ridiculous, and hence monstrous; that is, ugly and deformed. This he opposes to mixed or incongruous groupings, associated with nature and the living: A work, "if it be beautiful, and carries truth, must be a whole, by itself, complete, independent," and "particulars . . . must yield to the general design, and all things be subservient to that which is principal" (1:94). It remains, therefore, for the living and natural to be the subject of comedy—of Shaftesbury's ridicule, which will find out "what justly may be laughed at" "in everything"; that is, nature as opposed to "unity of design." This, of course, was opposed to the particolored costume traditionally worn by fools and by Harlequin in the commedia dell'arte.

The canon of Toledo concluded chapter 47 with the wish that it might be possible to combine "the epic, lyric, tragic, and comic genres and depict in turn all the moods that are represented by these most sweet and pleasing branches of poetry and oratory; for the epic may be written in prose as well as in verse" (1.47.428). At this point, as if in a hiatus, he is speaking for Cervantes himself.

Fielding sums up the positive tradition and returns it from the aesthetic to the moral register: In the introduction to book 10 of *Tom Jones* he cites Horace's *Ars Poetica*, referring to "those little Blemishes, *quas human parum cavit natura*" ("which human frailty has failed to avert").[34] On the one hand, a blemish in a good man or book can "raise our Compassion rather than our Abhorrence," and on the other they "can be of more moral Use than the Imperfections which are seen in Examples of this Kind; since such form [adapting the terms of Addison's novelty] a Kind of Surprize, more apt to affect and dwell upon our Minds, than the Faults of very vicious and wicked Persons. The Foibles and Vices of Men in whom there is great Mixture of Good, become more glaring Objects, from the Virtues which contrast them, and shew their Deformity" (10.1.527). Those "in whom there is great Mixture of Good" are "our favourite Characters," and so will be "not only taught to shew them [these blemishes or foibles] for our own Sake, but to hate them for the Mischiefs they have already brought on those we love." This is a remoralizing of Corbyn Morris's argument for humorous characters in the context of a book that redefines "character" itself in relation to conduct.[35]

In *Tom Jones*, Fielding makes his hero a "mixed character" and his book equally "mixed." He follows the defense of the flawed hero in the introductory essay to book 10 with the flawed book in the introductory essay to book 11; and in his dedication to *Tom Jones* he requests of his reader "That he will not expect to find Perfection in this Work; and secondly, That he will excuse some Parts of it, if they fall short of that little Merit which I hope may appear in others."

Thus we have a series of concepts—blemish, affectation, comic incongruity, mixed character, odd mixtures—that, for Fielding at least, takes off from the paragon Pamela/*Pamela* and ultimately substitutes the bastard "mixed character" Tom Jones, a quintessentially English hero and ethos. Here, at the center of his novel, he extends the analogy to epitomize, in the time of the Forty-Five, the last great threat of the "Young Chevalier," the English (Whig, Hanoverian) "mixed" system of parliamentary government. All of these elements, from author to hero to book, with their incidental flaws, he opposes to the Richardsonian paragon, the "perfectly" beautiful and virtuous Pamela on the one hand and, on the other, the "absolute monarch," the Stuart Pretender, supported by the papist absolute monarchy of France.

FIVE

Religion

The Parliament of Death
and the Puppet Show

Framing the story of the wine tasters are two scenes of spectatorship in which the question of taste is rephrased as an issue of appearance and reality. The more famous, the more influential in the eighteenth century, was Quixote's demolition of the Moors who are pursuing the maiden in Don Pedro's (Ginés de Pasamonte's) puppet show.[1] This episode, in chapter 26, is the central case of the impingement of the Secondary Imagination on life, by way of a new, a modern version of the old metaphor of life-as-theater: Quixote's attack on the puppet show addresses the question of which are real, the wooden puppets, the Moors of the story, or Quixote and the puppet-master, or (for that matter) the text of *Don Quixote* and its vexed authorship—and specifically what is *de*lusion and what reality, not simply appearance (or *il*lusion), because Quixote's response is not to *deceptive* appearances but to the effects of the human imagination.

The episode of the puppet show is preceded in chapters 11 and 12 by his encounter with a cart carrying the performers of the play *The Parliament of Death*, and this follows directly after the story of the enchanted Dulcinea, which, we have seen, was itself a sort of performance. The significant connection is that, as with the peasant maid to whom Sancho assigns the role of Dulcinea, the actors in this religious allegory also fail to deceive Quixote.

This is partly because, though still in costumes of Death, Devil, angels, and an emperor, the actors are between performances. "I perceive now," says Quixote, "that one must actually touch with his hands what appears to the eye if he is to avoid being deceived"—and he confesses a detail we have not hitherto known—that "as a lad I was very fond of masks and in my youth my eyes were fixed upon the stage" (2.12.576). His whole fixation, hitherto blamed on books, may be in part attributable to his "eyes . . . fixed upon the stage." It takes an actor to know one. Moreover, the usual confrontation and catastrophe does not follow in this case from Quixote but from a clown playing a demon who, *not* abandoning his role in the play, leaps and brandishes a stick and thereby "so frighten[s] Rocinante" that the horse dashes off with Quixote on his back. The reader will note that the clown has taken his "role" too seriously, carrying play into life, in much the way Quixote has taken his own "role." But now it is the theatrical world that is harassing the real. Sancho Panza persuades Quixote not to retaliate on the company for the clown's behavior by noting that the actors enjoy royal patronage—the same sort of patronage Quixote is soon to enjoy as a "clown" in the court of the pleasure-seeking duke and duchess, where he will supply them with the pleasures of the imagination.

There is another reason why *The Parliament of Death* does not deceive Quixote and the puppet show does. The former prompts him to discuss the topos of life as theater, which he easily recognizes: *The Parliament of Death*, he says, shows "what we are and what we ought to be"; what we are as opposed to what roles we play—"when life is done, death takes from each the garb that differentiates him, and all at last are equal in the grave" (580); and that on the stage, and *sub specie aeternitatis*, emperors' crowns are only "tinsel and tinplate" (579). The reason Quixote is not deceived in this case is that the figures of Death, Devil, angels, and emperor present the old theological version of life-as-theater as *vanitas vanitatum*, and presumably in this case the eschatological version of the topos based on rewards and punishments, which he is able to understand and expound to Sancho. It is only (as we are often reminded) when the performance is of chivalric romance that his imagination takes over and he cannot tell delusion from reality—or rather (as his focus on Dulcinea, as well as his discussion with the canon of Toledo, showed) he substitutes beauty for religion and morality. This is the world that, outside the confines of religious belief, can be validated by the imagination in a process that, in the context, is parallel to the enjoyment of wine tasting.

Before chapter 12—the encounter with *The Parliament of Death*—is over, Quixote has met the false Knight of the Mirrors (though he so far calls himself less-revealingly the Knight of the Wood), who brings news of a pseudo *Don Quixote*, Quixote, and Dulcinea, claiming that he has defeated this Quixote in combat, proving that his own lady is more beautiful than Dulcinea. The two following chapters compare the true and the false, the real and the play-acting squires and knights. The former highlights the tale of the wine tasting, in which the minutest difference in vintages could be detected by Sancho's connoisseur ancestors, and the second features the battle over the taste of the two knights in their ladies. The combat that follows between Quixote and the Knight of the Mirrors eventuates in chapter 26 in the combat between Quixote and the puppets, the Moors who are catching up with the Princess Melisendra. Taste in wine and in beauty, as in comedy and romance, projects a spectrum, at one end of which is disagreement and at the other physical combat; and all of these aspects of taste, we see, are presented as theatrical equivalents of, alternatives to, religion. The episode of the puppet show then is followed in chapter 30 by the entrance of the duke and duchess and the series of dramatic jokes and theatrical illusions in which Quixote and Sancho themselves become the actors.

The major episode between the two theatrical experiences, *The Parliament of Death* and the puppet show, is Quixote's vision in the Cave of Montesinos, the vision of a knight and not a saint (chapter 22); and the question that hovers over the rest of part 2 is whether the visionary's vision (like the wine taster's taste, like the pursuit of Melisendra by the Moors) is true or false. In the cave of Montesinos, the only time that Quixote is unaccompanied in his visionary state, he again sees only the peasant "Dulcinea."

The "enchantment" of Dulcinea hovers over the rest of part 2, until Quixote believes she is finally disenchanted, at which point (possibly for fear of encountering the paragon *now*, disenchanted) he receives the sacraments *and* repudiates the books of chivalry. In the final chapter he simply takes to his bed and dies. The motives attributed to him are "the defeat he had suffered" at the hands of Carasco and "the will of Heaven"; but the doctor's opinion ("that melancholy and depression were putting an end to his patient's life") supports the former (2.74.983).

The death of Don Quixote corresponds to—and balances—the dialogue of the canon, curate, and Quixote at the end of part 1. Returning to sanity is the locus for the double view of imagination, so strikingly at odds with Cervantes' final statement of intention on the last page. The return to the "true" Quixote—"Alonso Quijano the Good"—is both gain and loss, and produces a pathos that is cast back over the plot, at least the second part. Seen in retrospect from the ending, the elevation of Quixote's imagination, the image of the noble Quixote, appears validated.

But as significantly, by the logic of the continuing parallels between Dulcinea and the Virgin Mary, when Quixote repudiates knight-errantry he should realize that his folly was in putting his faith in a heroine of romance rather than in its proper religious object. Instead he merely tells his friends that his folly was in following knight-errantry rather than a life of good deeds—in being Don Quixote de la Mancha rather than Alonso Quijano the Good. We notice that he returns to being Alonso Quijano the Good, not the Pious. And although he agrees to stay home for a year, he refuses to deny Dulcinea's beauty.

When knight-errantry—or the imagination in *that* particular form—is repudiated, Quixote has nothing to do but die; but no mention is made of Dulcinea except for the claim by Carrasco and Sancho that she is now "as disenchanted as you could wish" (984, 986). It is at this point—reflected in the responses of his friends—that the gain of sanctity is balanced, or overweighed, by the loss of imagination. Thus if the hero without imagination has to die, the book *Don Quixote* (which has been equated with its hero, and on the last page is once again equated also with its author [Cid Hamete Benengeli]—"we two are one") has nothing to do but end. And yet the paragraph that begins with Quixote receiving "all the sacraments," expressing his "abomination [*después de haber abominado*] of books of chivalry," and "dying in his own bed so peacefully and in so Christian a manner," ends with the curate and notary needing to witness the fact that Alonso Quijano the Good "was truly dead," so "that some author other than Cid Hamete

Benengeli might not have the opportunity of falsely resurrecting him" in a sequel (987). In Spanish, Putnam's "resurrecting" is *resucitase*, which Shelton translated "to raise him from death again" (Jarvis: "raise him from the dead").[2]

Alexander James Duffield, writing in 1881, attributed the sacred parodies to Cervantes' anticlericalism:

> I do not contend that Cervantes was tilting at the Christian faith; it would be a gross libel to do so, but that he did fearlessly express his scorn for Romish ritual and priestly insolence, arrogance, and tyranny, would be folly to deny. One of the methods by which our great and sunny satirist abolished for ever the sham sages and mock knights was bringing them into the light of nature and common sense, making myth and fiction and lie to come in contact with reality; and when he makes rosaries out of shirt-tails, puts holy water into porringers, mitres and *sanbenitos* on asses's backs, and the bones of saints and the holiness of friars into Sancho's mouth, it is to bring all these to a like test.[3]

Duffield's phrase "the sham sages and mock knights" suggests that he thinks Cervantes used the harmless figure of the knight-errant to get safely at something more serious and controversial. Erasmus's *Praise of Folly* and such works had been popular at the court of Charles V and would certainly have been read by Cervantes; but with the ascension of Philip II they were placed on the Index, were not reprinted, and the Erasmian sort of ironic writing (for example, *La vida de Lazarillo de Tormes*) was prohibited.[4] How did Cervantes' book escape censorship? The Dulcinea-Virgin parallel might have been overlooked because it was so much at the heart of Cervantes' source of parody, the chivalric romance.[5] But the chivalric romances, as many scholars of the period have noted, were a dead horse for Cervantes to be beating; it seems possible that he was using the romances as a stalking horse (to continue my metaphor) for something else, more controversial and important. How such scenes were read in Spain, however, is less relevant than how, with the strain of deism in the 1720s, and Addison's epistemology of the Novel and Uncommon, they could have been read in England.[6]

In his formulation of Quixotism as mediated desire, René Girard noted that in the *Quixote* "[c]hivalric existence is the *imitation* of Amadis in the same sense that the Christian's existence is the imitation of Christ."[7] We can modify Girard's formulation to say that *Don Quixote* offered a new form of mediation that replaced that of the clergy, the apostolic succession that mediated between God and man, by direct contact with the Book. But, as Cervantes shows, as if ironizing Protestantism (specifically the Lutheran version with its emphasis on bringing the Book down to the people), one mediator is simply replaced by another—Christ by Amadis of Gaul, and, with even greater irony, the interpreter-priest by the Book itself. For Cervantes' purposes, this book is the Book of Chivalry, a book of manners and not the Book of God, which it has replaced with a more ambiguous and relaxed morality. Although he says he has destroyed the chivalric romances, he merely juxtaposes positive and negative interpretations, balancing them.

Religion Theatricalized: Addison

In his own way Addison aestheticized religion, but, as the spokesman of novelty, he required a practical model, whose comic locus was the two theatrical representations in *Don Quixote* part 2 and the problems they raised about the relativity of sense impressions relating to appearance and reality. The first, *The Parliament of Death*, Quixote saw through; the second, the puppets' performance of the story of Melisendra, Gaiferos, and the Moors, he did not. The first was religious allegory, the second romance. Addison chooses the second as his model in the *Spectator*.

Issue no. 335 directly recreates Don Quixote's response to the puppet show: Sir Roger de Coverley goes to the theater to see Ambrose Philips's *Distrest Wife*, an adaptation of Racine's *Andromache*. It interests him primarily because it reminds him of his own Dulcinea, the Widow who has rejected his advances. "These Widows, Sir," he says of Andromache, "are the most perverse Creatures in the World" (1:241). Sir Roger, unlike Quixote, makes no move toward the stage. Like other Tory gentlemen, he is obsessed with the memory of past defeats of a chivalric sort focused on a widow, who would have reminded Addison's readers of the rich widow pursued by the egregious Presbyterian Hudibras.[8] But the theatrical representation has distanced his experience, rendering it a harmless "pleasure of the imagination."

As its title indicates, the *Spectator* is based on the metaphor of life as theater. The disinterested Mr. Spectator and his "Fraternity of Spectators who live in the World without having any thing to do in it" are defined as "every one that considers the World as a Theatre, and desires to form a right judgment of those who are the Actors on it" (no. 10; 1:45–46). They are Sancho Panzas observing the behavior of Quixotes in relation to the puppet show; and even the Quixote, Sir Roger, can remain a spectator of his own devotion without involving himself in the performance.

If *Don Quixote* offered the comic model of life-as-theater, the religious meaning of the metaphor, Addison reveals in no. 219, is related to the operation of divine providence. Addison dismisses the traditional metaphor, from Scripture and dear to the Puritans and Dissenters, of life as a pilgrimage with a destination in an afterlife of rewards and punishments. He replaces it with Epictetus's metaphor of the world as "a Theatre, where everyone has a Part allotted to him" and is judged by how well he plays his part (2:353).[9] If the spiritual pilgrimage stressed teleology, the theatrical metaphor draws attention to the provisional structure of society itself. Implied is the arbitrariness, inscrutability, and incalculable distance from our everyday concerns of a transcendent rather than an immanent God, one who cannot interfere in terms of miracles or of rewards and punishments in this world and the next (the center of Shaftesbury's critique of the Judeo-Christian religion).

Don Quixote's explanation for the delusion that led him to take the puppets for real was, as usual, the enchantment of a malign magician who has changed these figures into what "seemed to [Quixote] very real indeed" (685). On the one hand, Cervantes suggests a parallel between the enchanter of romance and the God of the Corpus Christi play, and on the other, between Ginés de Pasamonte and his puppets and, in the following episode, the duke and duchess and the practical jokes they play on Quixote and Sancho. They create a spectrum from the religious to the secular, from priestcraft to charlatanry to politics and statecraft. These analogies are never far from the surface in the theatrical references of the *Spectator* and its offshoots (in the works of Fielding, Hogarth, and others).

Throughout, Addison presents the world of London as one of spectacle and spectators, and, when he stops to examine the metaphor,

it is as a way of understanding divine providence. Then in the "Pleasures of the Imagination" he elevates the spectator's response into the
knight's colorful imagination (which would include Sir Roger's memories of the widow) in contrast to the real, bleak world in which he lives.

In his commentary on Ovid's *Metamorphoses* (1704), Addison
took issue with his predecessors who (like the actors of *The Parliament of
Death*) turned the "persons of his [Ovid's] poems" into "virtues and
vices" or "discover[ed] in him the greatest mysteries of the Christian religion, and [found] almost in every page some typical representations of
the World, the Flesh, and the Devil." Accordingly he replaced Christian
allegorizing and moralizing with a description of Ovid's "beauties and
imperfections."[10] We can understand his description of the "beauties"
of *Paradise Lost* in the *Spectator* in the same light. The Ovid commentary reminds us that the sequence began with the aestheticizing of a religious reading—and that "aestheticizing" transforms belief in religious
doctrine into enjoyment of the senses, a secular sense of "worship."

Laughter as Release from Religious Gravity: Shaftesbury

Hume's aesthetics of the perfect circle explored the issue of taste
within the model of the Beautiful offered by Shaftesbury.[11] But this was
a model that, as Hume no doubt understood, was a replacement of the
Judeo-Christian deity with a platonic ideal.

Shaftesbury's aesthetics (which we can designate the aesthetics of
Don Quixote, as opposed to the aesthetics of Sancho Panza) replaced
the living woman with a Greek sculpture, idealizing her ultimately by a
geometrical form and a platonic idea. The platonic idea, however, prior
to that, replaced the deity itself. Shaftesbury expanded "love" and
"admiration" of "order, harmony, and proportion" into an aesthetic
equivalent of worship. The object of such "ecstasy and rapture" is the
deity. The "perfection and height of virtue" (and so of beauty), Shaftesbury concludes, "must be owing to the belief of a God," but this cannot
be a Judeo-Christian deity. In order to be disinterested, virtue must
replace the reliance on the ogre "god" of rewards and punishments
with a platonic idea of a god—in effect, a deist god—whose "divine
example" we can properly imitate.[12]

The penance Quixote does in the Sierra Morena is for love of

Dulcinea, not for his sins; the code of "punishment" he inflicts on Dulcinea's denigrators, usually redounding upon himself, recalls, if it does not parody, the Christian system of rewards and punishments. Sancho tells Quixote that one should love God "for Himself alone, without being moved by any hope of eternal glory or fear of Hell."[13] One comes to wonder whether corporal punishment in this world is not being opposed to the punishment in the afterlife promised by religious doctrine—as if to say, there's enough of it in *this* world. At the least, it stands in glaring contrast to the disinterestedness of Quixote's love for Dulcinea, which by contrast is called by ordinary people "madness."

When Quixote elsewhere tells Sancho, "You are a bad *Christian*, . . . for you never forget an injury that once has been done you" (1.17.160), he is also speaking words acceptable to Shaftesbury and the deists, who believed in the teachings of Jesus as against the orthodoxy of rewards and punishments, in this life as in the next, created by priests to ensure their power over their congregations. The progression in *Don Quixote* was from the pain of punishments to the indignity and ridicule of a practical joke—and to the putting in question of these practical jokes by the selfless idealism of Quixote's imagination, which was impervious to these "tests."

In fact, Shaftesbury regarded these risible scenes as testing the truth of Spanish chivalry and finding it wanting.[14] He does not go into the effects of chivalric obsession on Quixote or the virtue with which it endows his devotion to Dulcinea. These tests of chivalry could, however, have served as a model for his far more radical strategies for discrediting rewards and punishments as the symbol of a priest-ridden religion.

Shaftesbury laid the groundwork, in his *Letter concerning Enthusiasm* and *Sensus Communis: An Essay on the Freedom of Wit and Humour* (1708, 1709), for Addison's transformation of punitive satire into pragmatic comedy.[15] *Sensus Communis* was the locus for both his argument in favor of wit and humor as a test of truth and for his aesthetics of the beautiful and ugly. They join in the observation that "nothing is ridiculous except what is deformed; nor is anything proof against raillery except what is handsome or just" (beautiful and virtuous) (1:85).

The argument in the *Letter concerning Enthusiasm*, which connects a critique of enthusiasm with a defense of ridicule, is against

persecution of deviant religious belief; for "want of liberty may account
for want of a true politeness, and for the corruption or wrong use of
pleasantry and humour"; that is, their corruption into satire. And the
buffoonery will "fall heaviest where the constraint has been the se-
verest. The greater the weight is, the bitterer will be the satire. The
higher the slavery, the more exquisite the buffoonery" (1:51).

Shaftesbury draws on a tradition of positive laughter—a secular,
philosophical tradition, beginning with Hippocrates, the father of
medicine, who developed the idea of the therapeutic power of laughter,
and close after Hippocrates came Lucian's Menippus, the laughing
philosopher of "Dialogues of the Dead."[16] But Aristotle's own formula
in *De Anima* ("Of all living creatures only man is endowed with laughter") interpreted laughter as man's highest spiritual privilege, inaccessi-
ble to other creatures.[17] And in *Poetics* 6, immediately after his definition of the subject of comedy as the low and ugly (he promises to
develop the subject later), he turns to the beneficial effects of tragedy,
its purgation of the emotions of pity and fear. By implication, comedy
purges other equivalent emotions (on a lower level), presumably such
as pain, anger, and disgust.

We recall the passage in which Sancho cannot restrain his laughter at Quixote when he learns that the source of his terror was the
fulling hammers. In Shelton's striking translation, this reads: "[H]is
cheeks were swoln with laughter, giving withal evident Signs that he
was in danger to burst, if he did not permit that violent passion to
make a sally," and again he laughs "in such violent manner, to press his
sides hardly with both his hands to save himself from bursting."[18] In
the *Quixote* text this scene of the purgation of laughter is surrounded
by scenes of literal purgation—as the result of Fierabras's balm, on both
Quixote and Sancho, though it is restorative on the first and exhaust-
ing on the second. It is laughter that serves as Sancho's therapy.

Shaftesbury's cathartic theory of comedy could have served as
Addison's model for aestheticizing the transgressive emotions of satire
as positive laughter. Addison began his discussion of laughter in *Spectator* no. 249 by invoking the religious tradition—the Latitudinarian
discourse of "cheerfulness" and "mirth," which defended cheerfulness
as a reaction both to the moroseness of the Puritan ethos of the Civil

War and Interregnum and to the excesses of the court wits of the Restoration.[19] The discourse of "cheerfulness" and "joyfulness" Stuart Tave took to be the religious line on laughter. It was through Barrow and the divines, he argued, that "the way was prepared and the paths made straight for the appearance of Addison. And we may be certain that Addison knew Barrow, and Hacket, well enough." True enough, Addison does cite them in reply to Richard Blackmore's *Essay upon Wit* (1716).[20] The reference, however, which is in *Free-Holder* no. 45, is to Socrates—to the philosophical tradition; to any source that will support his reinterpretation of Hobbesian laughter.

Addison uses the religious tradition of cheerfulness (though hardly a transgressive category) to turn it away, like imagination and satire, from its religious associations toward the pleasure of aesthetic response. In *Spectator* nos. 381 and 384 he picks up the religious connotations of cheerfulness and opposes them to mirth: "I have always preferred Chearfulness to Mirth." His argument is that to "Men of austere Principles" (presumably Mr. Spectator) mirth is "too wanton and dissolute," filled with "a certain Triumph and Insolence of Heart" (again he evokes Hobbes). Indeed, mirth and cheerfulness, laugh and smile, are variant forms of comportment: Mirth is "an Act," a laugh; cheerfulness is "an Habit of the Mind. Mirth is short and transient, Chearfulness fixt and permanent" (3:429). Sir Roger has "a mirthful Cast in his Behaviour"; and Steele, in one of his *Spectator* pieces, distinguished laughter from "sober and polite mirth," summing up his attitude in the preface to *The Conscious Lovers* (1722), where he argued that comedy should elicit a "joy too exquisite for laughter."[21]

In no. 249, Addison subordinates both cheerfulness and mirth to the figure of Laughter himself in paroxysms (in Milton's words) "holding both his sides." He draws on the same tradition of therapeutic and cathartic laughter, defining man as "the merriest Species of the Creation" ("all above and below him are Serious"). He is going against the clerical line, which he associates with the Church of Rome but which as well fits English Puritans, "that Laughter was the effect of Original Sin, and that *Adam* could not laugh before the Fall." "Laughter is indeed," he writes, echoing Hippocrates, "a very good Counter poise to the Spleen." And he ends the quotation from "L'Allegro" asking Mirth to "admit me of thy Crue / To live with her, and live with thee, / In unreproved Pleasures free"—words that, of course point toward the "Pleasures of the Imagination." None of these responses is proscribed so long as it is pleasurable and not tendentious.

In Shaftesbury's hands the model of purgative laughter is closer to Cervantes' than to Addison's: Following the old hydraulic metaphor of the humors, his argument is that if the liberty of laughter is suppressed (censored) it will find an alternative vent, emerging as buffoonery or worse—perhaps civil disturbance.[22]

Shaftesbury's model is the balanced and harmonious system. With his formulation in which beauty equals virtue, based on the model of "a body and parts proportionable," it is difficult to say whether aesthetics or politics came first. His Whig idea of the English body politic was of a harmonious balance between monarch, aristocracy, and people. In his aestheticization of worship into taste he limits the aesthetic responders, however, "to those who have any knowledge or practice of the kind" (1: 279), pretty plainly referring to the aristocrats. These are the civic humanists whose ownership of property provides the disinterestedness necessary to judge beauty and govern the nation as well as to employ ridicule as a proper test of truth.

The worst restraint upon their liberty is "gravity." In *Sensus Communis* Shaftesbury cites an "ancient sage" to the effect "that humour was the only test of gravity; and gravity of humour. For a subject which would not bear raillery was suspicious; and a jest which would not bear a serious examination was certainly false wit" (1:52). Ultimately, gravity and all that "is contrary to good breeding is in this respect as contrary to liberty."

Ridicule then is an aspect of Whig "liberty." In the words of Shaftesbury's defender Charles Bulkeley (1751), "[n]othing can be plainer than that his Lordship uses the word *ridicule* as synonimous to *freedom, familiarity, good humour*, and the like"; that it is a social distinction, the "sort of freedom which is taken amongst gentlemen and friends who know one another perfectly well."[23] Shaftesbury defines this as "what passes in select companies, where friends meet knowingly, and with that very design of exercising their wit, and looking freely into all subjects, I see no pretence for any one to be offended at the way of raillery and humour, which is the very life of such conversations" (1:53). He is defining an ideal Whig community. As he explains, laying the groundwork for Addison's *Spectator*, he is writing "in defence only of the liberty of *the club*, and of that sort of freedom which is taken amongst gentlemen and friends who know one another perfectly well"—well off, therefore disinterested, gentlemen, free of religious scruples and monarchical subservience. Thus "good breeding" and "liberty" are aspects of conversation as opposed to the monological discourse of "men of slavish principles," who "affect a superiority over the vulgar, and . . . despise the multitude" (1:53). While we might be inclined to apply the last phrase to the gentlemen of the Whig club, Shaftesbury is thinking of the Hobbesian politics of the Tory-Jacobites, which includes in particular popish priests.[24] The Whigs, however superior to the vulgar and the multitude (as proved the case with Shaftesbury's privileged oligarchy), are the "lovers of mankind [who] respect and honour conventions and societies of men." Therefore, in the Whig "public space," conversation implies simply intercourse between equals—not, as among Tories, a grave priest talking down to inferiors:

> A freedom of raillery, a liberty in decent language to question everything, and an allowance of unravelling or refuting any argument, without offence to the arguer, are the only terms which can render such speculative conversations any way agreeable. For, to say truth, they have been rendered burdensome to mankind by the strictness of the laws prescribed to them, and by the prevailing pedantry and bigotry of those who reign in them, and assume to themselves to be dictators in these provinces. (1:49)

In this way Shaftesbury established the foundation for an aesthetics in which "mere will and power" are associated with absolute rule in politics, the Great or Sublime in aesthetics, and malicious satire in rhetoric; perfect balance and harmony are associated with the Beautiful or the civic humanist aristocracy.

Addison, by contrast, more realistically associated the shifting pragmatism of search, pursuit, and discovery with the middle area he calls the Novel, merging the best in the other two terms. Indeed, Addison recovers, along with satire, Shaftesbury's "liberty" of wit and ridicule as pure laughter (purged of Shaftesbury's deism) and his "test of truth" against possibly religious subjects as the discovery of novelty.

Two forms of the Whig ethos can be summed up as Whigs in power and out: Addison was a Revolution Whig, in office for all of his career except for the four years in which the Harley Whigs and Boling-broke Tories were in power—the period during which he constructed his ethos of Whigs in the ascendant. A fact to remember—which was already apparent in the importance of "enthusiasm" as a touchstone—is that religion was the central issue at the founding of the Whig party. As J. G. A. Pocock points out, "the First Whigs were a faction of former Presbyterians" whose aim at the Restoration was "the institutionaliza-tion of dissent," whose twin pillars were the Test Act and the Toleration Act—anticlericalism (anti-Catholicism) and toleration of dissent.[25] These First Whigs, led by the first earl of Shaftesbury, found their cause in Exclusion, and their essentially revolutionary politics was embodied in Locke's *Treatises of Government* (written c. 1680, published 1689). After the successful revolution of 1688 a splinter of these First Whigs re-mained dissatisfied and separate from the so-called Revolution Whigs who supported William III and his European wars right on into the reign of Queen Anne. Addison was one of the latter; Shaftesbury in important respects remained, following the doctrines of his grand-father, a First Whig. The distinction is clear enough in the difference between Shaftesbury's and Addison's treatment of the religious issue.[26]

Wit's Razor: Shaftesbury and Swift

The terms *enthusiasm* and *wit* were joined and redefined by Shaftesbury in his *Letter Concerning Enthusiasm* and *Sensus Communis; An Essay on the Freedom of Wit and Humour.* At this time Shaftesbury was accused of writing Swift's *A Tale of a Tub*, which had appeared just four years before, and Swift of writing Shaftesbury's *Letter Concerning Enthusiasm.* "Here," Swift wrote to Ambrose Philips on 14 September 1708, "has been an Essay of Enthusiasm lately publisht that has run mightily, and is very well writt, All my Friends will have me to be the Author, sed ego non credulus illis. By the free Whiggish thinking I should rather take it to be yours: But mine it is not; For tho I am every day writing my Speculations [on religion and the church] in my Chamber, they are quite of another sort."[27]

In a letter of about the same time to Lord Somers (the dedicatee of both *Tale* and *Letter Concerning Enthusiasm*), Shaftesbury expressed concern that the manuscript version of his *Letter* was about to be published as a work of Swift. He associated Swift's name with the names of Toland, Tindal, Collins, and John Asgill.[28] In his next work, *Sensus Communis*, however, he writes:

> But some gentlemen there are so full of the spirit of bigotry and false zeal, that when they hear principles examined, sciences and art inquired into, and matters of importance treated with this frankness of humour, they imagine presently that all professions must fall to the ground, all establishments come to ruin, and nothing orderly or decent be left standing in the world. They fear, or pretend to fear, that religion itself will be endangered by this free way. (1:52)

With these words he could be laying the groundwork for Swift's reply to the critics of the *Tale* in his "Apology" attached to the fifth edition, published one year after *Sensus Communis*.[29]

The cross-attribution of these works is not surprising. In order to explain the common denominators between their two texts, Shaftesbury has to have read either Swift's *Tale* or a mutual source. His argument rests on the observation that men "are wonderfully happy in a faculty of deceiving themselves," for which "a very small foundation of any passion will serve us." (He and Swift must both have known Rochester's lines in "Artemisa to Chloe" concerning a fool's "perfect joy of being well deceived.") Shaftesbury's sentence is significantly followed by the Quixotic formula: "Thus, by a little affectation in love-matters, and with the help of a romance or novel," a man will grow into a "*belle passion* in good earnest."[30] (Elsewhere, Shaftesbury associates travel narratives with the Quixotic romances: "These are in our present Days, what *Books of Chivalry* were, in those of our Forefathers"—connected by "faith.")[31]

Like Swift, Shaftesbury applies this pleasing delusion to religious belief: "Even a good Christian, who would needs be over-good, and thinks he can never believe enough, may, by a small inclination well improved, extend his faith so largely as to comprehend in it not only all scriptural and traditional miracles, but a solid system of old wives' stories."[32] The words "well improved," together with his reference (in a later passage) to "the evil as well as the good spirit of prophecy" and "the operation of this spirit is everywhere the same as to the bodily organs" (1:32), recall the argument of Swift's addendum to the *Tale*, "The Mechanical Operation of the Spirit."

In this way enthusiasm is born for both Shaftesbury and Swift, and of course also Addison, who in the "Pleasures of the Imagination" produces his own version of the "faculty of deceiving themselves" but with a positive rather than negative emphasis, under the Strange and the "faerie way," a strictly literary genre: "many [readers] are prepossest with such false Opinions, as dispose them to believe these particular Delusions; at least, we have all heard so many pleasing Relations in favour of them, that we do not care for seeing through the Falshood, and willingly give our selves up to so agreeable an Imposture" (*Spectator* no. 419; 3:571–72).

Shaftesbury's hydraulic metaphor echoes the metaphor Swift applies to enthusiasm in "The Digression on Madness" and, throughout his early work, serves as a basis for his model of politics and art:

> There are certain humours in mankind which of necessity must have vent. The human mind and body are both of them naturally subject to commotions: and as there are strange ferments in the blood, which in many bodies occasion an extraordinary discharge; so in reason, too, there are heterogeneous particles which must be thrown off by fermentation. Should physicians endeavour absolutely to allay [subdue] those ferments of the body, and strike in the humours which discover themselves in such eruptions, they might, instead of making a cure, bid fair perhaps to raise a plague, and turn a spring-ague or an autumn-surfeit into an epidemical malignant fever.

Shaftesbury unfolds the same story of the diverted vapors, which Swift focuses on the examples of Henry IV and Louis XIV, and concludes that once the worshipper becomes an enthusiast, "there follows always an itch of imparting it, and kindling the same fire in other breasts." "For inspiration is a real feeling of the Divine Presence, and enthusiasm a false one. But the passion they raise is much alike"—and he locates this need to impose one's madness on others, as Swift does, in "love" or sexual passion (1:36–37).

He offers the same warning about those "ill physicians in the body politic who would needs be tampering with these mental eruptions; and under the specious pretence of healing this itch of superstition, and saving souls from the contagion of enthusiasm, should set all nature in an uproar, and turn a few innocent carbuncles into an inflammation and mortal gengrene" (1:12). But these are not Swift's creators of new philosophies or religions but the clergymen and lawgivers, like Swift himself, who would control and contravene enthusiasm.

The chief form taken by the hydraulic metaphor in the *Letter Concerning Enthusiasm* is the deformity of "strong and healthy bodies which are debarred their natural exercise and confined in a narrow space":

> They are forced to use odd gestures and contortions. They have a sort of action, and move still, though with the worst grace imaginable. For the animal spirits in such sound and active limbs cannot lie dead or without employment. And thus the natural free spirits of ingenious men, if imprisoned and controlled, will find out other ways of motion to relieve themselves in their constraint; and whether it be in burlesque, mimicry, or buffoonery, they will be glad at any rate to vent themselves, and be revenged on their constrainers. (1:50)

Thus if "the natural free spirits of ingenious men" are blocked (along with the madness of enthusiasts) by religious censorship, they will "find out other ways . . . to relieve themselves in their constraint" and "vent themselves"; and these outlets take the form not of gentlemanly conversation but of "burlesque, mimicry, or buffoonery," terms he would doubtless have applied to Swift's *A Tale of a Tub*, as Addison does to Swift's Tory satire.

It must have been odd for the deist Shaftesbury to have found himself associated with a satire regarded as more subversive than his own, dedicated to the same great Whig, Lord Somers, but written by a Church of England clergyman who was attacking the position Shaftesbury was defending—liberty of the individual from the unnatural coils of priestcraft—and yet left the reader with a sense very similar to Shaftesbury's of the liberty and power of wit to sweep away follies. But Swift's follies were the corruptions of a true church, whereas Shaftesbury's were to be found in the Christian religion itself.[33] They would have agreed that ridicule is especially effective against "gravity"—but by "gravity" Shaftesbury meant, above all, priests and priestcraft, and

Swift meant enthusiasts, Dissenters, and Nonconformists. If Swift's version of ridicule as a test of truth shows the corruption at both extremes of popish and Dissenter enthusiasm, Shaftesbury's exposes the folly of a religion and a god of rewards and punishments—as opposed to disinterested—that is, freely chosen—virtue. Shaftesbury's call is for toleration.

Both Swift and Shaftesbury draw on the hydraulic metaphor and the disequilibrium of humors in the body caused by a proper vent being blocked, but Shaftesbury invokes Hippocrates' theory of the therapeutic power of laughter. (If Swift also invokes this, he does not let on.) In Swift's scenario, liberty (sexual energy) blocked will find an outlet in the brain and through the mouth in enthusiasm—and so in "new" philosophies, religions, and politics that lead to insurrection. In Shaftesbury's scenario, "the natural free spirits of ingenious men" permitted their natural exit will produce laughter—and a test of truth. Blocked they will be diverted into Tory satire as well as civil insurrection.

This "free spirit" can also produce poetry. Indeed enthusiasm, without the shackles of religion, may produce sublime poetry. An important aspect of Shaftesbury's critique of enthusiasm is the balancing of a positive sense of the term in poetry against religious enthusiasm, and in effect projecting something close to Addison's Great, though in terms of his own image of the body-vessel: "[W]hen the ideas or images received are too big for the narrow human vessel to contain" "enthusiasm" is used "to express whatever was sublime in human passions" (1:38). Addison writes: "Our Imagination loves to be filled with an Object, or to grasp at any thing that is too big for its capacity," such as "unbounded Views," which becomes one version of "an Image of Liberty." The remains of Shaftesbury's image of a "vessel" appears in the sense of "Confinement, when the Sight is pent up in a narrow Compass" (3:540–41).

According to one of Archbishop Tillotson's anti-wit formulations, "Wit is a very commendable quality, but then a wise man should always have the keeping of it. It is a sharp weapon, as apt for mischief as for good purpose if it be not well manag'd." "For wit is a keen instrument, and every one can cut and gash with it."[34] Swift draws upon the religious interpretation of wit, for example Tillotson's razor, and rewrites it in *A Tale of a Tub* as the reminder that "it is with *Wits* as with *Razors*, which are never so apt to *cut* those they are employ'd on, as when they have *lost their Edge*."[35] For Swift the danger of the razor depends on the astuteness of the wit, but he shows that he is aware of the problem, from which he was destined to suffer.[36]

In *A Tale of a Tub*, one of the wittiest books ever written, Swift devotes his preface to an attack on the wits who are regarded as so dangerous to church and state that, in the image of the Hobbesian Leviathan, they are seen to be attacking the ship of state.[37] Swift's "author" ironically echoes the proposal of the Moderns to delay and divert the whale with a tub, the wits with this Grub Street hack's "tale of a tub," on which the wits can be expected to expend their efforts, while the Moderns construct an academy in which to lodge and effectively neutralize them all (much as, years later, Swift proposed a madhouse in Dublin to house—or contain—the Irish Parliament). The preface itself is a "diversion" from the treatise, *A Tale of a Tub*, as the *Tale* is intended to be from the ship of state. This scenario is followed by an attack on ironic wit, by which is meant satire, and defense of its opposite panegyric, which leads eventually to the extremes of witty analysis and self-delusion that cancel each other out in "The Digression on Madness." On one side, the wit that flays and dissects ("I saw a woman flayed . . .") and on the other the delusion that creates the sense of felicity of being a fool among knaves.

Swift was playing a dangerous game. As he wrote *A Tale of a Tub* around the turn of the century, empiricism and Restoration wit joined in the extension of empirical philosophy into freethinking and deism, and wit came in for increasing suspicion from the pious: "Nothing," wrote Tillotson, "is so easy as to take particular phrases and expression out of the best Book in the world and to abuse them by forcing an odd and ridiculous sense upon them."[38]

With Swift, wit, irony, and burlesque were all capable of being mistaken for impiety. William Wotton, one of the protagonists of the "War of the Ancients and Moderns," drew particular attention to "our *Tale-teller's* Wit" (for example, in "the *Glosses* and *Interpretations of Scripture*"), claiming that Swift's *Tale* "is of so irreligious a nature, is so crude a Banter upon all that is esteemed as Sacred among all Sects and Religions among Men," that he feels he must expose it. "In one Word,

God and Religion, Truth and Moral Honesty, Learning and Industry are made a May-Game, and the most serious Things in the World are described as so many several Scenes in a *Tale of a Tub*."[39]

Was the joke of the three brothers, their three ladies, and the three "oratorial machines" a parody of the doctrine of the Trinity? From Swift's point of view it was obviously a Satanic parody of true Christian doctrine, like Milton's of Satan, Sin, and Death. But it was not taken kindly by "grave" orthodox readers;[40] and he responded in his "Apology" to the fifth edition, defending himself from accusations of freethinking, claiming, with tongue in cheek, that the original manuscript had had four machines and one was dropped without his authority. The satire is presumably aimed at the confused and confusing controversy over the Trinity, which raged at this time, but Swift's critics can be forgiven for reading it as a cut at the folly of the doctrine itself as well as the controversy.

Swift repeats the scenario of Quixote's "piece of bread as black and moldy as the suit of armor he wore" in *A Tale of a Tub* when Peter, the representative of Roman Catholicism, declares that brown bread is a shoulder of mutton, to the dismay of his brothers Martin and Jack, who see, smell, touch, and taste only a crust of bread. When one of the brothers objects to his interpreting "Silver Fringe [signifies] *Broomstick . . .* in a *Mythological*, and *Allegorical* Sense," Peter excoriates him "as one that spoke irreverently of a *Mystery*, which doubtless was very useful and significant, but ought not to be over-curiously pryed into, or nicely reasoned upon" (88). In order to make his brothers believe in his mysteries, Peter must treat them as Quixote treats various people he encounters, by attempting to impose his delusion by force.

Wotton argued that "Images in the Church of *Rome* give our *Tale-teller* but too fair a Handle" for an attack on Christianity itself: "The Author, one would think, copies from Mr. *Toland*, who always raises a Laugh at the Word *Mystery*, the Word and Thing whereof he is known to believe to be no more than a *Tale of a Tub*" (53). Wotton and others noted that Swift and the Toland of *Christianity Not Mysterious* (published in 1696, just as Swift was writing, and eight years before he published, the *Tale*) agreed on certain basics. They both began from the same assumption that (in Swift's later words) "Religion was invented by cunning Men to keep the World in Awe"; that is, by an unscrupulous priesthood that turns plain doctrinal statements into mysteries, thereby ensuring their position of power while misrepresenting the true conditions of individual salvation. They all draw upon a common Protestant and Whig heritage for the terms of their critique.

In his "Sermon on the Trinity" Swift summed up the way the deists looked to an orthodox Church of England man: "[T]hey can believe that the World was made by Chance; that God doth not concern himself with Things below; will neither punish Vice, nor reward Virtue; that Religion was invented by cunning Men to keep the World in Awe."[41] Swift's satire on allegorical interpretation is, like Addison's, aimed primarily at the papists—it is Peter who uses exegetical techniques that corrupt the original text; and he echoes the Protestant belief that to interpret Scripture in any other than the literal sense is to "add to, or diminish" the text without divine sanction. On this point overlaps with the deists who also believed that words must be interpreted according to their common, literal usage.

Swift's excuse in the "Apology" was that he attacked the corruptions of religion, not religion itself—or, it could have been thought, more basic than "corruptions," superstition itself. As Fielding wrote, in his obituary of Swift in the *True Patriot* (5 Nov. 1745), he "employed his wit to the noblest purposes, in ridiculing as well superstition in religion as infidelity." And in his poem "The Author upon Himself," Swift himself sees the problem of wit from both perspectives, outsiders' and his own: "Swift had the sin of wit, no venial crime" and "He reconcil'd divinity and wit" (ll. 9, 12).

In many ways Swift's antipapist satire complements that of the Whigs in the 1690s. We need to recall that he began as an Old Whig and believed that he remained one when he joined the Tory ministers, Harley and Bolingbroke, in 1710. He has certainly adapted in *A Tale of a Tub* a point of view not inconsistent with the anticlerical wing of the Whigs—as laid out, for example, in Harrington's attack on "priestcraft."[42] But, of course, he is also satirizing the enthusiasts, the Dissenters, for whom the Whigs urged toleration (as they urged penalties for papists).

One result was the attack on Swift as a freethinker and infidel, and indeed the question: Did the *Tale* show Anthony Collins how to apply wit to biblical typology and Thomas Woolston to Christ's miracles? How is the wit of Swift's *Tale* different from that of Woolston's *Discourses of the Miracles of our Saviour* (1727–29)?[43] At Woolston's trial for blasphemy in 1729 the attorney general argued that "this was the most Blasphemous Book that ever was Publish'd in any Age whatsoever, in which Our Saviour is compared to a Conjurer, Magician and Imposture, and the Holy Gospel, as wrote by the Blessed Evangelists, turn'd into Ridicule and Ludicrous Banter." The defense argued, much as Swift had in his "Apology," that Woolston had not written "with a Blasphemous Intent, to bring Our Religion into Contempt, but to put Our Religion upon a better Footing, and shew, That the Miracles of Our Saviour were to be understood in a Metaphorical Sense, and not as they were Literally Written."[44]

Contrary to Swift's and Shaftesbury's essentially polemical ends, Addison's aim (at least for rhetorical purposes) was to turn wit from a weapon that can cut both ways (Swift's distinction was only between a skilled and unskilled wielder of the razor) into a tool of enquiry, an epistemology of the Novel or Uncommon. The origins of Addison's position are nevertheless in Shaftesbury. Certainly "test" is as important a word for Shaftesbury as "search" and "learn" for Addison: terms that enabled Addison to connect wit with learning and his aesthetic category, the Novel—the search for the new. But "a liberty in decent language to question everything" carries wit beyond Addison's more polite and politic model.

Following Shaftesbury's defense of enthusiasm, Addison turns enthusiasm from a religious to an aesthetic response—from a response to religious doctrine (or a Dissenter preacher) to a response to beautiful stimuli, whether in nature or in the writings of Milton and Shakespeare, purged of religion and politics. For Addison the lapse into allegorical interpretation, defended by the Papists and some High Churchmen and ridiculed by both Swift and the deists, can only be recovered by the process of turning the allegory into a search for, a definition of, beauty—or, more specifically, by way of wit a search for the new and surprising. Addison makes gestures toward orthodoxy (as he did toward composition with the Tories), but he generally follows the interpretation of Locke that assumes reason and sensory perception to be the only means of gaining knowledge. For Swift, on the other hand, empiricism represents only one means of gaining knowledge, and an undependable one at that.

Quixote showed how to question *and* validate imagination in place of mystery—imagination being the appreciation of beauty in nature (and secondarily in art). In terms of sacred texts, Swift's position is that because human reason is unable properly to interpret the literal meaning of the Bible "mysteries," it must be superseded by belief. Addison's position is that this belief, questionable as it is, should be superseded by—can be recovered as—aesthetic pleasure.

In the quarrel of the Ancients and Moderns, the Ancients read the classics for their ethical content, as ideals of *humanitas* and models to live by. The Moderns—the Richard Bentleys and William Wottons—regarded them as objects of scholarship, determining the text's authenticity by reconstructing its original historical context, calling for precise definition in terms of time and place.[45] The Modern position came to mean scholarship, or the reliance on "learning," and could be regarded by Swift as the secular branch of the deists. In this case, the Ancients' classicism was parallel with Christian orthodoxy: both wished to allegorize the ancient text in a pragmatic attempt to accommodate it to the morals of contemporary society. From a deist perspective, Pope's Homer "New-dressed" was, therefore, merely a corruption of the original text, a distortion of its actual sense in its particular time and place. The same, therefore, was true of sacred texts.

Substitute romance for classical text and, seen from the Modern perspective, Quixote is living by models and ideals of the imagination (in Hobbes's sense of the word) in a Modern world of precise historical time and place—but which preserves *not* the ideality or efficacy of the romance but the poetry, the pure form or the pleasure of the pure form, which is aesthetics. Thus Addison, whom we might call the Whig (or orthodox) deist, recovers the text (whether Ovid or Milton) from both the ancient Scylla and the modern Charybdis by aestheticizing it—replacing both Christian allegory and historicity with its "beauties." As a document of the Moderns, Addison's "Pleasures" metamorphoses ancient morality into the Novel; religious worship into the Beautiful—enthusiasm into the Great (here and now, in the present moment).

But if Shaftesbury laid the groundwork for Addison's "Pleasures," he and Swift agreed that the categories of imagination, satire, and wit are as potentially dangerous as the utilization of a razor in the wrong hands. The areas Addison recovers or vindicates remain problematic for them, as they did above all for Cervantes.

The Aesthetics of Sancho Panza: Hogarth

Thirty years after his print *The Mystery of Masonry* (fig. 10) Hogarth rematerialized Sancho's response to Quixote's attack on the puppet show in the second plate of his *Analysis of Beauty*, applied now to the problematics of aesthetics (fig. 13). Again, the puppet show itself is absent, and Quixote as well: only, in a marginal diagram on the right, the same Sancho (Coypel's) who appeared in *The Mystery of Masonry* is responding with surprise to (in the opposite left margin) a beautiful woman. In the text Hogarth explains that his pose of "the comic posture of astonishment"—signified by a "plain curve"—is taken from Don Quixote's attack on the puppet show, and he contrasts this with "the effect of the serpentine lines in the fine turn of the Samaritan woman, . . . taken from one of the best pictures Annibal Carrache ever painted" (103).[46] The reference is to *Christ and the Woman of Samaria* (Milan, Brera),[47] and the implication is that for Sancho the equivalent of Quixote demolishing the puppet show—his attack on the Moors who are pursuing the "beauteous" Princess Melisendra—is Jesus exposing the beautiful Woman of Samaria as an adulteress. The group inside the picture, immediately under Sancho's nose, and so equally an object of his astonishment, consists of a young lady (more serpentine lines), who is in the process of committing adultery (exchanging a note with) a young man behind the back of her elderly husband (paralleled, in plate 1, by the adulterous triangle of sculptures, of Venus, Apollo, and Hercules).

In both cases a young lady formed by Hogarth's serpentine Lines of Beauty is proving herself to be an adulteress. By implication it is Shaftesbury's Platonic aesthetics, with its equation of beauty and virtue, that is being labeled Quixotic by the astonished Sancho. Hogarth's dissociation of beauty and virtue is radically heterodox. The common view was expressed a few months later by John Hawkesworth (who subsequently wrote a favorable review of the *Analysis* in the *Gentleman's Magazine*): "[T]hose who wish to be LOVELY, must learn early to be GOOD."[48]

Hogarth asks us to see from Sancho's position and so replaces the hypothetical Dulcinea with a living and blemished woman, putting also in question the corollary, posited by both Shaftesbury and Don Quixote, that beauty is accompanied by high rank and social status. The adulterous Samaritan Woman, in the margin, is formally parallel to the dancing nobleman, adjacent inside the picture, also consisting of the same Lines of Beauty (joined to his equally aristocratic partner by the spread legs of Henry VIII, in a niche above, whose royal virility is being admired by a plebeian man and woman standing between his legs and the two dancers); while filling the center of the scene is the mob of clumsy, "comic" shapes of the plebeian "country" dancers.

The question of which is real, the text (the dance) or the marginal comments (Sancho and the Woman of Samaria) represents a graphic equivalent of the problematization of textuality in the *Quixote*. There the texts of Cervantes/Cid Hamete Benengeli, including marginal comments and illustrations and even the quoted comments of a friend at the beginning and Cid Hamete at the end, distance and put in question the represented action.

In the margin immediately above Sancho's head is a small figure (no. 70) that juxtaposes two Latin crosses. In the text (66) Hogarth discusses them together with a Greek cross (no. 69) as a schema for "the figure of a man." In order to "produce a figure of tolerable variety," in the illustration he shows one Latin cross made of straight lines, the other of serpentine Lines of Beauty. The Latin cross is of course the Christian crucifix, which he has therefore rendered beautiful; that is, aestheticized as well as humanized. A few pages later in the text Hogarth remarks that "A man must have a good deal of practice to *mimic* such very *straight* or round motions, which being incompatible with the *human* form, are therefore *ridiculous*" (106, emphasis added).

The two crosses are Hogarth's symbol for the way he arrives at aesthetics. On the title page of the *Analysis* his logo is the traditional triangle of the Trinity, but Hogarth has replaced the Tetragrammaton (the four Hebrew letters that form the name of God) with the Line of Beauty, once again naturalized but this time with the head of a serpent. The epigraph from *Paradise Lost*—Satan, "Curl'd many a wanton wreath, in sight of Eve, / To lure her eye"—argues for a fleshing out of the line into a particular serpent, or a translation of Satan's negativity into an image of beauty related to the pleasure of pursuit, discovery, surprise, and the other elements associated with the Beautiful in the *Analysis*, illustrations and text.

Opposite the title page, the frontispiece, *Columbus breaking the Egg* (fig. 14, earlier used as subscription ticket for the *Analysis*), burlesques the composition of a Last Supper in order to celebrate Columbus's messianic discovery of a "new world"—analogous to his own *living* "discovery" of the principle of Beauty in a serpentine line. In this case Hogarth uses the Last Supper to indicate that religion is demystified only in order to be recovered as natural beauty. To illustrate his point he replaces the Host in the Last Supper with two serpentine eels, which form "Lines of Beauty," and two eggs. In the story of Columbus's jest at the expense of his detractors who said *anyone* could have made his discovery (a story connected by artists with Brunelleschi), he challenges them to stand an egg on end. When they cannot, he does so by breaking the egg and standing it on its broken end—showing skeptics *how* he discovered a new world. (In the text of the *Analysis* he asserts that the perfect oval of a female face is more alluring when broken, for example by a lock of hair.) In the last plate of *A Harlot's Progress* he had burlesqued the composition of a Last Supper to satirize a brutal society that uses harlots to atone for its sins. In the *Analysis of Beauty* he again burlesques a Last Supper, but now in order to celebrate Columbus's (Hogarth's) aesthetic discovery.

It cannot be an accident that in Columbus and his dinner table, Hogarth recalls Sancho and his, which he represented in his one independent illustration for *Don Quixote* (to judge by its size, shape, and composition modeled on Coypel's *Don Quixote* plates) (fig. 15).[49]

It depicts Sancho's attempt, as governor of the island of Barataria, to enjoy dinner: A "truly magnificent board was spread," but at every dish Sancho is stopped by the court physician with his wand, who, from Hogarth's point of view, is a figure of the connoisseur or art critic, rationalizing Sancho's starvation, while Sancho's position is expressed by the words, "I am dying of hunger" (2.47.809–10).[50]

Sancho represents the plain common sense of the Panzas in a

situation of taste that has been set up by the duke and duchess, who are entertaining, and being entertained by, Quixote and Sancho. (And is Hogarth recalling the duke and duchess with the aristocratic couple who dominate, and may be hosting, the country dance?) Sancho is being bullied by the physician (Hogarth would call him "quack") who will not permit him to follow his own *instinto*, arguing that he must eat "only in accordance with the usage and custom in other islands" or "only what is good for him" (rabbits because they are "a furry kind of food"; veal, "if it were not roasted and pickled"; here "too much moisture," there "too hot and filled with spices") based on the authority of Hippocrates—because, he tells Sancho, "I hold the degree of doctor from the University of Usuna."

I hesitate to make the connection between the courtiers and Lord Carteret, but *Sancho's Feast*—given its date of publication[51]—might also be read as an allegory of Hogarth's experience trying to make illustrations to please Carteret and Oldfield. The timing and the examples of Hogarth's later self-consciousness such as *Columbus breaking the Egg* would support such a hypothesis.

Hogarth's method of aestheticizing, like Sancho's, fleshes out a diagram into a representation of living humans, preferably a woman (women, he notes, are more beautiful because they consist of more serpentine lines than men), as the plain curve and the serpentine line are fleshed out into the representations of Sancho and the Samaritan woman, respectively. Though far more adventurous than Addison's aestheticizing of Milton and Ovid, it begins with the same assumption: religious allegory can be made viable by the critic by turning his attention to its "beauties." Nevertheless, to carry out his demystification Hogarth retains Addison's version of Quixote's metaphor of life as theater, and he regards the figure of Quixote and his confusions of illusion and reality through the eyes of Sancho.

If he idealized the tall Quixote in terms of the plebeian Roundheads of the Model Army, he nevertheless associates himself more accurately with the short, earthy Sancho. Contrasted with the combination of nobility and folly in his idealistic master, Sancho is the character who sees and judges truly. Hogarth's aesthetics (based on the accessibility of the living, flawed woman) is the aesthetics of Sancho.

[handwritten note:] Hogarth's aesthetics is the aesthetics of Sancho

Indeed, he associates himself, as well as his stance of plebeian common sense, with Sancho. He seems to have felt that he physically resembled Sancho (as he also resembled his pug, whose face he juxtaposed with his own in his best-known self-portrait). After his death his widow told visitors that the Sancho of *Sancho's Feast* was a self-portrait.[52]

It is also worth noting that the Sancho of Cervantes' text constantly spouts appropriate and inappropriate folk wisdom—old saws from oral tradition, obviously contrasted with the written and printed sources parroted by the educated Don Quixote. To Hogarth this would have meant that Sancho's discourse is based on common sense and is preferable to Quixote's upper-class romance-reading. Sancho reminds us that as *Don Quixote* epitomized the distinction between literary and existential experience, so in the early eighteenth century in England the stage (much to the dismay of Addison as well as Pope and the Tories) was dominated by popular, pre- or subliterary entertainment, shockingly removed from the literary representation of the classics, Shakespeare, Jonson, and Congreve.[53] The puppet shows, harlequinades, and rope-dances were absorbed into the relatively high literary form of satire—in the theater itself by Gay in *The Beggar's Opera*, in the mock-epic *Dunciad* by Pope, and in satiric prints by Hogarth. Gay showed how the demotic language of beggars can be absorbed into the discourse of opera, and Hogarth's earliest paintings were of a performance of *The Beggar's Opera* and its aristocratic audience. One of the functions of Hogarth's graphic art was to bridge these two areas and show a way for the demotic to be absorbed into something that he, if not Shaftesbury, would acknowledge to be high art. The literary model for this procedure was *Don Quixote* and its fiction in which the popular, common sense, and the proverbial (the world of Sancho), as well as the hard and gross reality of windmills and chamber pots, are absorbed into the literary imagination, or vice versa.

Between *The Mystery of Masonry* and *The Analysis of Beauty*, plate 2, the scene of Sancho watching with astonishment as Quixote demolishes the puppet show became the model for Hogarth's "progresses" and his "modern moral subjects." These are scenes that appear to be taking place on a stage with a central action responded to by spectators, usually in ways reminiscent of the way Quixote is treated by innkeepers and shepherds, dukes and duchesses. But always we assume Sancho's plebeian, empirical presence, which functions particularly in the face of "mysteries," aesthetic and moral.

Immediately following the *Hudibras* and *Don Quixote* illustrations, at the end of 1726, Hogarth published two political prints, coordinated with the launching of *The Craftsman*, as part of the opposition campaign to unseat Walpole. One alluded to *Gulliver's Travels*, which had appeared in October. (At about this same time Hogarth's friend Nicholas Amhurst, editor of *The Crafstman*, linked *Gulliver* and *Don Quixote* referring to "the same Manner that *Cervantes* exposes Books Books of *Chivalry*, or Captain *Gulliver* the Writings of *Travellers*.")[54] The second print, *Cunicularii: or the Wise Men of Godlimen* (fig. 16), was a popular reportorial image of Mary Toft, the so-called "Rabbit Woman" who had given birth to seventeen rabbits. London physicians, conspicuously including court physicians, had been taken in by the hoax. The print invokes Caleb D'Anvers' (Amhurst's) analogies in *The Craftsman* between quackery in medicine and in politics, hoaxes on the stage and in politics. The print shows the Sancho figure from *Mystery of Masonry*, at far left, his mouth hanging open, expressing amazement at the scene of rabbit-birth. He is labeled "The Rabbet [sic] getter," by which Hogarth means *be*getter, Mr. Toft. The composition recalls Sancho, Quixote, and the puppet show, but the story evokes Sancho's little play in which he attempts to pass off the country wench as Dulcinea.[55]

Cunicularii depicts, as one of the doctors exclaims, "A great birth," and the composition resembles a traditional scene of Wise Men bearing gifts to the Christ Child, but in this case arriving fortuitously at the moment of birth: They are there to witness a "Nativity" like the famous one in which the birth, as the deists complained, had precisely gone *un*witnessed. The wit lies in combining the "Miracle" of the Birth of Christ with the "hoax" of Toft's litter of rabbits—and the distant echo of Sancho's "Dulcinea" hoax. Hogarth has replaced the three Wise Men with the three "Wise Men of Godlimen," who are quacks (according to Hogarth's epigraph from *Hudibras*, "They held their Talents most Adroit / For any Mystical Exploit"), Mary the Mother with *Mary* Toft, and Jesus with the rabbits. The Mary-Mary analogy is made unmistakable by Toft's identification in the "key" as "The Lady in the straw," as if in a manger though no straw is in evidence. The Latin title plays on the pun of *cuniculus* (rabbit) and *cunnus* (vulva); and the foremost Wise Man is "An Occult Philosopher searching into the Depth of Things." The rabbit birth is, of course (like, it is implied, the Virgin Birth), fraudulent: yet another rabbit carcass ("too big") is being offered for sale at the door.

Besides being on a wavelength with the *Craftsman*'s satire of Walpole, suggesting that Toft is a Mary of our time, corrupted and Walpolean, *Cunicularii* is a parody, in the manner of Collins and Woolston, which "historicizes" the New Testament story in order to demystify and "allegorize" it. In 1724 Collins, in his *Discourse of the Grounds and Reasons of the Christian Religion*, had started his demystification of Scripture with the example of the Virgin Birth—always, among freethinkers, the miracle that evoked the most mirth. (Common sense said the story of Mary's virgin conception was a hoax and the aged Joseph a cuckold.) He had sought to uncover "the plain drift and design" of the story, "literally, obviously, and primarily understood," which he therefore was forced to interpret in "a secondary or typical, or mythical, or allegorical sense."[56]

In Woolston's *Discourses on the Miracles of our Saviour* this sense proved to be Jesus' attack on priestcraft. In his *First Discourse*, published early in 1727, Woolston satirized the Nativity, remarking of the "Wisemen" that had they acted "as wise as well as good Men," they would have brought gifts of not gold, frankincense, and myrrh but soap, candles, and sugar. In the same passage, as if he had seen Hogarth's *Cunicularii*, he refers to Mary as Jesus' "Mother in the Straw."[57] *Cunicularii* permitted Hogarth to go a step beyond Amhurst's satiric analogizing in *The Craftsman* to the mode of Collins and Woolston. On top of the political coding of court-ministry as quack doctors he adds the religious coding of Wise Men as quack doctors and the Virgin Mary as Mary Toft. A few years later he fleshed out *Mary* Toft into *M[ary]* Hackabout, the Harlot, which in a pre-publication state of Plate 2 included a portrait of Woolston. Hackabout progresses through parodies of a Visitation, Annunciation, and Flagellation. By the final plate, a Last Supper, the Harlot and her son have become the 1730s reality beneath the fiction of the Eucharistic Sacrifice.

The new element, introduced with the *Don Quixote* illustrations

and *Cunicularii*, was the politics of opposition. Hogarth imbibed opposition satire in a general way from the work of Swift, who regarded
himself as an Old Whig, always part of a Country Party, but more
directly he learned from his friend Amhurst and the opposition to
Walpole. By this time, the late 1720s, anticlerical satire was being
applied to Walpole, whose chief assistant in matters of religion was the
High Church Bishop of London, Edmund Gibson, known as "Walpole's Pope" because he was responsible for dispensing ecclesiastical
preferment and so control of the House of Lords. Gibson represented
the position that ecclesiastical authority should extend into civil affairs;
primarily, as it developed in his practice, in the case of prosecutions of
vice and heterodoxy—which also figure (related to Gibson) in the
Harlot's Progress.[58]

Gibson offered Hogarth an opportunity to indulge in anticlerical
satire. Plainly, however, he and Amhurst held a set of beliefs that were
not easily accommodated to those of their colleagues in the Walpole
opposition such as Arbuthnot, Swift, Gay, and Pope.[59] It is well known
that the opposition to Walpole was by no means of a piece—by no
means limited to, or distinguished by, the Jacobite-Tory nostalgia of
Swift himself (or Bolingbroke or Pope).[60] The first-mover of the *Craftsman,* the first person to reinterpret *Gulliver's Travels* as an anti-Walpole
satire, was a freethinker and Hanoverian Whig, and certainly no "Ancient." Bolingbroke, also a freethinker, was otherwise temperamentally
one with the exiled Swift and the Roman Catholic outsider Pope. For
Amhurst and Hogarth the past was not a Golden Age, a country-house
idyll, but Jacobite, tyrannical, priest-ridden, and (in Hogarth's case)
dominated by academic and Continental (in effect, Roman Catholic)
models of painting. Hatred of ecclesiastical tyranny was the element
shared by Amhurst, Bolingbroke, and Hogarth. Bolingbroke, the figure who bridged the two groups, kept his deism to himself, and both
Amhurst and Hogarth kept theirs under the umbrella of Hoadlian
latitudinarianism and Erastianism.

The strands of anti-Trinitarianism (Arianism and Socinianism)
within the church hierarchy, embodied in Bishop Hoadly (greatly admired by Hogarth and Amhurst, as well as Fielding), naturally served
as one challenge to the authority of the ministry, in particular to
Bishop Gibson's control over ecclesiastical patronage. The opposition

cry of "liberty" referred not only to freedom of property but freedom of thought, conscience, and speech, particularly in religious matters. This was a rhetoric that began in the Restoration but by the end of the century, in certain of its forms, had accrued traces of deism.

Hogarth's prints following his *Don Quixote* illustrations asked to be read as a bold extension of the Protestant attack on the particular emphases of counter-Reformation popery, and, in its context of Whig opposition anticlericalism, on the supposed acceptance of these by High Church Anglican prelates: the role of priests and their spiritual primacy, the nature of the Holy Sacrament as the Body of Christ, and the worship of the Virgin as Mother of Christ.

Hogarth may have intended to imply degeneration when he showed Mary reduced to a Walpolian Toft; but a cross that is "beautified" is a very different thing. What for Swift and Pope was a negative process, for Hogarth is a positive one. Toft was a living, contemporary Mary, consisting of serpentine lines and a face that Hogarth has in fact beautified beyond that of the real Toft.[61] The "demystification" or reduction of Mary to Mary Toft (or, in *Harlot,* to M[ary] Hackabout) involves the preference for the second (as in the Calvinist redefinition of the Eucharist as a friendly meal, the altar as a dinner table), because it contains the principle of natural beauty, which was excluded from the straight lines of such religious symbols as the Tetragrammaton and the Latin cross. The contrast is between religion (a clerical religion of what were held to be ridiculous doctrines such as the Trinity and the Eucharist) and Nature, in its deist sense of God.

Addison, in his "Notes on Ovid," had contrasted Virgil's and Ovid's representations of a goddess assuming the body of an old woman. "*Virgil's Iris* could not have spoken more majestically in her own shape; but Juno is so much altered from her self in *Ovid,* that the Goddess is quite lost in the Old Woman." Virgil's Iris raises the old woman to the level of a goddess, as in the georgic the poet as farmer endows dung with grace; the elevated style is an expression of the poet who turns even the lowest into the most elevated (or, in Addison's term, beautiful) poetry. Ovid (whose style Addison associates with "a low middle way of writing") shows the divine "lost in," or becoming, or embodied in, the ordinary—"the Goddess is quite lost in the Old Woman." In this respect Hogarth is, once again, drawing on Addison's

Novel, which invokes Ovidian metamorphosis; but also reminding us that if "the surprising Adventures" of Milton's Satan are Ovidian, Ovid and Cervantes also share an aim. Cervantes finds a way to embody romance in the everyday; that is, in the only form it can take, "the Goddess . . . quite lost in the Old Woman," as knight-errantry is in the mad old man Quixote. Most of all, seen in the perspective of Ovid, he shows the goddess of chivalric romance *becoming* the peasant maid, Dulcinea as "Dulcinea."[62]

The "female Quixote" of *A Harlot's Progress* is also Sancho's Dulcinea in the sense that she is the real, living Mary, not the religious myth. In this way Hogarth makes quite clear that it is the spectators of the "puppet play" in which she performs who see her in the Dulcinea position, as Mary *manquée* or the living "Mary."

If the miracles of the Nativity and the Eucharist were not normative in Hogarth's satires (as they were in Swift's and Pope's), what was? In truth, there was little that was positive in his works from the *Harlot* onward: primarily isolated and unproductive acts of charity, in the Harlot administered by her noseless servant woman, but thereafter by young women who tend to be pretty.[63] There was not, as expected in satire, an ideal—either religious, political, or moral—until in the later 1730s he denominated an aesthetic ideal: a young woman who mediates between extremes of unity and variety, order and disorder. Like Sancho's Dulcinea she becomes the aesthetic substitute for the deity, and in the specifically Christian terms of Atonement. She is a young actress, a milkmaid, a poet's wife, and finally the Venus of the *Analysis of Beauty* and the Thalia of *Hogarth Painting the Comic Muse.*

Hogarth's move toward aesthetics was, at least in part, a despairing inability to find any positive value, let alone ideal, in political or moral life—or any efficacy in religion—except for the isolated acts of charity he associates with a young plebian woman. Thereafter it is precisely and only an aesthetic ideal that survives for him in a world that is bankrupt in terms of religion, politics, and morality.

As he moves from the rational explanation for a "Virgin Birth" to the rational explanation for transubstantiation, he substitutes in the deist (indeed, Shaftesburian) way the artist for the deity in his "discovery" of a "new world," whether in geography or art. In terms of morality, wit replaces simple denunciation with the curiosity, surprise, and laughter that reveals error where least expected; which means in the terms of Hogarth's aesthetics, the variety hidden in uniformity. The aesthetic and the moral join insofar as Hogarth's aim in aestheticizing religious symbols is, first, actually to humanize them—to assimilate them to Sancho's aesthetics of the living Dulcinea; second, to demystify what he regards as aesthetic assumptions that are both erroneous and immoral, merely turning his attention from priests and politicians to their equivalent in critics, connoisseurs, and judges of art. His aesthetics remains moral in its focus of guilt upon these false judges and the false art they foist, in the manner of the romances of chivalry, on contemporary Quixotes. (The judges of society and of art are equated in his print *The Bench* of 1759.) As in *Analysis*, Plate 2, the spectator responds with surprise and laughter to the confusion of beauty and vice embodied in art, religion, and society.

Fielding in the preface to *Joseph Andrews* had written that "The only Source of the true Ridiculous (as it appears to me) is Affectation." Mark Akenside, in his revision of Addison as *Pleasures of Imagination* (1744), uses the word ridiculous, gives a definition based on pure incongruity, but offers examples that correspond to Fielding's affectation. Corbyn Morris continues to include the ridiculous in his formulation of wit and humor.[64] In the *Analysis* Hogarth does not use the word, and his definition is of formal incongruity, and yet he arrives at it through burlesque and the result is, once again, affectation.

He follows his chapter "Of Intricacy" with one "Of Quantity"; his progression is from the mental pursuit, which Addison defined in terms of the subject's faculty of wit, to the object and a formal explanation of the cause of laughter based on incongruity: "When improper, or *incompatible excesses* meet, they always excite laughter; more especially when the forms of those excesses are inelegant, that is, when they are composed of unvaried lines" (31). This is the opposite of satire, where one "incompatible excess" is normative and used to condemn the other. But he first introduced "quantity" as a version of Addison's Great: "quantity . . . adds greatness to grace." Opposite this phrase in the margin of his first draft he introduces his aesthetics of laughter by transforming greatness into the ridiculous: quantity exaggerated becomes "a burlesque." The example that opens the discussion is the juxtaposition of a robe or full-bottomed wig with the person who wears it.

Were "an improper person to put it on, it would then too be ridiculous." He alludes to the magistrate in Plate 1, figure 16, related in the illustration to hanging justice, in the text to bad aesthetic judgment. The ridiculous lies in Hogarth's connecting the idea of incongruity with "burlesque" and "contrivance" and locating them "at Bartholomew-fair"—in an actor *plus* a wig or a dancing master plus the stage role of a deity.

In this way Hogarth posits a beautiful object discovered by an epistemology of novelty, but unsurprisingly given his credentials, the latter is grounded, implicitly and explicitly, in the response of laughter. The risible discovery of variety in unity (of similarity in difference, of difference in similarity) is based on wit. Hogarth alludes to Morris's theory in his manuscript notes, and his examples are two of Morris's three—Falstaff and Don Quixote (*Analysis*, 126).

Theorists of comedy have tended to distinguish the laughter of ridicule from the laughter of sympathy, and one locus has been Addison's aestheticizing of satire into a disinterested laughter related to spectatorship.[65] But when Addison aestheticized laughter it was at least in part a political strategy for discrediting Tory satire. Addison's humane, sympathetic laughter is not pure as he claims, any more than was Shaftesbury's disinterestedness. As Fielding, Akenside, Morris, Murphy, and Hogarth all realized, there *is* no purely comic incongruity; some sort of judgment is being passed on the object by the incongruity (which, in Hogarth's word, is "improper"). Adams *is* being ridiculed; though we also laugh with and love him. The pure forms, the lines and shapes, Hogarth cites are not comic in themselves. More than the pure forms are necessary, as for example the trylon and perisphere of the 1939 World's Fair; they have to be embodied in a Quixote and Sancho Panza, in the conjunction of Quixote's spiritual excesses and Sancho's earthiness. Rather, the satiric (or moral) contrast of good and evil has been replaced by what can be called an aesthetic contrast of nature and art. The metamorphosis is not from ridicule to pure comedy but from ridicule based on right and wrong, good and evil, to ridicule based on nature and art, with nature privileged and art condemned as affectation.

In the *Analysis* Hogarth is attempting to create an aesthetics that acknowledges that if we place a beautiful woman on a pedestal we will inevitably and appropriately desire her and may discover, moreover, that she is not strictly virtuous. This is an anti-aesthetics, or a practical aesthetics, in relation to the theoretically pure aesthetics of Shaftesbury, where the human body can only be beautiful if divorced from function, fitness, and utility. Hogarth says that in the real world (again, the daily world of the *Spectator*'s novelty) the beautiful object cannot be separated from any of these—only that the moral judgment is replaced by a subtler, more "disinterested" (in his reinterpreted sense of Addison's word) "pleasure," the "pleasure of pursuit."

The Cathartic Laughter of Mr. Punch: Fielding

Fielding responded to the Quixotic immersion he read in *Pamela* by returning to the Cervantean model of fiction; and the particular scene he recalls, like Addison and Hogarth, was Don Quixote's attack on the puppet show. Beginning with his first characteristic play, *The Author's Farce* (1730), he had used it as the model for his "rehearsal plays" in which an empirical Sancho, a deluded Quixote, and other spectators (critics, actors, authors, and audience) respond in comically divergent ways to the "farce" (which in *The Author's Farce* was literally a puppet play). These spectators mystify and demystify, allegorize and historicize the "play." But it was in *Tom Jones*, five years after *Joseph Andrews*, that Fielding produced his direct imitation of the puppet show.

On his way to London, Tom attends a puppet show, a version of Colley Cibber's *Provok'd Husband* (1728), in which laughter has been censored by the decorous (and fashionable) puppet-master, who has eliminated the low rustic characters of Vanbrugh's original play—Aristotle's subject of "comedy"—leaving only the high-life characters of Cibber's sentimental revision, "without anything that could provoke a Laugh" (an equivalent of Steele's "joy too exquisite for laughter"). Laughter takes the emblematic form of Punch, the most elemental (and English) figure of burlesque. The puppet-master "improved" his show "by throwing out *Punch* and his Wife *Joan*, and such idle Trumpery," and Tom calls for the return of "my old Acquaintance Master *Punch*," who for Fielding is a comic *and* an erotic figure—indeed a figure of Tom, as when "*Cupid*, who lay hid in [Sophia's] Muff, suddenly crept out, and, like *Punchinello* in a Puppet-shew, kicked all out before him" and alters her pious resolve to stay with her father (7.9.360).

It is the servant Grace's Quixotic confusion of Lady Townley's behavior on the stage with her own in life that carries her over the edge from illusion into reality. Immersed in the play, Grace "affects" the model of Lady Townley as Polly Peachum imitated the style of a "lady" by reading romances; although in Grace's case (like the other characters in *The Beggar's Opera*), she uses Lady Townley as a rationalization for her concupiscence.

Melisendra and Lady Townley are both high-life romance heroines burlesqued by being played by puppets; they call for the low-life antics of the puppet Punch, withdrawn from the play only to be recovered by the antics of Grace and the Merry Andrew. Quixote's physical attack this time is not on the puppets but on the human transgressors, the couple who have assumed the roles of puppets. The landlady beats Grace and the Merry Andrew whom she finds copulating on the stage, and then the puppet-master himself and her husband the landlord, very much as Joan batters Punch in their conventional comic agon (itself a parody of heroic combat).

The puppet-master expresses the distrust of theater that began with Plato's warning in *The Republic* that by imitating base behavior actors were liable to become what they mimed; by attending plays, the audience was equally liable. Fielding evidently accepts this assumption about human nature, especially cogent to him since the appearance and popularity of *Pamela*. He supposes *Pamela* to be an *Amadis*, read by everyone and acted upon because its fantasy world invites immersion. All of this is because, as Tom would say, the comedy, the low and ugly, have been excised, leaving nothing to distance the spectator from immersion in Lady Townley's behavior. And the laughter of Punch, the symbolic figure who has been suppressed, now bursts out in antisocial behavior. The threat will be avoided, Fielding believes, by the presence of Punch—a comic ethos—which will permit the spectator to judge the action; for example, to distinguish the difference between the spectator Grace and the puppet Lady Townley.[66]

In *Shamela*, Fielding satirizes the paragon Pamela (in burlesque fashion) by revealing her as in reality the strumpet Shamela, who has conquered Mr. Booby by her hypocrisy. But he makes Shamela a Quixote who learns how to play "Pamela" by reading or listening to the advice of her mother and her lover Parson Williams. The crucial insight is embodied in one of Shamela's Pamelian *sententiae*, after frightening "the poor Booby . . . out of his Wits": "O what a Difficulty it is to keep one's Countenance, when a violent Laugh desires to burst forth."[67] She recalls Cervantes' description of Sancho Panza: "his cheeks were swoln with laughter, giving withal evident Signs that he was in danger to burst, if he did not permit that violent passion to make a sally" (Shelton, 1:166).

Sancho's irrepressible laughter (which he prudently learns to control with tightly closed lips) was one model for Fielding's reliance on the therapeutic theory of comedy. But his own version of laughter is the reader's natural response to the consequence of censorship; and this derives from the familiar hydraulic metaphor of Shaftesbury and Swift. Fielding quotes Roger L'Estrange to the effect that "if we shut Nature out at the Door, she will come in at the Window."[68] In the preface to *Joseph Andrews* he cited Shaftesbury's comment on burlesque as a bad reaction to "spiritual tyranny," the diversion of a good reaction and not to be found in the politer ages, in which free discourse was encouraged. This citation of Shaftesbury is in proximity to his remark that burlesque can "contribute more to exquisite Mirth and Laughter than any other; and these"—he adds, substituting the cathartic for the satiric explanation—"are probably more wholesome Physic for the Mind, and conduce better to purge away Spleen, Melancholy and ill affections, than is generally imagined."[69] It is Punch who bursts out when nature is repressed, and the laughter is liberating.

For Fielding this comic catharsis is parallel to Shamela's inability to withhold her passion, beginning with her mother's admonition, "Why will you give way to your Passion?" (281), and ending with her inability to restrain her passion for Parson Williams, which from one point of view is her downfall, from another her humanizing.

Fielding's particular version of the cathartic theory of comedy uses the terminology of the humors (to "purge away Spleen, Melancholy and ill affections"), but in a particular way. As a type Shamela is a hypocrite (the ridiculous equals affectation); but as a character, her humor is the passion of love (for Parson Williams). As to her hypocrisy,

Shamela has learned this by reading the letters of her mother. Although her mother, when disowned by Shamela (again, as instructed by Williams), produces the authentic Shamela letters to contradict the forged "Pamela" letters, the definitive exposure is brought on by the living Shamela herself: she cannot stay out of Williams's arms and is discovered by Booby.

Pamela, Parson Adams, and Scripture

Pamela Andrews is a heroine who, if she does not apparently read novels, certainly reads the paternal admonitions (die rather than lose your virginity) that reflect a religious ethic, embodied presumably in religious texts her father has had her read. Richardson shifts the emphasis from profane to sacred texts. This may be Richardson's way of replacing the novels of amorous intrigue with his new, improved novel. But from Fielding's point of view Richardson has tacitly retained the plot, setting, and assumptions of these amorous novels and associated them with religious texts. From the perspective of romance, in an un-Quixotic manner, Pamela's fantasy comes true and she is married and elevated by Mr. B. to become mistress of the house in which she was a servant. Seen in terms of her religious discourse, her marriage and elevation fulfill (receive the sanction of) a providential pattern.

In *Pamela*, Richardson has introduced the religious text as the object of imitation; and by opening the door to the suspicion that he has conflated Scripture with romance (supported by the promoting of *Pamela* by clergymen) he has permitted Fielding to make *Pamela*, itself essentially a religious text, the object of scrutiny by clergymen in *Shamela* and to introduce religious texts as themselves the source of imitation in *Joseph Andrews*.

In one of the many inns in which people in *Joseph Andrews* gather, Parson Adams *sees* Fanny faint after *hearing* Joseph's voice, and unthinkingly he throws his book of Aeschylus into the fire.[70] Adams's Aeschylean authority is, in fact, biblical authority—the "scriptural" authority of *Pamela* reflecting popish priestcraft contradicted by the real, spontaneous, and good actions of a human being. By making Quixote a clergyman Fielding has both found an equivalent for Quixote's spiritual dimension and problematized the clericalism of *Pamela*. Parson Adams's Quixotism reaches to his religion, too, with the usual Quixotic ambivalence. Fielding has turned Quixote into a clergyman, but he has not (as Eric J. Ziolkowski believes) turned madness into religious faith.[71] Rather he has focused on the issue of the reading of texts, and being converted, governed, and effectively dehumanized by their authority. In Joseph's case (noted at the beginning of the novel) he has turned Quixote's reading of romances into Joseph's reading of his sister Pamela's letters. Fielding indicates the "religious" devotion attached to Richardson's text (which was preached from pulpits and recommended by clergymen): he parallels the devotion of Joseph to his sister Pamela's letters and to Parson Adams's sermons. But in Adams's case (more pervasively) he has turned Quixote's romances into the Scriptures.

The effect of Quixotism on the English reader, brought up on empirical philosophy, as well as (by the time of Hogarth and Fielding) its extension into such forms of freethinking as deism, raises the question of whether an innocent reading was possible when a clergyman was based on Don Quixote. Fielding deflects the Quixotic sense of Adams's reading to his Aeschylus and the miniature auto-da-fé (compared with the fire that destroyed Quixote's whole library) to which he consigns it, and limits Adams's citations to the Old Testament. But the fact remains that Adams's primary reading is the Bible and that he acts upon an interested reading of that text, and his better nature (what Fielding calls his "perfect Simplicity") emerges spontaneously in order to contradict his devotion to texts, secular *and* sacred.

As Fanny is the true, blemished Dulcinea of *Joseph Andrews*, appropriately her lover is Joseph, the Sancho of the story. In Fielding's first version of Cervantes, *Don Quixote in England*, it was Sancho the poor squire, and not Quixote the knight-errant, who was Fielding's spokesman, the unchanging center of the play, representing the proverbial Nobody (the poor) versus the Somebodies, the men of quality, who include Quixote himself as well as Sir Thomas, Badger, and Brief.[72] It is Sancho who knows there is no Dulcinea and who goes along with Dorotea's plan to pass off her maid Jezebel as Dulcinea. Of

Sancho, Fielding noted at the end of his career, in his review of Charlotte Lennox's *Female Quixote* (1752), that he "is perhaps a Masterpiece in Humour of which we never have, nor ever shall see the like."[73]

In *Joseph Andrews*, it is Joseph himself, though he fills the position vis-à-vis Adams of the sensible Sancho Panza, who draws out Fielding's primary emphasis, which falls more on the necessary and prudent adaptation to the society through which Quixote and Sancho travel than on the impracticality of Quixote. The Sancho figure (essentially the living Fielding himself, down to his "Nose a little inclined to the Roman") is tall, husky, handsome, and normative. (Hogarth, who also associated himself with Sancho, employed a short, plump Sancho, resembling himself, to expose, wittily explore, and elucidate his various Quixotes.)

Joseph's affectation of Pamelian and Old Testament chastity, with which he wards off Lady Booby, covers the "perfect Simplicity" of his real love for Fanny Goodwill (unlike the "love" of Macheath and Polly, the one unfixed and the other mimetic). Beginning as a sort of priapic nature figure in the English countryside (an aspect of Addison's *faerie*), Joseph travels to London with Lady Booby and momentarily affects the foppishness of his peers. Discharged by Lady Booby after his refusal to accede to the fashionable image of a footman, he is stripped of his livery, then of his clothes (Pamela is threatened with stripping only to titillate her readers). Joseph's stripping coincides with the revelation that his love of Fanny, not his imitation of Pamela's letters and Adams's sermons, kept him from sleeping with Lady Booby.

In the passage in book 2 where Joseph's struggle with the hounds is represented through epic similes, Fielding announces that Joseph himself transcends any simile: this is to say that Joseph is like *no* classical Ajax, biblical Joseph, or even living Parson Adams; he is not an epic hero, not even a fictional "book" hero (emphasized in the last sentence of the book), but in fact a "living" man like Hogarth's "living woman." What specifically makes him "living" is that his motive is simply his love of Fanny. Further, this (in Pamelian terms) "foible" is not a flaw but a driving, undiverted passion that defines him positively. Joseph, in his love of Fanny, in fact, is another, positive version of Shamela.

Joseph is also, minimally, a reader of books. Even before he met

Parson Adams, he had read *The Whole Duty of Man,* as well as Baker's *Chronicle* and the Bible. Shamela excised, at Parson Williams's urging, the part of *The Whole Duty of Man* that has to do with duty to your neighbor, as opposed to the parts on duty to God and oneself, which she keeps, and yet it is a passion for one neighbor that returns, like the repressed, to destroy her hypocritical stratagem. Fielding's irony suggests that we can do without the duties to God and ourselves, but not to our neighbors, even if it is only Parson Williams. Chastity (which Fielding associated with Pamela) is one of the duties to ourselves, along with temperance in drinking; whereas, "The great rule of Charity" is "that grand rule of *Loving our Neighbours as our selves.*"[74] (Loving thy neighbor, to the extent of violating chastity, will be the subject of *Tom Jones.*)

We might say, on the basis of the few normative literary models in *Joseph Andrews* (Jesus' parable of the Good Samaritan; *The Whole Duty of Man*; Bishop Hoadly's *Plain Account of the . . . Lord's Supper* [1735]; Hogarth's painting *The Good Samaritan* [1736–37]), that Joseph follows the New Testament and the teachings of Jesus. In this way he is defined as a Sancho to Adams's Quixote; therefore as an un-Quixotic character—and therefore also as a noncomic hero. Or rather comic in a slightly different sense: he is defined in terms of fictions and models that he is not *and makes no attempt to imitate,* as opposed to the other characters (except Fanny), who attempt to define themselves in terms of more or less inappropriate models. Lady Booby, on the other hand, *is* like (or rather imitates, or thinks she is) Dido—though she is actually closer to Joseph's perception of her, as Potiphar's wife.

The author's assertion that Joseph transcends any simile is preceded by Joseph's speech on charity (book 3, chapter 6). This speech, which puts Adams to sleep (and brackets his version of the biblical text), would appear to be proof of Joseph's independence of models and comparisons, classical and biblical, specifically of charity. And the argument Joseph offers is that one's fame is not established by the collection of riches and art objects (they establish the fame of their makers) but by the dispersal of charity.

In the context of Shaftesbury's civic humanism, Joseph would seem to be defining charity against the "disinterestedness" of the property owners, who need feel no hunger or thirst (precisely the position taken by Hogarth—and in this passage Hogarth is invoked as the last in a series of great artists who, rather than the collector, deserves the fame of their paintings), against which he places the satisfaction of fame and reputation resulting from charitable acts. The collector, Fielding agrees with Hogarth, represents another form of doing one's duty to God or to oneself rather than to one's neighbor.

Fielding himself has a literary model in this passage—Pope's "Epistle to Bathurst," from which he takes the example of the Man of Ross, implicitly contrasted to the earl of Bathurst, the great landowner, builder, and collector, whom Pope associates with classical as opposed to Christian ideals. The Man of Ross in particular is living an *imitatio Christi*, which from Fielding's point of view would include the practice of Joseph. But he is also a character in Pope's "Epistle to Bathurst," and, as Fielding states on the title page, his own book is "Written in Imitation of" *Don Quixote*. The artifice of an author (of the text itself—of *any* text), as opposed to Joseph's "character," is called for by the anti-Pamelian novel. In a passage of "no other Use in this History, but to divert the Reader," "divert" means to entertain but also to distract and distance the reader from the event of Fanny's dangerous situation, one of rape, which is clearly contrasted with the Richardsonian situation in which there is no "diversion" but only Pamela's relentless self-engrossment and self-dramatization, in which Richardson immerses the reader (3.10.259).

The Hobby-Horse: Sterne

The first two volumes of Sterne's *Tristram Shandy* were published at the end of 1759. Sterne at once invokes the Quixote model, turning Quixote's madness-foible into everyone's hobby-horse, which "so long as a man rides [it] peaceably and quietly along the King's highway, and neither compels you or me to get up behind him," is harmless.[75] Like Quixote's madness, these hobby-horses run up against "the World" (a world that will not accommodate Quixote's particular skewed vision) with consequent disasters. These are, however, as Tristram classifies them, "small evils" (624); one aspect of Sterne's comedy is based on small misfortunes, which are risible because they are *not* great.

Tristram focuses his concept of the hobby-horse, however universal, on three chief characters. First is Parson Yorick, who rides "upon a lean, sorry, jack-ass of a horse, . . . who, to shorten all description of him, was full brother to *Rosinante*" (18). His hobby-horse is literally his horse, which he lends to all and sundry rather than replace it with the handsome horse with which he began his parsonic career. Like Quixote, Yorick has the "spare" figure of his decrepit horse. In his "sallies" about his parish he "never could enter a village, but he caught the attention of both old and young" (19). Sterne is recalling the formulations of Quixote in Morris's *Essay* and echoing them in his invocation of Quixote. He compares Yorick to "the peerless knight of *La Mancha*, whom, by the bye, with all his follies, I love more, and would actually have come further to have paid a visit to, than the greatest hero of antiquity" (23). *Follies, love,* and *paid a visit to* are, of course, Morris's terms.

Being a clergyman, Yorick also draws upon the "simplicity" of Parson Adams: he is "utterly unpractised in the world"—with "world" as threatening a term as it was for both Quixote and Adams (27). Shaftesbury also remains a primary influence, though filtered through Fielding's preface: Yorick "had an invincible dislike and opposition in his nature to gravity"—not "gravity as such" but "the affectation of it" (28). Yorick is, of course, a "living" character, who coincides with Sterne himself in the writing and publishing of a sermon on Conscience, in the hobby-horse of satiric jesting, and in the sad consequences of riding such a hobby-horse.

His last words, a reference to Sancho Panza's (not Quixote's) suffering, are spoken "with something of a *cervantick* tone" (34). Tristram's (or Sterne's) frequent references to "*Cervantick* gravity" (200) or (in letters) to "Cervantic humour" or "Cervantik Satyr" suggest that it is less precisely the analogy between Quixote's madness or foible and the hobby-horse than the irony of Cervantes' reconstruction of Quixote's situation.[76] Tristram's references show that he has read *Don Quixote* and sees the hobby-horse and its rider as somehow Quixotic; that is, a superimposition of Quixotic delusion on, and as his interpretation of, the characters' hobby-horses.

Like Hogarth and Fielding, Sterne seems to associate himself more with Sancho than with Quixote. When Yorick is dying he quotes Sancho, and other references come at crucial moments (34, 347, 639). In the passage in volume 9, introducing the story of Maria, in which

Tristram invokes Cervantes, he calls *Don Quixote* the story "of Sancho and his master" (780). He associates Yorick with Sancho because he is a truth-teller, not a deluded Quixote in the sense that the other characters are. And Tristram associates himself, spiritually and genealogically, with Yorick, not with Walter or Toby. Long after his death Yorick keeps returning, always to point toward the truth (as about Tristram's paternity), and he has the last word in the novel: "A COCK and a BULL, said Yorick——And one of the best of its kind, I ever heard" (809).

Walter Shandy is a second Quixote. Both Quixote's and Cervantes' "seriousness" are used to define Walter as we are introduced to his theory of names (58). But Walter, the system-builder, derives from Swift's version of Quixote in *A Tale of a Tub*; in any other book he would be a villain. So he was in Hogarth's Earl Squander, who in *Marriage A-la-mode* (1745) represented the effect of his folly upon his children in his paintings as well as in the possessive stamp of his coronet. Walter's hobby-horse is his "attempt to create a perfect child by begetting, rearing and educating it upon principles of 'reason' and 'science,'" one consequence of which is the maiming of Tristram.[77] Walter is comic rather than satiric only because of the ineluctable failure of each of his attempts to control his family and surroundings and so the consequences to him as well as to Tristram.

If Walter's hobby-horse is system-building (and we can only suppose its source was reading too much), Uncle Toby's is war—but war reduced from the War of the Spanish Succession (corresponding to the Seven Years' War) miniaturized and imposed on a peaceful bowling green. Toby's chivalric romances are books of military science—an eighteenth-century Quixoticism in which real events (the siege of Namur) are appropriated into the "romance" world of fortification. In fact, prior to all the manuals of fortifications, Toby's Quixotic reading went back to his immersion in his reading of the *Iliad* in school. With Toby comes his "non Hobby-Horsical" Sancho Panza, Corporal Trim, who goes along with his humor, adopts it himself, and, like Sancho, is "voluble" in converse (109).

Toby's hobby-horse, a positive (harmless) version of Walter's, is an analogue or emblem for the central one of Tristram himself, whose writing of *The Life and Opinions of Tristram Shandy* is a Quixotic quest: the reconstruction along the lines of Toby's recreation of the Siege of Namur of the early traumas that have defined his life, which is at the same time the therapy for dealing with them. This is Tristram's writing project (hobby-horse), which operates according to the same process as Toby's, advancing from words to signs to gestures and spatial re-creations of the experience.

Toby's hobby-horse and Tristram's bring out an aspect of Quixote's madness that we have not hitherto noticed. In the dedication to William Pitt (whose own hobby-horse, if designated, would have been as military as Toby's) Tristram-Sterne places the emphasis on the therapeutic nature of laughter: his aim is the "constant endeavour to fence against the infirmities of ill health, and the evils of life, by mirth," and to have "beguiled you [the reader] of one moment's pain"; and the crucial line of volume 1, on nearly the last page, of Uncle Toby is "The history of a soldier's wound beguiles the pain of it" (88). Sterne picks up the therapeutic rather than the imitative-absorptive aspect of Quixotism.[78] This is essentially recovery through reconstruction. The hobby-horse is neither imitative nor imitable; it is divorced from burlesque or deflation, except in Walter's case, and even Walter's delusion is not related to affectation. Yorick, for example, uses his hobby-horse to laugh at affectation, consequently bringing retribution upon his head.

Tristram begins by defining Yorick's hobby-horse as his riding an old, broken-down nag; this is in fact his stratagem for dealing with the dilemma that he loves this beautiful steed but cannot refuse a request for the use of it by any of his parishioners. His parishioners, with hobby-horses of their own, misunderstand his conduct and laugh or censure him. He ruefully sees the comedy of his continuing to ride the broken-down nag. This is, in Morris's terms, his foible: his jesting, satiric temperament. Consequently he is wounded like the other characters, but his wounding is fatal; he has no opportunity to recover through reconstruction. This may be because Yorick's particular "character" is defined according to Morris's model of Falstaff rather than Quixote, in that when he sallies through a village and is ridiculed he is able to join the laugh at himself (20).

Tristram seems to carry on for Yorick after his early death in volume 1; Yorick's wounding specifically anticipates Tristram's, both involving smashed heads, one literally, the other metaphorically. The "blow" that finishes off Yorick follows from jokes like the one Phutatorius, the "lecher" and author of a book on concubinage, believes he carried out on his codpiece. Yorick's death may be interpreted as the result of his unwillingness or inability to cope with his wounding; the coping is elaborately worked out by Tristram, also a jester, but on a wound that, following the analogue of Toby's war wound, is in no sense self-inflicted. Yorick with his satiric foible is a screen for Tristram, whose punishment follows from no possible crime of his own.

Toby's wounding in war is another screen. Tristram's hobby-horse is simply the reconstructing of "where"—in all of Uncle Toby and Widow Wadman's senses—he was wounded. All of the Shandy hobby-horses can be summed up as showing "where you were wounded"—even Walter's, since each new system he builds is his attempt to fend off the disaster of an earlier one.

With more than one Quixote the hobby-horse not only collides with the "world" but with other hobby-horses, creating a comedy of incongruity: "——He was a very great man! added my uncle *Toby*; (meaning *Stevinus*)—He was so; Brother *Toby*, said my father, (meaning *Piereskius*)" (493).

The exceptions are the infrequent cases when the brothers' love of each other overrides the laughter of ridicule or anger that results from the collision of hobby-horses. The hobby-horse itself serves both to defend its owner from and to seek empathy with others—joined in a moment of rupture in laughter followed by pain followed by empathy. The Quixote-Sancho encounter following the experience of the fulling hammers (see chapter 1, page 16) is the model for the scene in which Walter ridicules Toby's hobby-horse: "My uncle *Toby* would never attempt any defence against the force of this [Walter's] ridicule, but that of redoubling the vehemence of smoaking his pipe." This produces so much smoke that it causes Walter to go into a "suffocating fit of violent coughing," which causes Toby to leap up, despite the pain in his groin, "with infinite pity" to help his brother; which gesture "cut my father thro' his reins, for the pain he had just been giving" Toby—and produces a rare moment of sympathy (249).

Sterne is the first of Cervantes' English imitators to explore the element of pain in *Don Quixote*, which so worried Nabokov. Smollett had done so but only in the slapstick consequences of picaresque jests (*burlas*). Fielding developed only Cervantes' comedy of incongruity—

Lady Booby and her affectation of Dido; Adams and his adherence to sacred texts. Sterne plays with the incongruity of multiple hobby-horses colliding; but he also depicts the wounding and the pain that make the hobby-horses necessary. The result is a new combination: the comedy of incongruity, the pain of wounding, and then the consequent laughter followed by pain and sympathy.

Throughout, death is the real subject of *Tristram Shandy*. By volume 6 and the story of Le Fever, Sterne has progressed from the comedy-sympathy of the Walter-Toby and the responses to the death of Bobby (in volume 5) to the pathos-comedy of dying and death. The alternation of tones leading up to Le Fever's death ("the pulse fluttered———stopp'd———went on———throb'd———stopp'd again——— moved———stopp'd———shall I go on?———No" [513]) expresses the effect in one way; the question of "Whether Bridget should laugh or cry" (798) expresses it in another. Laughter, release, pain, and potential death join in Tristram's plight when he has "a fit of laughter" so hard that he breaks a blood vessel and hemorrhages. What produces this release—therapeutically, a form of phlebotomy—was "seeing a cardinal make water like a quirister (with both hands)" (663).

This laughter of release is related to Shaftesbury's response to gravity and to Fielding's Master Punch emerging from Sophia's muff or from the respectable high life of Lady Townley's provoking behavior; but, when it focuses on an anticlerical image, it is release or liberation from intolerable pressure. Sterne's context is not only "wounding" and death but the laugh within the restraining context of church, schoolroom, court, or battle. It is also a form of play—of fun without rules and relief from the restraints of society; the form it takes, again based on the two-sided comedy of *Don Quixote*, is the pun.

Walter, the representative of judgment, detests and abhors a pun ("or the insinuation of a pun"—any doubleness or wit, here in the dubious context of curtins and hornworks): "*Dennis* the critick could not detest and abhor a pun, or the insinuation of a pun, more cordially than my father" (128). Toby always reads his own hobby-horsical sense of any word with no awareness of the second (or the third) sense; Tristram and his audience, who have read *Don Quixote*, catch both, and so enjoy the comic reaction to wit (unconscious wit) in others. While Tristram insists that wit without judgment (like the knobs on the back of a chair) is aesthetically unpleasing, he clearly favors wit, the chief principle of composition in *Tristram Shandy*. Judgment uncorrected by wit, as in the "narrow confines" of the Laplanders' winter caves, is the opposite of the hobby-horse.

The use of books and any form of text is not absorptive as in *Don Quixote* or *Joseph Andrews*, but oppressive, closing, forcing a unity upon variety. Wit is to judgment in the preface to *Tristram Shandy* (vol. 3) as conscience was to religion in the "Sermon on Conscience" (another formulated and written text) that brought volume 2 to a close. Thus in volume 4 the secular interpretation of the hobby-horse is summed up by Walter, while Uncle Toby serves as spokesman for the religious interpretation. Walter tells Toby: "[W]hen one runs over the catalogue of all the cross reckonings and sorrowful *items* with which the heart of man is overcharged, 'tis wonderful by what hidden resources the mind is enabled to stand it out, and bear itself up, as it does against the impositions laid upon our nature." " 'Tis by the assistance of Almighty God, cried my uncle *Toby*, looking up, and pressing the palms of his hands close together—'tis not from our own strength, brother *Shandy*"; to which Walter replies, "That is cutting the knot, said my father [recalling Dr. Slop's attempt to cut Obadiah's knot, his cutting himself instead, and his reading of Ernulphus's excommunication on the knot], instead of untying it" (332).

Sterne seems to contrast Toby's hobby-horse and his religion (Toby is the advocate of religion in *Tristram Shandy*), as if they are alternative reconstructions: "[R]eligion inclined him to say one thing, and his high idea of military skill tempted him to say another; so not being able to frame a reply," he says nothing (751). Religion fills much the same position in *Tristram Shandy* that it did in *Don Quixote*, where it was replaced by the provisional and comic construction-deconstruction of the Dulcinea story. Sterne's clergyman is destroyed because he refuses to be a grave clergyman in an overformalized religion. The idea of religion is embodied in contracts, opinions, and charters, associated with the Church of Rome, crazy saints' lives, excommunications, and the Inquisition (so stressed in Trim's memories of his brother as he reads the "Sermon on Conscience" that in the contrast of conscience-religion the latter term becomes contaminated with the associations of Inquisition).

Tristram's genealogical play, which always points away from Walter to Yorick, includes the argument of the theologians of the cathedral chapter who get into the intricacies of the Trinitarian controversy, followed by the wry comments of Yorick and Toby on the nonrelationship (in these theological terms) of Tristram and his father: The question of Tristram's paternity is stretched out to include Yorick's jest that it may be an Immaculate Conception, in the context a memory of the deist jest, with which Hogarth played in his *Harlot's Progress*, that any sensible Joseph (another old man like Walter) would look elsewhere than to God for the father of his son.[79] Not God but, in all probability, Parson Yorick (whom Tristram resembles both physically and spiritually much more closely than Walter) is his father.

Tristram evokes the discussions in *Don Quixote* comparing religious relics and the relics of romance heroes: Rather than "the pillar to which Christ was tied" or "the house where pontius Pilate lived" Tristram prefers to visit "the *Tomb of the two lovers*," Amandus and Amanda (626–27)—which proves to be nonexistent, or, in short, as dubious as the two religious shrines (or Lippius's clock and the *History of China*, other landmarks of Lyons). The story of Amandus and Amanda is a typical romance plot, "a story *read* of two fond lovers, separated from each other by cruel parents, and by still more cruel destiny" (627, emphasis added).

Later, when he is recalling the "love" of Widow Wadman and Toby, Tristram refers to the plan of Bouchain with "the marks of [Wadman's] snuffy finger and thumb" and the marks of Toby's pins as "this precious relick, with it's *stigmata* and *pricks*"—preferring these to "the pricks which enter'd the flesh of St. *Radagunda*" (679): a scene that again plays on Cervantes' alternation of sacred and profane love.

It may be significant that Toby, with "the loss of his hobby-horse" at the Treaty of Utrecht, is left vulnerable to the attack of the Widow Wadman. We recall the eating scene in *Tom Jones*, where the food diverted attention/energy from love-making; when it was used up, Tom's attention turned to Jenny Waters and they went to bed. Suppressed or deflected in one place, it turns up in another, in Sterne's version of the comedy of hydraulic mechanism.

Toby's hobby-horse diverts him from the pain (real and metaphorical) of his wound, and when it is finished the pain of the wound returns. It is then diverted into "love"—a "love" that is as distanced from experience (as Quixotic) as the hobby-horse, but then exposed by the "blow" of the Widow Wadman's physical desire. The "blow" of Toby's wounding at Namur and the "blow" he suffers in his love affair with the Widow Wadman prove to be homologous.

Hobby-horses are thus distinguished from asses: the former is what one mounts "to canter it away from the cares of solicitudes of life—'Tis as useful a beast as is in the whole creation—nor do I really see how the world could do without it"; whereas the ass (or at least Walter's conception of the ass, via St. Hilarion) is of "a beast concupiscent—and foul befall the man, who does not hinder him from kicking" (716).

All in all, Sterne treats religion and love, Mary and Dulcinea, as alternatives much as Cervantes appears to do in *Don Quixote*. The sacrament of the Eucharist—the "real Presence"—he compares with talking as opposed to making love (787). In this context, Toby's mind—with which Toby himself has associated the movement of a smoke-jack—may be associated with religious belief and Walter's judgment with conscience.

Defoe and "the quixotism of R. Crusoe"

As opposed to the genres of the classical tradition (epic, tragedy, georgic, pastoral, and on down to satire), the Christian tradition offered on the one hand the Roman Catholic "Saints' Lives," or the *Imitatio Christi*, together with the litany and sacraments and biblical commentaries, and on the other, opposed to this "formalism," the Protestant sects' personal, unmediated forms of the diary and spiritual autobiography. To these English Protestants the story of Don Quixote could have been read as a spiritual pilgrimage: Quixote is an individual who practices outmoded forms—a veritable formalist—but who suffers through his violent adventures, mostly comic, toward a conversion and return to Christian virtues. Quixote could be read as a Christian drawn away from God to Dulcinea and false chivalric ideals and returned by all the lost skirmishes with the real world to God in his conversion at the end. To an English Protestant this would have seemed a personal conversion away from High Church formalism; to a Spanish Catholic it would be only a return to sanity and orthodoxy.

Although *Robinson Crusoe* would seem to be an unlikely offspring
of *Don Quixote*, Defoe himself (writing as Crusoe) thanks Charles
Gildon for the compliment of referring to "the quixotism of R. Crusoe"—not a satire, as Gildon thinks, but "the greatest of panegyrics."[80]
What Defoe means is that Don Quixote's story (as he apparently
believed) was an allegorical representation of the life of the duke of
Medina-Sidonia in the same way that Robinson Crusoe's story was an
allegory of Defoe's own life. This remark shows that Defoe knew *Don
Quixote* (and he indicates its popularity—"which thousands read with
pleasure"). But it also points to the common element that makes
Robinson Crusoe the first English novel in the manner of Cervantes,
even though it is only a comedy in the sense of *comedia*.

Crusoe, of course, has his Sancho Panza in Friday; but more
significant, his story is the Quixotic one, of a man on a mad quest in
the face of hostile nature and elements, reconstructing as best he can
his lost Eden. *Robinson Crusoe* was a melding of *Don Quixote* and its
sacred equivalent, *Paradise Lost*, connecting the practical "how to"
aspect of home rebuilding with the story of the Fall and Redemption of
Man (with, inevitably, a secular strain of georgic renewal adapted in
Milton's religious fable).

It is surprising that there were no explicit allegorizations or allegorical interpretations of *Don Quixote*, as there were of Virgil and
Ovid. But to Defoe *Pilgrim's Progress* (1677) would have seemed one
equivalent—an allegorical version in which Bunyan's Christian is a sort
of Quixote. Christian is first seen with "a Book in his hand"—"I
looked, and saw him open the Book, and read therein," and this
reading sends him away from his family and out into the world on his
quest for salvation: "I seek an *Inheritance incorruptible, undefiled, and
that fadeth not away*," much like the Dulcinea Quixote seeks. His
family's conclusion (like that of Quixote's family) is "that some frenzy
distemper had got into his head" (they hope "that sleep might settle his
brains").[81] Evangelist lends him a paper that tells him to leave the City
of Destruction and points the way, and when he flees, some neighbors,
like Quixote's curate and barber, "resolved to fetch him back by force"
(10). To outsiders he seems as mad as Quixote, and his adventures are
often as disastrous, beginning with the Slough of Despond and including Vanity Fair.

Christian's encounters tend to be with tempters or alternatives, but their responses are often those of the world to Quixote. The significant difference is that Bunyan acknowledges the relationship between the Book and the burden: Worldly Wise-Man asks, "How camest thou by the burden at first?" Christian answers: "By reading this Book in my hand"; to which Worldly Wise-Man replies, in words the Tory Swift could have used: "I thought so; and it is happened unto thee as to other weak men, who, meddling with things too high for them, do suddenly fall into thy distractions; which distractions do not only unman men, (as thine, I perceive, has done thee) but they run them upon desperate ventures, to obtain they know not what"(18). It is not likely that Bunyan would have read a book like *Don Quixote*, but readers of *Pilgrim's Progress* would have, and indeed these two books, with the Bible, were among the most read books of the century. There is no need for Bunyan to have known *Don Quixote*; but a reader like Defoe could triangulate from Quixote and Christian—as the book shifts from books of chivalry to the Bible—to Robinson Crusoe and, later, to Fielding's Parson Adams and Sterne's Parson Yorick.

English Protestants would have been drawn to *Don Quixote* for other reasons than the narrow Whiggish one of its satire on chivalry. Writers in the Protestant tradition would have found a sanction for a kind of fictional writing that attracted them and that, in this comic form, was available nowhere else.

SIX

The Female Subject

Marcela Discourses on Beauty

The two plots of *Don Quixote*—comic and romantic—are usually connected by a figure like Marcela who rhymes with Quixote's particular folly, acting out what she reads in a book. Thus Fielding's *Don Quixote in England* includes, alongside Quixote and Sancho, the she-Quixotic reader Helena, the love intrigue of Fairlove and Dorothea, her father Sir Thomas Loveland, and his enforcement of a mercenary marriage with Squire Badger. *Joseph Andrews* includes, as well as the story of Adams and Joseph, the inserted tales of Leonora and Horatio, Leonard and Paul.

Cervantes' tales are not, strictly speaking, interpolated. When Fielding has one of the ladies in the coach carrying Parson Adams and others tell the story of Leonora the Jilt, there is simply a tale and the responses of an audience; no one ever meets Leonora or Horatio or Bellarmine, who exist in another world. In *Don Quixote*, although Quixote first hears their story, he actually encounters Grisóstomo and Marcela, as also Cardenio, Dorotea, and Don Fernando. The responses of Quixote and Sancho to their stories and their characters intertwine with the responses of most of these characters to them. The connections are elaborate and what makes these tales "interpolated" is the fact that they come from another tonal range—of pity and fear rather than laughter.[1]

These love stories—first with a tragic plot, then with romantic plots—are laid not in the past with chivalric romances but in the present, in the time of Quixote, and so are situated on the scale of reality somewhere between the chivalric romances he reads and the comic, "modern" world he experiences. In Fielding's terms they are the equivalent of the contemporary "novels" of amorous intrigue by Behn, Manley, and Heywood that he was correcting in his "new" type of Cervantean writing, partly by incorporating them into, and subordinating them to, his central comic plot.

The first and most cited of the romances in *Don Quixote* is the story of Grisóstomo and Marcela. In part 1, chapter 2, Quixote and Sancho meet some goatherds, one of whom (Pedro) tells them the story of Grisóstomo, who has died for unrequited love of Marcela. Marcela fills various analogical roles in the Quixotic story: she is the beauty who, having read pastoral romances, has left society to become a Quixotic shepherdess; she also projects the mad ideal of another Dulcinea, and her lovers are the Quixotes who don shepherd's attire and follow her into her pastoral world.

Just before he hears this story Quixote has held forth on the pastoral Golden Age (when all "was peace, all was concord and friendship," and, as to women, "that which modesty requires and always has required should remain covered" [81–82]). The goatherds listen "in open-mouthed wonderment, saying not a word," while Sancho keeps quiet by munching acorns and drinking wine. In chapter 12 the story of Grisóstomo and Marcela leaves Quixote "thinking of his lady Dulcinea, in imitation of Marcela's lovers" (91). In the morning, in chapter 13, he meets Vivaldo, the shepherds, and the mourners on their way to the funeral of Grisóstomo.[2] This melancholy group sets the tone for the funeral, but Quixote is also taken by them for a madman, and Vivaldo decides "to give him a further opportunity of displaying his absurdities" by introducing the comparison of Quixote's worship of Dulcinea with worship of God. But he fails to see that the men dressed as shepherds and idealizing Marcela represent their own displacement of deity-worship. When Quixote asserts that "there can be no knight-errant without a lady," he might have added, "or shepherd." Quixote's description of the knight-errant's devotion to his lady falls only a little short of Grisóstomo's fatal devotion. At Vivaldo's prodding, Quixote names his Dulcinea and proclaims: "Her beauty is superhuman, for in it are realized all the impossible and chimerical attributes that poets are accustomed to give their fair ones"; he follows with her attributes of golden locks, rainbow eyebrows, sunny eyes, and so on (96).

This company then meets another group of shepherds carrying Grisóstomo's body. The central scene in chapters 13 and 14 is Grisóstomo's funeral, with Ambrosio and Vivaldo delivering funeral orations, one on love as the cause of Grisóstomo's death, the other on art and the survival of Grisóstomo's spirit in his poems (despite his dying wish to have them destroyed). Suddenly there appears Marcela herself, who delivers *her* oration. In the context of Quixote's impossible devotion to the "superhuman" beauty of Dulcinea, it becomes a discourse on aesthetics.

We could say that the whole funeral is aestheticized in that there is no mention of God or rewards and punishments or an afterlife; the discourse is of love, art, and—with the arrival of Marcela—beauty. Ambrosio's speech at least remains within the discourse of Christianity: not Satan but Marcela, according to Ambrosio, is the "mortal enemy of the human race" (13.97); he associates her beauty with pride and temptation, fall and damnation, and this offers one ground for the aesthetic terms of her response. The other is offered by a discourse of desire, which was that of Grisóstomo and the other suitors.

The story itself was told from Grisóstomo's point of view, expressed by Pedro the goatherd. In chapter 13, following Pedro's recounting of the story, the discussion of Vivaldo and Quixote (aimed at ridiculing Quixote's devotion to Dulcinea) simply elaborated on this version in which Grisóstomo is the subject and Marcela the unapproachable object in an erotic exchange. But in chapter 14, precisely interrupting the funeral that celebrates Grisóstomo, Marcela retells the story from her own point of view, changing the terms from those of desire to those of aesthetics. A critic of Marcela could argue (as I have of Addison) that her aesthetics is a rhetoric, used to defend herself against the shepherds. She places herself in the aesthetic position while her suitors are addressing her from the high ground of morality and religion.

However, for the first time Dulcinea's point of view is expressed: the beautiful object shows itself to be a subject, expounding how it feels to be the beautiful object.[3] And this transpires in the space between the defense and description of Dulcinea by Quixote in chapter 13 and, in chapter 15, the equally unrequited and unfortunate lust of Rocinante for the Galician ponies of the Yanguesian carriers. Foreshadowing the great scene of the two Dulcineas in part 2, Cervantes brackets the funeral with the delusive aesthetics of Quixote and the realistic aesthetics of Sancho; but here he fills in the middle by letting "Dulcinea" speak for herself. This is "Dulcinea," not the "living" origin of Dulcinea, Aldonza Lorenzo, who will make her brief appearance in chapter 25.

Marcela, "more beautiful even than she was reported to be," begins by acknowledging the suitors' (Grisóstomo's) point of view: "Heaven made me beautiful, you say, so beautiful that you are compelled to love me whether you will or no; and in return for the love that you show me, you would have it that I am obliged to love you in return" (1.14.104).[4] She knows ("with that natural understanding that God has given me") that "everything beautiful is lovable," but—turning the object of beauty-love into a subject—she maintains its integrity as an aesthetic subject in its own right. There is no reason why she should love and admire in return, even if the male subject were himself a beautiful, therefore lovable, object.

In fact, "not all beauty inspires love, but may sometimes merely delight the eye and leave the will intact"—otherwise "all [men] would wander vaguely and aimlessly with nothing upon which to settle their affections." Grisóstomo and the other suitors have confused love and admiration, desire and the disinterested contemplation of beauty. Indeed, while Marcela was born an aesthetic object, she has also made herself one by withdrawing (distancing) herself from the desires and attentions of men. By this effort to escape men's attention she has in fact idealized herself as Swift's Chloe idealized herself up to the fatal moment when she climbed into bed with Strephon.

Then picking up the discourse of morality from Ambrosio's oration, Marcela argues that beauty and virtue are equated because both are based on distancing. "Beauty in a modest woman is like a distant fire or a sharp-edged sword: the one does not burn, the other does not cut, those who do not come near it."[5] Thus Marcela's intention "to live in perpetual solitude" means that not interested men but "only the earth should enjoy the fruit of my retirement and the spoils of my beauty." The admiration of only the earth, Marcela believes, removes her from the status of aesthetic object as well as object of desire; but of course, as with Dulcinea, the idea (in this case memory) only increases her allure. She has retired to the country, and made her appearance before her admirers, in order to explain that she wishes to remain only an *aesthetic* object; which, however, means that she wishes not to be an object of desire *or* of aesthetic contemplation but a subject in her own right. By expressing her position she has in fact declared herself to be such: her withdrawal and speech turn her into a subject theorizing the situation that is at the heart of *Don Quixote*. At the same time we balance her individual freedom against the death of the obsessed Grisóstomo and discover not a comic but a melancholy affect.

The case of Grisóstomo shows that disinterested or distanced admiration (the aesthetic experience) can be corrupted into desire and then, separated from its object, can lead to despair and death. But another alternative is implied: disinterested admiration, *because* it is separated from its object, can turn into desire, and certainly is intensified by distancing. Grisóstomo's fate might have been Strephon's if Chloe had withdrawn into (in her case) the myth of deity she was acting out for his benefit.

As an aesthetic object that combines beauty and virtue, Marcela is a living manifestation of Quixote's idea of Dulcinea, but not by enchantment (as Quixote requires) but by distancing. As long as Quixote can remain at a distance from Dulcinea he can pursue her, but the moment he meets "Dulcinea"-Dulcinea his illusions begin to crumble (as Strephon's do in "The Lady's Dressing Room," before he becomes a Sancho Panza in "Strephon and Chloe").

Supplementing Marcela's aesthetics of beauty is an implied aesthetics of the "ugly." Suppose, she says, "that the lover of the beautiful were ugly" (*que clamador de la hermoso fuese feo*); if the beautiful deserves to be loved, the ugly must "deserve to be shunned," and therefore, as the beautiful attracts, the ugly repels. Or supposing heaven had made the beautiful object (Marcela) ugly instead, she would have no right to complain if beautiful or ugly men were repelled by her.

Repelling, however, is one form of distancing, and, in the terms of Swift and Sancho, lack of distance reveals the Ugly in the form of a "blemish." The suggestion is that Marcela's "ugly" is therefore a close-up particular. If we judge Marcela's speech from the perspective of

Sancho's accounts of the real Dulcinea (1.25, 2.10), the implication is that real human desire (as opposed to the desire of Quixote, Grisóstomo, and the suitors) requires a particularity, in effect a foible or blemish, or in Corbyn Morris's terms humorous "character."

Marcela starts with a distinction between distance and disinterestedness: distance idealizes, whereas disinterestedness requires the absence of desire. Distance of necessity creates disinterestedness, but distance is also a necessary component of disinterestedness. Distance can mean unattainableness and so despair, but—so long as there is "hope," a man's Quixotic unwillingness to accept the fact of distance—it can also stimulate desire. (Recall Strephon's groping for "hope" at the bottom of the close stool.) Distance can also, by concealing the blemish, create the illusion of perfect beauty. Marcela is herself disinterested and so distances herself physically, but as an object rather than a subject; or as a subject who implicitly regards the men as "ugly."

After her speech Marcela withdraws into "the thickest part of a near-by wood" and all present are "lost in admiration of her wit as well as her beauty." Some, however, "were of a mind to follow her, taking no heed of the plainly worded warning they had just had from her lips," and so Quixote stops them. He speaks out, we are told, "thinking to himself that here was an opportunity to display his chivalry succoring a damsel in distress"; yet he also notes that Marcela "has shown with clear and sufficient reasons that little or no blame for Grisóstomo's death is to be attached to her" and that "in place of being hounded and persecuted she should be honored and esteemed by all good people in this world." His concluding words are: "as the only woman in it who lives with such modesty and good intentions," but we might add: as an object of purely aesthetic interest. Her words have had no effect on Ambrosio, whose epitaph for Grisóstomo is still in the old misogynist terms: "a faithless maid," a "cruel, heartless hand."

Quixote has the last word, which validates Marcela's position, though only from his own, mad perspective: he defends her as a good knight-errant should a lady. Cervantes' last word, however, further qualifying Marcela's position on disinterestedness and beauty, is in the following chapter (chapter 15), in Rocinante's uncontrollable lust for the Galician ponies, which foreshadows the real, living Aldonza Lorenzo in chapter 25.

In his dramatic version of *Don Quixote*, D'Urfey accepts Grisós-tomo's story and Ambrosio's interpretation. When Marcela appears she merely rants and serves as an object of conventional antifeminist satire: "But know that I was born to plague your Sex. . . . I know my Power, and Men shall Obey." Sancho responds that "this Woman is too much a Tatler to be of any great Quality" and Quixote's defense of her ("I find she does but Justice to her Sex") is merely another ridiculous response of the deluded knight-errant.[6]

All three English illustrators—Vanderbank, Hogarth, and Hay-man—illustrate the scene and show Marcela speaking over the bier of Grisóstomo (figs. 17, 18) . Vanderbank's and Hayman's Marcela rises above the shepherds on a high rock, as if to emphasize her isolation and superiority—in beauty and discourse, moral and spiritual—to the group of suitors, including Quixote and Sancho, beneath. They are illustrating the lines: "[F]or on the top of the rock, under which they were digging the grave, appeared the shepherdess *Marcela*" (Jarvis, 1: 65); she "appeared upon the top of the rock, just above the grave they were digging" (Smollett, 1:75). Hayman's illustration, more dramatic than Vanderbank's, has the grave at the bottom, so that the elevation of Marcela vis-à-vis the living, the dead, and the grave, suggests a hierarchy of values.

In Hogarth's version the details, including Grisóstomo's jaw cloth and his hand on his sheaves of poetry, are more realistically portrayed. His Marcela, though foregrounded and the most prominent figure in the composition, is on a level with the men. Choosing the moment following the one chosen by Vanderbank and Hayman, Hogarth suggests that Marcela has come down from the rock to the men's level to speak to them. He places the bier in the center, Marcela in the foreground to the left of it (emphasized by her large shepherdess's hat), and the men, virtually merging into anonymity, on the right. Quixote stands out from this crowd and balances Marcela, who appears to be addressing him. Hogarth sets Marcela in a tableau of beauty, death, and a spectrum of responses to it that roughly corresponds to the rich variety of Cervantes' text, but keeps the charismatic woman on a level with her besotted men (not in any sense celestial or a "goddess dyed in Grain"), facing Quixote, as if she is of chief importance to him (much as he later portrayed the wife and milkmaid in relation to the poet and musician).

Hogarth's Marcela is both aesthetic object and subject because she is seen in both ways and her perspective does not (literally) override the men's and, especially, Quixote's—partly because hers is a self-defense and partly because it concludes with Quixote taking her side but for the wrong reason. The comic incongruity resides in the moment at which the romance of Grisóstomo and Marcela intersects the madness of Quixote.

The Female Quixote

Charlotte Lennox's *The Female Quixote* (1752), one of the most popular novels of the second half of the century,[7] arrived with the blessing of Henry Fielding, who had announced his own *Joseph Andrews* as an "imitation" of Cervantes' novel. Fielding's official interpretation of *Don Quixote* appears in his review of Lennox's *Female Quixote* in the *Covent-Garden Journal* (no. 24, 24 March 1752), and, of course, echoes Cervantes' own words:

> Cervantes is to be considered as an Author who intended not only the Diversion, but the Instruction and Reformation of his Countrymen; With this Intention he levelled his Ridicule at a vicious Folly, which in his Time universally prevailed in Spain, and had almost converted a civilized People into a nation of Cutthroats.[8]

Therefore, it is "the Humour of Romance, which is principally ridiculed" in Lennox's novel—as, he might have added, it was in his own *Joseph Andrews*. *The Female Quixote* begins as a commentary on the unreality of the French romances Arabella reads. She sees everything through their eyes, and Lucy, her Sanchoesque maid, points out the reality.

Fielding's remarks take the form of a series of comparisons. In respect to the satire of romance, he says, Cervantes was more successful than Homer, Virgil, and Milton in their epics—and certainly more successful than Lennox. He also prefers the characters of Quixote and Sancho to those of Arabella and Lucy, but, he adds, "this may possibly be rather owing to that Advantage, which the Actions of Men give to the Writer beyond those of Women, than to any Superiority of Genius":

Don Quixote is ridiculous in performing Feats of Absurdity himself;
Arabella can only become so, in provoking and admiring the Absurdi-
ties of others. In the former Case, the Ridicule hath all the Force of a
Representation; it is in a Manner subjected to the Eyes; in the latter it is
conveyed, as it were, through our Ears, and partakes of the Coldness of
History or Narration.

By "provoking and admiring the Absurdities of others" he refers to
Arabella's suitors. A woman, in short, cannot herself be ridiculous but
only a subject that responds to the ridiculousness in men and records
her response. This is because, we must assume, she is beautiful rather
than comic, the center of an aesthetics of the Beautiful rather than of
the Novel.

He defines her character in the familiar terms of the Quixotic
foible: Like Quixote, Arabella is a person of good sense, "and in all
Cases, except one, of a very sound Judgment"—and that one is "the
Humour of Romance, which is principally ridiculed."[9] (At the end he
adds, completing the formula, that "Some Faults" may perhaps be
found in the book itself.)

He finally explains the ways in which she is an improvement on
Don Quixote: It is more probable that a young lady (indeed, "Most
young Women of the same Vivacity") than an old gentleman should
be "subverted by reading Romances"—and influenced by the circumstances of family, class, and background that Lennox assigns her heroine. She is conditioned for her reading of romances by her mother's
library of French romances, collected "to soften a Solitude which she
found very disagreeable" (that is, her husband, the marquis's retirement from the court); and by the misanthropy of her father following
his fall from court favor and retirement to the country. She inherits
"the natural Haughtiness of his Temper," his "secret Discontent," and
his belief in "the Baseness and Ingratitude of Mankind" (7, 5).

She is more endearing than Quixote because she is "a beautiful
young Lady," more interesting because the readers' "hearts are engaged" in her courtship—because, once again, she is "a beautiful young
Lady." Finally, because of her gender and therefore the courtship situation, there is a greater unity of action, as opposed to "the loose uncon-
nected Adventures in Don Quixote," and the adventures "are much

less extravagant and incredible" than the romances of Cardenio and Dorotea and the rest. Only the behavior of Arabella herself "is carried beyond Common-Life; nor is there any Thing even in her Character, which the Brain a little distempered may not account for"; that is, only the confusions of a young female brain, which "conceives indeed somewhat preposterously of the Ranks and Conditions of Men; that is to say, mistakes one Man for another; but never advances towards the Absurdity of imagining Windmills and Wine-Bags to be human creatures, or Flocks of Sheep to be Armies."

Therefore, Fielding concludes, since it is the "Humour of Romance" that is being ridiculed, Lennox exposes "all those Vices and Follies in her Sex which are chiefly predominant in our Days, that it will afford very useful Lessons to all those young Ladies who will peruse it with proper Attention." The author of *Joseph Andrews* presumably sees that, as William Warner has noted, "By gendering the novel reader female, Lennox incorporates the fantasm of the woman novel reader into her narrative."[10]

Fielding neatly describes the originality and importance of *The Female Quixote* for the development of the form he felt he had originated (the "kind of writing, which I do not remember to have seen hitherto attempted in our Language"). But when he compares Arabella with Quixote he is comparing her with his own Parson Adams. Though speaking by now as the sober Bow Street magistrate, the old Harry Fielding still condescends to women, especially those (like Slipslop at one extreme, Mrs. Atkinson at the other) who read too many books. Arabella's reading of romances, in the eighteenth century, gives her (as Fielding was quick to remark) the aura of a bluestocking. In *Don Quixote* the illiterate innkeeper's daughter and Maritornes merely listened to the romances read aloud. Marcela and Dorotea read pastoral romances, and this led to their retirement into the wilderness to escape the unwelcome attentions of men. The duchess and her ladies read romances as well as being familiar with *Don Quixote* itself, and this led them to satiric rather than romantic enterprises. These women, by their reading, knew what to expect of Don Quixote, and so made him both a butt of jests and the source of pleasure. In short, they opened up the problem of the aesthetic object who, by reading and imitating her text, becomes a subject as well. This was the figure whose problems were outlined by Marcela in her address to her suitors over the body of Grisóstomo.

Lennox's radical departure is to have Dulcinea change places with Quixote and become the protagonist.[11] In appearance, "Nature had indeed given her a most charming face, a Shape easy and delicate, a sweet and insinuating Voice, and an Air so full of Dignity and Grace, as drew the Admiration of all that saw her"; and there is no discrepancy between her "beauty" of mind and that of her body (or her dress—"perfectly magnificent") (6–7). But since it is Arabella who has read the romances, and knows the etiquette of romance, she "often consulted" her mirror and, "not finding herself engaged in such Adventures as were common to the heroines in the Romances she read, she often complained of the insensibility of Mankind, upon whom her Charms seemed to have so little Influence" (7).

Who then assumes the emptied Dulcinea position? Arabella is both Quixote and Dulcinea—the roles being not exchanged but combined; and for this reason she worships herself. Like Pope's Belinda, she admires herself in the mirror—and this leads her to complain of "the Insensibility of Mankind" for *not* pursuing her (7). Arabella's object is herself; her system is closed, and *should* be broken at the end by her finding a beautiful male object. But then this is an accidental aesthetics—and the story ends only with her discovery (written by Samuel Johnson or some other older mentor) that some fictions *can* be trusted.

Arabella, of course, embodies the two Dulcineas—the ideal and, in the manner of the ideal travestied, the real. Quixote envisioned his ideal Dulcinea (of the romances he read) as a mirror image of himself the knight-errant and therefore when he saw what she really looked like he began to see himself as he really was and to shed his madness—and to die.

In the ideal Dulcinea position, Arabella is the maiden who, as Fielding noted, distinguishes herself by "provoking and admiring the Absurdities of others." She must remain ostensibly at least passive. Her actions are largely blocking and thwarting ones rather than active and questing. There cannot be much danger of Arabella's falling for the wrong man since, as the romance forms dictate, his period of service requires that he save the life of her father, hazard his own life for him, suffer and be faithful over a long period of time, do some "great and generous action," and so on.

Lennox has only duplicated more schematically Cervantes' Marcela, who was both aesthetic object and subject and was comic because she reflected both points of view; she is the subject who carries the Quixotic sensibility but is also an aesthetic object. In a full-fledged courtship situation, however, Arabella cannot merely retreat like Marcela; her reading of romances is subsumed under a thematics of form and feeling, the emphasis falling on the rigidity of her behavior, which happens to be parallel with Quixote's, though at the other end of the telescope. In the central instance of Mr. Glanville, the romance forms intervene between Arabella and her feelings and thwart Glanville's feelings toward her; in the case of the opportunistic Hervey these forms act as a protection necessary to a naive girl who knows nothing of the world; and in the case of the gardener ("Edward"), to whom they draw her attention, the forms demonstrate her lack of perception. If Glanville, the true lover, brings out the defensive passivity of Dulcinea, Edward the gardener brings out the crazy agency of Quixote.

The Quixote fiction permits Lennox to render comic the straightforward first-person narrative of her earlier novel, *The Life of Harriot Stuart, as Written by Herself* (1750). There Harriot had no enabling factor or fiction to justify her self-assertiveness in the face of male courtship; her actions were only somewhat mitigated by being located in the uncivilized American colonies.[12] The rigidity of her behavior was forced on her by her parents and the image society had of daughters— and indeed by the Richardsonian fiction of Pamela and Clarissa in relation to their society. In *The Female Quixote* Lennox presents a young woman who is socially elevated, without the hindrance of a father or mother, and with a comic justification for the aggressive behavior of Harriot in her Quixotic reading of romances.

The incongruous juxtaposition of Quixote and Dulcinea, the subject and object, in a single character ought to have been comic. Substituting Dulcinea for Don Quixote could have been a brilliant satiric device in the hands of Swift or Fielding. In *Don Quixote* the object of laughter was, initially, Quixote. Responded to by bystanders and readers, he was an object both ridiculous and ludicrous—a model for a problematics, and thus an aesthetics, of laughter. Dulcinea was equally a model for an aesthetics, either of beauty (the ideal "Dulcinea") or of novelty (the real Dulcinea), depending on whether she was responded to by Quixote or by Sancho Panza. Dulcinea represented the usual model for aesthetic experience: the male subject responds to a female object. *The Female Quixote* shows what happens when these roles are exchanged and Dulcinea becomes Quixote. She may become the object of laughter or of aesthetic contemplation; or, therefore, an example (of a new, post-Quixote kind) of the aesthetics of laughter.

In the event, however, Arabella is often tiresome and irritating. She manifests no doubt as to the correctness of her perception and the error of everyone else's—her favorite word is "questionless." Glanville first interprets her Quixotism as snobbery; then, evoking Quixote's duke and duchess, he exploits it (as opposed to the marquis who, like Quixote's barber and curate, would burn the books). The characteristic reaction to her, from the people who are closely related to her or are close friends, is sympathy and annoyance, not the combination of laughter and astonishment, satire and wonder, directed at Quixote from his first adventure. As Sir Charles Glanville says, "I should be sorry to have a Daughter-in-law for whom I should blush as often as she opened her Mouth" (64).

It is possible that the oddness of *The Female Quixote* may partly be explained by the revaluation of chivalry following the Forty-Five. For Arabella's life independent of her reading, chivalry is a subtext. Her father is a great man who is toppled by envy and retires to a remote country estate; his daughter merely extends his misanthropy—or fulfills his Quixote function—by living according to the old chivalric ideals associated with the Stuarts, a mixture of folly and idealism (or, according to the view, stubbornness and inflexibility). Lennox's beleaguered Harriot Stuart cannot carry her Jacobite name by accident; and another indication that she was at least what Fielding was referring to in 1747 as "Jacobite," may be the fact that in *The Female Quixote* she satirizes George II's fat German mistress.[13]

The effect of transplanting the female half of the courtly love code in eighteenth-century England is to produce a monster of egotism and self-sufficiency, who can say, and believe, that "[i]t is impossible to think" that Sir George won't die "since he has not so much as received a Command from me to live" (191). As a Quixote, Arabella attempts to impose her own fiction of herself as goddess on the men who enter her life. The latter is a Swiftean enterprise: the modern whose imagination produces a new religion or philosophy must then impose his delusion on others.[14]

In this sense, Lennox thematizes and exposes the Quixotic subtext in gendered rather than religious terms, but with the Quixote message of superiority to his/her surroundings.[15] Arabella, Swift would have concluded, is using the romance forms (doubtless unconsciously) in order to stave off sexual experience—or, we might speculate, to aestheticize sex as Quixote used romance to replace religious belief. Given what we know of her relationship with her father (of whom she is clearly a chip off the old block), we may wonder whether her utilization of the romance forms was not a way to mourn for his loss.

Lennox comes from the camp of Richardson, and her heroine Arabella derives not from Parson Adams but from Richardson's feminine heroines. Arabella is a woman with the sense of inwardness associated with her sex and substantiated by the conventions of inwardness so strongly implanted in *Pamela* and *Clarissa*. As this suggests, looking back from Lennox's female Quixote, there is no way of avoiding the fact that Pamela was a prototype of the solemn Quixote—and that Lennox thematizes the Pamela model or uncovers the Quixote in her. The comic incongruity of Marcela was lacking in the monocular figure of Pamela, who was only comic when Fielding subjected her to the second (the suitors') perspective.

Presumably because he wished to declare the filiation between Lennox's novel and his own, Fielding did not read *The Female Quixote* as he read *Pamela* and conclude that Arabella embodies the female attitude that he would call prudery: the refusal to recognize one's feelings, desires, or humanity—the destruction of innocent people who do not conform to the stereotype Arabella carries in her head.

One intermediary novel calls for mention: Sarah Fielding's *David Simple* (1744) crossed her brother's Quixotic novel with *Pamela*. David's quest is for friendship, as Sarah Fielding acknowledges in book 1, chapter 3:

This was the Fantom, the Idol of his Soul's Admiration. In the Worship of which he at length grew such an Enthusiast, that he was in this Point only as mad as *Quixotte* himself could be with Knight Errantry; and after much amusing himself with the deepest Ruminations on this Subject, in which a fertile Imagination raised a thousand pleasing Images to itself, he at length took the oddest, most unaccountable Resolution that ever was heard of, *viz.* To travel through the whole World, rather than not meet with a real Friend.[16]

One expects the last clause to be "in search of a real Friend"; whereas "rather than not meet with" implies at the outset the impossibility of the quest. David is one of the Quixotes whose madness follows from a disillusionment (with his brother) and so his impossible quest is for a true friend. His first adventure is with a Dulcinea whose behavior extends his disillusionment from siblings to lovers.

In the sentimental novel a protagonist with a delicate feminine sensibility (imagination) comes into contact with a real, unsentimental world. The emphasis shifts decidedly onto the unfeeling world in which the sensibility of the feeling hero is beleaguered if not destroyed. Insofar as his character is based on a Quixote, on a derangement (a foible), as in his disillusionment with all men, David Simple is something of a humorous character. Though caught in a sentimental plot, though largely a female in men's clothing, David is still gendered male and so lacks the complexities and potentials of a female Quixote with her agenda of courtship. He is a Pamela without credentials.

Arabella is Richardson's Pamela (or Clarissa) with her Quixotic apparatus showing. "Truth," says the divine to Arabella in the speech that returns her to sanity, "is not always injured by Fiction. An admirable Writer of our own Time [Richardson], has found the Way to convey the most solid Instructions, the noblest Sentiments, and the most exalted Piety, in the pleasing Dress of a Novel, and to use the Words of the greatest Genius in the present Age [Samuel Johnson], 'has taught the Passions to move at the Command of Virtue'" (377). The divine's advice to Arabella is to replace romance reading not with reality but with the reading of novels, a different kind of fiction, defined here in terms of Richardson's practice and Johnson's theory in

Rambler no. 4 (the words cited are from no. 97). Therefore, in Lennox's terms, *The Female Quixote* itself becomes a "novel" in the proper Richardsonian-Johnsonian sense. We may assume that this is the way she read *Don Quixote*—as substituting not reality but the novel itself for the chivalric romance.

Arabella is placed, as the experiencing woman, within the Quixotic aesthetics of idealism versus the living body, in this case the body of a man—of reading versus experience (or the doctrines of connoisseurs or priests versus the experience of the common man). As an example of taste, she invokes the responses of Quixote versus Sancho, or of the blinkered connoisseurs versus those who see for themselves. Her opinions are twice removed from reality, for the texts she reads are "not in the original *French*, but very bad translations" (7). And yet a scene such as the one with Miss Groves and her woman, Mrs. Morris, contrasts the artificial book-learned manners of Arabella with the realistic, cynical ones of Mrs. Morris, who thinks she can get money out of Arabella for the information about her mistress, and the city sophistication and shallowness of Miss Groves, which are as artificial as Arabella's. The same sort of comedy of manners follows in the scenes with Charlotte Glanville, for example in their different interpretations of the word *adventure:* to Arabella a romantic love affair, to Charlotte a sordid affair, probably like Miss Grove's. Again, Sir George is not rebuffed on his first meeting with her because, with Charlotte pressing all her attentions upon him, he has no opportunity to attempt "a piece of gallantry which would undoubtedly have procured him a banishment from her presence" (87).

At the opposite pole from Quixotic madness is a return to the Quixotic vision of his society as a falling away from the Golden Age, embodied in Arabella's old books. Charlotte Glanville's "favours" are a kiss or worse, while to Arabella they are merely giving a scarf or a bracelet as a token to her "servant." Charlotte's self-centeredness, pride, and insincerity are contrasted with Arabella's Quixotic idealism, presumably to indicate how far we have fallen from the idealism of courtly romance (as well as how inappropriate such ideals are in the present). The comedy or satire of manners comes down to the subject of how *should* courtship be carried out, what *is* decorous and how much form should give way to feeling, and so to the subject of "taste" and issues of disinterestedness and passion.

If there is not much laughter in *The Female Quixote*, nevertheless Lennox thematizes laughter as a crucial aspect of manners as related to class: the déclassé Henry laughs to forestall the servant Lucy's laughter at his mistaking Arabella's return of his letter for a reply; to Lucy, as acolyte of Arabella, Henry's laughter means that he did not take Arabella's rejection tragically, but to the naturally gentle Arabella, who in this case reads the sign correctly, it was a way to cover his embarrassment. The comedy itself arises from these multiple misunderstandings. Arabella talks on one level, Charlotte on another—as Don Quixote and Sancho did, and much as the representative of one class talks with that of another.

Catherine Morland

Arabella's madness is related to that special quality of imagination that sets her off from the other women in *The Female Quixote*. This is, in Corbyn Morris's sense, a foible, but Arabella, a woman who comes across to the reader as far more "living" (in Ian Watt's sense of "formal realism") than comic, demonstrates that a woman's foible can be confused with the blemish that confirms or improves her beauty. Following *The Female Quixote* it is easy to see how in the right hands a woman can be as complex a figure as Quixote himself.

The social blindness that goes with Arabella's madness is at least analogous to the blind spot in a Catherine Morland, Elizabeth Bennet, or Emma Woodhouse. Glanville resembles a Darcy who perseveres in the face of the heroine's misunderstanding (the annoying quality of her prejudice); and the other woman, here Charlotte Glanville, anticipates Bingley's sister, who is after the man who loves the heroine and is both jealous and unable to believe that he can really love her rival, whether Arabella or Elizabeth. Once Quixote is embodied in a woman, Austen can create a novel that is centered on the woman who is cleverer than those around her but deluded in one area.

The moment in which Quixote is feminized leads in one way to the heroines of Anne Radcliffe's novels and in another to Austen's—

both of which are about sensitive young women who are wrong about one thing; and the effect is either sublimity or novelty. The latter, however, requires an aesthetic standard that is "tested" by laughter. And, of course, Austen makes the Radcliffe novel serve as the romances of chivalry in her specifically Quixotic novel *Northanger Abbey* (begun c. 1798–99, published posthumously in 1818). The basis for Austen's imitation is Cervantes' use of one sort of fiction or fictional character to set off the relative verisimilitude of his own, with the earlier fiction heavily conventional by contrast. The effect is summed up in Catherine Morland's remark on the windows of Northanger Abbey: "To be sure, the pointed arch was preserved—the form of them was Gothic—they might be even casements—but every pane was so large, so clear, so light!"[17]

Like Arabella, Catherine also "was in training for a heroine; she read all such works as heroines must read to supply their memories with those quotations which are so serviceable and so soothing in the vicissitudes of their eventful lives" (15).[18] The delusion is, of course, based on her reading: Catherine expects that Blaize Castle will be "like what one reads of" and Bath the same as "what I have read about" (85, 106). She has read sentimental works (broadly, including select passages from Shakespeare) and so has "reached the age of seventeen, without having seen one amiable youth who could call forth her sensibility; without having inspired one real passion, and without having excited even any admiration but what was very moderate and very transient. This was strange indeed!" The reason, the Austen narrator intrudes as her opinion, is that "[t]here was not one lord in the neighbourhood; no—not even a baronet. There was not one family among their acquaintance who had reared and supported a boy accidentally found at their door—not one young man whose origin was unknown" (16). Catherine's reading places her, as both Quixote and Dulcinea, in the confusing world into which Arabella was introduced at the beginning of *The Female Quixote*.

There are, however, major differences. Unlike Lennox's Arabella, Catherine (like Fielding's mock heroes) always falls short of romantic expectations—in beauty, in sensibility. Commonsense empiricism distinguishes her from Arabella (who recalls the unpleasant Isabella

Thorpe more than Catherine). The Gothic flourishes are the author's. One is followed by the concession that Catherine, however, is "undisturbed by presentiments of such an evil" (131). Seeing Henry Tilney with a young lady, Catherine infers that it is his sister—"thus unthinkingly throwing away a fair opportunity of considering him lost to her for ever, by being married already" and "of turning of a deathlike paleness, and falling in a fit on Mrs. Allen's bosom": "But guided only by what was simple and probable, it had never entered her head that Mr. Tilney could be married; he had not behaved, he had not talked, like the married men to whom she had been used; he had never mentioned a wife, and he had acknowledged a sister. From these circumstances sprang the instant conclusion of his sister's now being by his side" (53). And when she falls in love, "[h]er passion for ancient edifices was next in degree to her passion for Henry Tilney" (141). Her problem then is that "she soon began to see beauty in every thing admired by [Tilney]" (111).

Austen is also, unlike Lennox, a master of irony. The contrast between the young woman's image of the world and the actual world is conveyed by a witty author. For Austen irony is a form of wit, and her voice throughout this early novel addresses the problem of wit formulated by Addison and Morris: that wit focuses attention on the poet rather than the character. We cannot, Addison wrote, "at the same time be delighted with the wit of the Poet, and concerned for the person that speaks it." Thus he concluded that Ovid "employs his Invention more than his Judgment, and speaks all the ingenious things that can be said on the subject, rather than those which are particularly proper to the person and circumstances of the speaker."[19]

In Austen the wit is normative; it designates an area related to the novelty of Addison, Hogarth, and Fielding; and the wit that begins as the narrator's irony ends suggesting the character's psychological defense system. When the wit is associated with a character within a work of fiction, it becomes an aspect of that character; specifically, her ability to see wittily (that is, as a test of truth) the novelty in which she lives. In *Northanger Abbey* the author's wit, which takes the form of burlesque, measures Catherine against something she is not—which becomes something she *thinks* she is, and which then someone else, Tilney or

Thorpe in different ways, jestingly makes her become in social situations that have moral consequences.[20] By moral consequences Austen means feelings of discomfort and pain.

In *Pride and Prejudice* (1813) then the wit, quizzing, and rattling are transferred from the author and other characters to the protagonist herself, a combination of the wit of the author and the empiricism of the heroine in *Northanger Abbey*—and the discomfort and pain to others as well as herself. The wit of the heroine resolves the problem Lennox fell into in *The Female Quixote*: Elizabeth Bennet's "country town indifference to decorum" (36), her freedom of spirit, explain her wit—"I expected at least that the pigs were got into the garden, and here is nothing but Lady Catherine and her daughter."[21] Elizabeth does happily merge Quixote and Dulcinea, combining wit and humor in a single character—blemish and foible seen by a witty intelligence, herself or an author very close to her. The most significant case of the thematization of wit is, of course, Emma Woodhouse's jest at the expense of Miss Bates.

In the famous authorial digression on the "novel" at the end of chapter 5 of *Northanger Abbey*, the author's irony flashes this way and that, at one moment suggesting double irony, at another an ironic dialectic. As I read the passage, by "novel" the author specifically refers to the "novel" Catherine and Isabella Thorpe have been reading just prior to this authorial disquisition—Radcliffe's *Mysteries of Udolpho*. While here and elsewhere in *Northanger Abbey* Austen associates "novel" with all sorts of fiction, from *Tom Jones* to *Camilla*, the common element is a romance plot with the conventions of romance fiction most blatantly embodied in *Udolpho*. I also read this dense passage as a miniature reproduction of the discussion of the curate, the canon of Toledo, and Quixote, where romance is said to be lies but pleasureful (beautiful) lies, and this is contrasted with *comedia*, which is as untruthful but lacks the saving grace of beauty.[22]

Austen's "polyvalent irony" in fact masks a dialogical discourse, leaving the reader to conclude which of the discourses is employed in *Northanger Abbey* itself.[23] The author cites first the "abuse" of "such effusions of fancy" as novels, and then asserts that "our productions have afforded more extensive and unaffected pleasure than those of any other literary corporation in the world." She could be echoing Swift's Grub Street hack's claims for "our" modern works in *A Tale of a Tub*:[24] "From pride, ignorance, or fashion, our foes are almost as many as our readers . . . there seems almost a general wish of decrying the capacity and undervaluing the labour of the novelist, and of slighting the performances which have only genius, wit, and taste to recommend them." The hyperbole, which does not survive the grave irony that runs consistently through these chapters, rises to a climax in the author's response to "the common cant," the young lady's exclamation, "Oh! it is only a novel!"—"It is only Cecilia, or Camilla, or Belinda"—

> or, in short, only some work in which the greatest powers of the mind are displayed, in which the most thorough knowledge of human nature, the happiest delineation of its varieties, the liveliest effusions of wit and humour are conveyed to the world in the best chosen language. (38)

Although "the greatest powers of the mind" is surely ironic, the formulation—in the context referring to the novels of Burney as well as Radcliffe, but also to "our" novel—includes words that clearly designate the Austen novel only: *human nature*, its *varieties*, and *effusions of wit and humour*.[25]

If one pole is the discourse of *Udolpho*, the other, from which, one would think, are drawn *human nature*, its *varieties*, and *effusions of wit and humour*, is the discourse of the *Spectator*:

> Now, had the same young lady been engaged with a volume of the Spectator, instead of such a work [as these novels], and told its name; though the chances must be against her being occupied by any part of that voluminous publication, of which either the matter or manner would not disgust a young person of taste: the substance of its papers so often consisting in the statement of improbable circumstances, unnatural characters, and topics of conversation, which no longer concern anyone living; and their language, too, frequently so coarse as to give no very favourable idea of the age that could endure it. (38)

"Improbable circumstances" and "unnatural characters" are terms that apply better to *Udolpho* than to the *Spectator*, except perhaps in the case of a "young person of taste." The latter is evidently Catherine, and what she has learned by the end of *Northanger Abbey* is what she would have learned more easily had she read the *Spectator* rather than *Udolpho*.[26]

Austen presents *Udolpho* on one side and the *Spectator* on the other, reversing the adjectives we would ordinarily expect to see attached to each—and implying what we will find at the end of the novel, that the qualities of the Gothic are as significant as those of the Novel, and that Catherine's favorite adjective, *strange*, carries the connotations of both Burke's Sublime and Addison's Novel, Uncommon, and Strange.

As Addison (as well as Steele) frequently asserted, one purpose of the *Spectator* was to recover, elevate, and instruct women—usually ignored in such a male, club-oriented society as Mr. Spectator's. In the "Pleasures" essays he turned the unruly (we might say masculine) imagination into a pleasurable way of seeing; and in the Quixotic context of his comic theory, this sensibility that lives on secondary qualities (color, odor, taste) runs up against harsh primary qualities of extension and movement in a perpetuation of Addison's Quixotic knight wandering in an enchanted forest. It is important that the sensibility be regarded as a delusion, though a pleasing one. For insofar as morality remains, the story is of an aesthetic sensibility coming into contact with a harsh world, and the result is, as in *Don Quixote*, a moral judgment equally on the character's delusion and on the world. It is easy to see how Addison's aestheticizing of the Quixotic imagination could function best in the person of a female subject.

The joining of *Udolpho* and the *Spectator* involves a dialectic of female and male sensibilities as well as romance and satire. This passage, the only one in which Austen gives us something like an *ars poetica*, situates her novel at a juncture of the discourses of the Gothic novel (which, as with Quixote's knight-errantry, is largely recovered by the end of *Northanger Abbey*) and the novelty defined by Addison in the *Spectator*. The terms that surround it in the adjacent chapters make the connection between spectatorial laughter and Quixotic reality.

In the novel itself this chiasmus takes the form of the crossover of Gothic and modern (or Sublime and Novel) perception as embodied in Catherine. As it turns out, this Quixote's perception is, of course, correct: The general, "enraged with almost every body in the world but himself," is "furious in his anger," and he and Henry "parted in dreadful disagreement"—Henry "in an agitation of mind which many solitary hours were required to compose." And "Catherine, at any rate, heard enough to feel, that in suspecting General Tilney of either murdering or shutting up his wife, she had scarcely sinned against his character, or magnified his cruelty" (247–48). The character who embodies the Gothic is Montoni in *Udolpho*, General Tilney in the present of *Northanger Abbey*. Austen's point is not only that Catherine is correct to see Tilney as a Montoni but that they are merely two of a kind. Tilney is one of those banal, secondhand villains, poor shadows of the real ones, created by Swift in the 1700s. Tilney also draws attention to the banality at the heart of Montoni, who is merely another Tilney with an Italian name, whose basic instinct beneath Radcliffe's trumpery was focused on money, estate, and family.[27]

He is another version of the "something very shocking indeed" that Catherine says she has heard "will soon come out of London . . . more horrible than any thing we have met with yet." She means a new Gothic novel; but Miss Tilney thinks she means a riot, and Henry then explains the discrepancy between a book and "a mob of three thousand men assembling in St. George's Fields; the Bank attacked, the Tower threatened, the streets of London flowing with blood," and so on. Tilney's reference is to what he calls his favorite subject, "history," and so to the Gordon Riots of 1780 and the French Revolution of 1789, perhaps to the crowd of one hundred and fifty thousand that gathered at the meeting of the London Corresponding Society in Copenhagen Fields in 1795, and the riots of 1794–95 with their death toll, and the naval mutinies at Spithead and the Nore in 1797.[28]

"The Age of Chivalry is gone"

When Addison aestheticized imagination it took the form of his memory of Quixote's story of the Knight of the Lake.[29] In that early "Pleasures of the Imagination" essay he focused on the pleasure of sight (the sense that Quixote stressed in the knight's experiences); in the last of the essays Addison recovered chivalry itself, along with related fancies, as the Strange. This, however, was the aspect of his "Pleasures" that was longest taking hold in England. It was not until the mid-1740s that Collins made the recovery of imagination including chivalry itself into the subject of a new poetics, one of sublimity.

The turn toward the side of *Don Quixote* that supports romance, imagination, and defeat at the hands of the crass world coincides with the Forty-Five, the possibility of sympathy for Scotland, its chivalric clans fallen in battle and outlawed in their own countryside (less so for the final defeat of the Jacobites). With the Forty-Five came associations with lost causes and a poetics of the primitive, defeated, and mythic.

Hogarth's *March to Finchley* (1750) employed the comic balance of military order (the troops marching toward combat in the far distance) and, up close, the geometrical order of the windows in the brothel; but, overflowing the windows and the military order, the human disorder of Sanchoesque hunger, lechery, beautiful women, and wandering children. Hogarth shows no more sympathy for the chivalric ideal than he had in his *Hudibras* illustrations. Only the subscription ticket, which shows a pile of combined British and Scottish standards and weapons, may refer to chivalry, balancing the Scottish swords, shields, and axes against the English rifles and canon. Hogarth's emphasis is primarily on the primitive and unequal weapons of the Scots.[30] In *Finchley* he epitomizes his (and Fielding's) aesthetics of the "mixture," the Beautiful as the greatest variety to be discovered in apparent uniformity (the greatest number of different parts in a whole), but grounds it in the Forty-Five, *Tom Jones,* and the moral disinterestedness (but morality still) of the novel and wit, reflecting the "mixed" character of English Whig politics. The aesthetics of Shaftesbury/Quixote he would have associated with the Cavaliers and Jacobites of the Forty-Five.

After the Forty-Five, in fact, the defeated Scottish Highlander begins to assume the Quixote role, standing for outmoded chivalric ideals defeated by the more modernized military forces of England. In this sense, Collins's reference to Don Quixote in "The Manners," though brief, is a telling detail. If there is a correlation in the early 1740s between the fall of Walpole, the rise of *Pamela,* and the development of the "humorous character" based on Quixote's one foible, there may also be a correlation between the political events of the later 1740s and the turn away from the comic to the heroic and idealizing Quixotes of

Smollett. The new Quixote emerges from the traumatic events of the Forty-Five, especially for the Scotsman Smollett, who had always felt himself isolated in London by his nationality. Smollett's nominal Quixote was Sir Launcelot Greaves (in the eponymous novel of 1760), a handsome and idealized descendant of the Hogarth-Vanderbank illustrations, who is driven Quixotic by the loss of his beloved Aurelia to the schemes of villains. His Sancho, Timothy Crabshaw, carries all of the burlesque elements upon his (as if he were a cross between Maritornes and Hudibras) humped shoulders.[31]

In his *Letters on Chivalry and Romance* (1762), the book that sought to revalue romances of chivalry and the Gothic as the superior source of poetic inspiration, Richard Hurd singles out "the Spaniards, of all the Europeans, . . . furthest gone in every characteristic madness of true chivalry" and notes "the discredit into which the stories of chivalry had now [by the end of the seventeenth century] fallen by the immortal satire of Cervantes."[32] His conclusion: "In a word, you will find that the *manners* they [chivalric romances] paint, and the *superstitions* they adopt, are the more poetical for being Gothic" (55).

Hurd refers disdainfully to the period just prior to Addison's *Spectator* papers, citing Shaftesbury as an egregious example of the preference for the classical over the Gothic (82). His Addisonian recovery of chivalry and romance starts from Addison's Strange, but it goes on to combine the two modernisms, historical and aesthetic, of Bentley and Addison. First he historically contextualizes the peculiarities (the "imagination") of chivalric romance, explaining why knights went "in quest of adventures" or hastened "to run to the succour of the distressed" (13–14): it was, he says, because the historical situation called for such activities, and these, in turn, could be mythologized in fictions. This is, in fact, a form of euhemerism such as the Abbé Banier had applied in the 1740s to the classical gods and heroes, showing that they were mythologized versions of historical figures, kings and soldiers.[33] Hurd makes this clear by turning from the historicizing of the heroes of romance back to analogies with the heroes of classical epic.[34]

Having established the historical argument, Hurd turns to the aesthetic, which began with Addison's recovery of the imagination and madness associated with chivalric romance—a development that was first guardedly embodied by Addison in Sir Roger de Coverley (the

Tory opponent) and then more openly, and positively, in the "Pleasures" essays. Hurd notes "that the *love of God and the Ladies* went hand
in hand, in the duties and ritual of Chivalry" (19). And he singles out
the Spaniards, explaining "why the Spaniards, of all the Europeans,
were furthest gone in every characteristic madness of true chivalry" as
"their [religious] fanaticism," which had been "kept alive by the memory and neighbourhood of their old infidel invaders," the Moors (22).
Thus, if chivalric romance replaced the worship of the Virgin with the
worship of one's "lady," Cervantes, as he turned Quixote's madness to
the positive side that was his chivalric idealism (his powerful imagination), replaced religion with aesthetics.

By questioning the authority, validity, and authenticity of the text
of *Don Quixote,* Cervantes questioned the haphazard composition of
all texts, including implicitly the Bible. The scholarly Modern did
the same—Bentley on Phalaris (and, less successfully, on Milton) by
historical contextualizing, justifying the text in terms of its historical
sources. This is what Hurd does, not to discredit romances but to
augment the aesthetic with a historical justification. He shows why
such strange practices came about; that they were historically factual;
and that even such apparent vagaries as giants and monsters were
mythological versions of facts. "These giants were oppressive feudal
Lords, and every Lord was to be met with, like the Giant, in his strong
hold, or castle" (28).

Hurd was a clergyman who justified romances on the same
grounds that Woolston discredited the Scriptures. But while the latter
detached the miracles of Christ from a historical context and therefore
was forced to allegorize them—morally, but in effect only aestheticizing them—Hurd established *both* the historical and the aesthetic. He
showed that the strange conventions of romance do have a historical
origin *and* that they are aesthetically pleasing—in both cases in lieu of
being read as moralities; but, perhaps to compensate, he raised the
stakes: Though he cites Addison's case for *faerie* and the Strange out of
"the darkness and superstition of later ages" (53), like Collins he now
designates the area as the Sublime. "Gothic manners and machin-
ery . . . have, by their nature and genius, the advantage of [the classical]
in producing the *sublime*" (60).

It follows that Hurd also attributes to the romances of chivalry a principle of unity the contrary to that of the "classical ideas of Unity, which have no place here; and are in every view foreign to the purpose, if the poet has found means to give his work, tho' consisting of many parts, the advantage of Unity" (66). This sense of sublime form essentially corresponds to the canon of Toledo's definition and equation of form in popular romance and *comedia*.

Edmund Burke begins his *Reflections on the Revolution in France* (1790) with the anti-Quixote position. Speaking of the revolutionaries in Paris, he asks rhetorically whether he should congratulate the "madman, who has escaped from the protecting restraint and wholesome darkness of his cell" (recalling Swift's madmen as well as Swift's imagery of "effervescence") or, directly invoking Quixote, the "highwayman and murderer, who has broke prison, upon the recovery of his natural rights? This would be to act over again the scene of the criminals condemned to the galleys, and their heroic deliverer, the metaphysical Knight of the Sorrowful Countenance."[35] Burke first sees the French as Quixotes whose delusion of liberty led him to release the prisoners on their way to the galleys (as they released the prisoners of the Bastille); but then he becomes himself, without noticing an inconsistency, the spokesman for "antient chivalry" (92)—a Quixotic position with which he was associated by his opponents. At the heart of his *Reflections* he compares the French constitution to "a noble and venerable castle," and France itself is "a generous and gallant nation, long misled to [its] disadvantage by [its] high and romantic sentiments of fidelity, honour, and loyalty" (40–42).

The notorious passage about Queen Marie Antoinette pursued and (theoretically) stripped and violated by the rough plebeians who break into her bedchamber is followed by his fond memory of the queen in her glory

> in a nation of men of honour and of cavaliers. I thought ten thousand
> swords must have leaped from their scabbards to avenge even a look that
> threatened her with insult.—But the age of chivalry is gone.—That of
> sophisters, oeconomists, and calculators, has succeeded; and the glory
> of Europe is extinguished for ever. Never, never more, shall we behold
> that generous loyalty to rank and sex, that proud submission, that

dignified obedience, that subordination of the heart, which kept alive, even in servitude itself, the spirit of an exalted freedom. (91)

In her response, *A Vindication of the Rights of Man* (1790), Mary Wollstonecraft focuses her criticism on Burke's image of the queen as a passive image of beauty and love, threatened by irrational (sublime) forces. Women readers of Burke's *Philosophical Enquiry* "have laboured to be pretty, by counterfeiting weakness." In the context of the *Reflections on the Revolution in France*, they are the Marie Antoinettes of the greater world, convinced by Burke's aesthetic that "*littleness* and *weakness* are the very essence of beauty" and that "Nature, by making women *little, smooth, delicate, fair* creatures, never designed that they should exercise those feelings." In Burke she sees the civilization that uses the search for beauty to replace the correction of crimes against the people, that sees experience in aesthetic rather than moral categories— that, in short, "refines the manners at the expense of morals" or makes them "a painted substitute for morals."[36]

Burke's Beautiful, she makes clear, is only a prettifying, as when reason "is only employed to varnish over the faults which it ought to have corrected" (4), and the stripping of Marie Antoinette, which he deplores, she sees as an essential act: "is hereditary weakness necessary to render religion lovely? and will her form have lost the smooth delicacy that inspires love, when stripped of its Gothic drapery?" (120). "Gothic" is Wollstonecraft's favorite word for Burke's aestheticizing of politics: "These are gothic notions of beauty," she says, "—the ivy is beautiful, but, when it insidiously destroys the trunk from which it receives support, who would not grub it up?" (10). Her remark that "You mourn for the idle tapestry that decorated a gothic pile" (152) anticipates Paine's more famous formulation in *The Rights of Man* (1791), "You pity the plumage and ignore the dying bird."

Wollstonecraft opposes "gothic gallantry" to a woman's "humanity," which "should have been better pleased to have heard that lord. George Gordon [inciter of the Gordon Riots] was confined on account of the calamities which he brought on his country, than for a *libel* on the queen of France" (89).

Emily St. Aubert in Catherine Morland's favorite Gothic novel, *The Mysteries of Udolpho*, includes in her aesthetic of the Beautiful-

Sublime the memory of Burke's Marie Antoinette pursued by the plebeian mob. In this sense Austen is making a political statement that is closer to Wollstonecraft's than to Burke's formulation. For Wollstonecraft and, following her, Austen, "gothic" summons up ideas of chivalry and courtesy but also castles, cells, locked rooms, high walls, contracted marriages, and all the customs that make women fit into Burke's Beautiful and that inform the novels of Austen. Burke's image of aestheticized woman, according to Wollstonecraft, is precisely the one that Austen challenges in *Northanger Abbey* and her other novels: God gave women beauty so that they would *not* be inclined "to cultivate the moral virtues that might chance to excite respect, and interfere with the pleasing sensations they were created to inspire" (112). Wollstonecraft's central insight is that beauty and seductiveness are men's fiction imposed on women to keep them weak and submissive.

Claudia L. Johnson's argument is that from beginning to end Austen makes the Gothic the mirror image of the ordinary: "*Northanger Abbey* does not reflect, but rather clarifies and reclaims, gothic conventions in distinctly political ways."[37] While plausible in a retrospect of the novel, this overlooks the Quixotic model in which the romance's illumination of the ordinary is progressive; in fact, it is the climactic immersion of Catherine in Northanger Abbey itself (she never reached Blaize Castle) that causes the reader to rethink earlier episodes. In the abbey Catherine's Gothic reading is replaced by Henry's Gothic scenario (by this time she has turned her allegiance of imitation from Radcliffe's novels to Henry's words because she is falling in love with him); this scenario is obviously untrue in its details of black cabinets and mysterious manuscripts, but in a larger sense the plot of *Udolpho* is proved to have been rewritten in contemporary England: not only is General Tilney a contemporary Montoni but Mrs. Tilney *was* a contemporary version of the nun, equally "injured and ill-fated" (141).

The test of character in *Northanger Abbey*, as in Austen's subsequent novels, is aesthetic: the responses of the heroine and her friends to the estates and gardens they visit are as significant and telling as those of the characters in Pope's "Epistle to Burlington" or Hogarth's *Marriage A-la-mode*, where art, paintings, and architecture wittily defined character as well as taste (or character *as* taste).[38] After Catherine stands up the Tilneys for a visit to Blaize Castle (with the help of

Thorpe's lie) "she meditated, by turns, on broken promises and broken arches, phaetons and false hangings, Tilneys and trap-doors" (87).

It is important that it is a woman who responds; hence, it is an aesthetics whose subject is the woman and whose object is nature, art, and men, as well as other women. In the Austen world, Catherine always falls short of the ideal: she is "almost pretty" (in this case versus Isabella Thorpe, who is a "beauty" [15]), and even Tilney, "if not quite handsome, was very near it" (25). Short of the ideal of the Beautiful, Catherine is the real Dulcinea rather than the ideal Dulcinea (as we were led to believe Lennox's Arabella was). Because it is a woman "almost pretty," her position is closer to the spectator of Addison's Novel than the object of his Beautiful.

The plot of *Northanger Abbey* allegorizes the different aesthetic positions at the end of the eighteenth century: If Catherine, despite her yearnings for the Gothic, is the spectator of novelty, the Beautiful is embodied by the fiction of Radcliffe's Emily St. Aubert and her beautiful counterpart Isabella, who urges the reading of *Udolpho* on Catherine. The Beautiful in this story is threatened by the Sublime in its various forms—the villain Montoni, the power he holds over Emily, the confinement he threatens, and the rugged mountains into which he has taken her.

In chapter 14, where Tilney admits that he reads and enjoys novels, he also reveals himself to be an advocate of the Picturesque. This is, first, "viewing the country with the eyes of persons accustomed to drawing"—the framing of nature and seeing it through the eyes of paintings by Claude or Salvator Rosa—and as such parallel to Catherine's attempt to see society through the eyes of Gothic novels (unsuccessfully because of her strong empirical bent); and second, it is the natural version of Addison's Novel or Uncommon, which appreciates the untended and overgrown, the accidental and flawed, and appreciates surprise and astonishment (110–11).[39] Tilney himself is, like Catherine, "almost handsome," and combines her (the humorous character's) foible with the witty intelligence of the "author." Catherine also imitates Tilney: after listening to his disquisition "she soon began to see beauty in every thing admired by him," and "voluntarily rejected the whole city of Bath, as unworthy to make part of a landscape" (111).

Austen's plot of aesthetics—the struggle of Beautiful, Picturesque, and Sublime—recalls the fiction with which Hogarth had brought his career to a close thirty-five years earlier. Between 1757 and his death in 1764, he combated the privileging of the Burkean Sublime over the Novel, Uncommon, and Strange. In his reading of Burke's Sublime, the woman who began as a harlot and became a figure of beauty, a Comic Muse and normative, becomes in the late 1750s a beleaguered, gothicized woman. Briefly he tried out the Burkean Sublime in two monumental paintings, *The Lady's Last Stake* and *Sigismunda* (both 1758–59), two young ladies about to lose honor or life. They were an interim stage—whether experiment or accommodation—between his own aesthetics and the Burkean, before the genuine signs of reaction against Burke appear in *The Cockpit* and *Enthusiasm Delineated* of 1759, leading into the last prints of the 1760s. In the process, he was himself shown by at least one caricaturist as the visionary Don Quixote—not his self-image of the commonsense Sancho—riding a goose and following his crazy theories in a quest for Beauty.[40] He identified sublime chaos with Bedlam in his revision of *Rake*, plate 8, and with the "end" of all things in *Finis: or The Tailpiece*, which shows his Line of Beauty distorted, broken, and destroyed by the aesthetics/politics of Burke's Sublime; but this Sublime was clearly as mocking of the politics of 1763 (the year he inscribed on the wall of Bedlam) as Catherine's "Montoni" is of General Tilney.

Austen's is a comic version of Hogarth's losing battle with Burke's Sublime and the chaotic political world of 1763. In her aesthetic fable a moral judgment is being passed on the Burkean Sublime. In Austen's reference to "broken promises and broken arches," the promises are not aestheticized; rather the Gothic arches are moralized—or moralized by being banalized. The joining of *Udolpho* and the *Spectator* means that the aesthetics of the Radcliffean Gothic is demystified and remoralized. Austen introduces aesthetic terms in order to code her recovery of morality—a morality, as Johnson has shown, that cut against the grain of much of the counterrevolutionary fiction of the 1790s. Austen's solution remains Quixotic because the story is about Catherine's imagination, as contrasted with her own essential empiricism, and yet also the degree to which there is an equivalent in the world to her imaginary constructs. The story is finally about how laughter—even or especially at General Tilney—is the final criterion and experience on which her imagination depends.

Hogarth's point in *Analysis*, plate 2, was that Beauty is *not* detachable from desire, seduction, and (at worst) deception: against a "pure" aesthetics he demonstrated that aesthetics is indistinguishable from rhetoric. He also demonstrated that aesthetics, once it has replaced religion and religious morality, must be *re*moralized. Obviously there can be rhetoric that has nothing to do with morality (as in Addison's rhetorical use of aesthetics for Whig ends). But by posing the question as he does, by showing that Beauty (both Shaftesbury's and Addison's) is a form of interestedness and of rhetoric, Hogarth does in effect *re*moralize aesthetics.

Thus while aesthetics replaces religion and priestcraft with pleasure based on the senses, it replaces Christian morality with a disinterested morality—one without bias. Hogarth's argument is that one should replace a partisan morality with an epistemology of the "pursuit" of understanding. Addison in his aesthetics of novelty subordinated understanding to enjoyment—pursuit, curiosity, surprise are elements that contribute to the "pleasures of the imagination." This aesthetics, learned from Hogarth's *Analysis of Beauty*, defines the comic world of Sterne's *Tristram Shandy*.

Hogarth, and then Austen, subordinate enjoyment to understanding, and the understanding does not lose its moral (as opposed to, in Addison's case, its rhetorical) dimension. Every time Hogarth's or Austen's wit reveals another case of variety in apparent uniformity (and unlike Sterne), a moral judgment is made. Even if the norm and the satiric object keep changing places, there is never a Kunderian sense of being above judgment—even though judgment itself (in the sense of conventional, priestly morality) may be put in question.

Historically this reflects a perspective (again, interested) from the direction of Whig opposition politics, and its antiestablishment and anticlerical position. Thus if Addison aestheticized laughter, which had been resolutely moral, Hogarth remoralizes it; and Austen also redefines morality in terms of Addisonian aesthetics. She uses a moral standard against an aesthetic one—or at least what she regards as a pseudo-aesthetic one, or an aesthetics used as a rhetoric in favor of a false position.

At the end of book 7 of *Tristram Shandy*, in the south of France in his flight from Death, Tristram pauses to dance with a nut-brown maid with a "cursed slit in [her] petticoat." He cannot pause for enjoyment of her "Viva la joia!" ("Why could I not live and end my days thus?" or "sit down in the lap of content") but must "dance off . . . so changing only partner and tunes, I danced it away from Lunel to Montpellier—from thence to Pesçnas, Beziers—I danced it along through Narbonne, Carcasson, and Castle Naudairy" (650–51).

In chapter 10 of *Northanger Abbey*, Henry Tilney offers Catherine his witty analogy between the country dance and marriage: "Fidelity and complaisance are the principal duties of both; and those men who do not chuse to dance or marry themselves, have no business with the partners or wives of their neighbours" (76). Tilney's analogy exfoliates into a most Quixotic dialogue. Catherine replies, Sancho-like: "But they are such very different things!——" "——That you think they cannot be compared together," replies Tilney. "To be sure not," Catherine returns. "People that marry can never part, but must go and keep house together. People that dance, only stand opposite each other in a long room for half an hour."

I see in Tilney's analogy an inference Austen has drawn from Hogarth's "Country Dance" in *Analysis*, plate 2, that the young man passing a note to the wife was her dancing partner prior to her husband's insistence that they depart. For Hogarth the dance provided an opportunity to illustrate the transitions between attitudes, the interrelation of nature and art, but in the context of a critique of beauty and virtue. By discovering the adultery within the dance, Hogarth's parable of aesthetics recovered aesthetics for morality.[41]

From this aesthetic model Austen has Tilney infer the tension between dancing partner and husband—between the "people that dance" (Sterne's Tristram) and the "people that marry" in her own novels. The difference, he acknowledges, is that, "in marriage, the man is supposed to provide for the support of the woman; the woman to make the home agreeable to the man; he is to purvey, and she is to smile. But in dancing, their duties are exactly changed; the agreeableness, the compliance are expected from him, while she furnishes the fan and the lavender water." The passage is about wit, about the formal, purely aesthetic (though seductive) relations in dance as opposed to the practical ones in marriage. The country dance is metamorphosed by Tilney's wit into a play version of marriage—a purely aesthetic experience and yet, in Tilney's case vis-à-vis Catherine, with the intention and the rhetoric of seduction. Catherine is correct: play is not the same as living, courtship as marriage. This interplay of aesthetics and morality culminates in the reality of Henry's house, Northanger Abbey, and General Tilney's "tyranny." Beneath the aesthetic agon Austen has recovered morality; she has found the fiction in which (as if to dramatize Hogarth's illustrations to his *Analysis*) to remoralize subjects that have been aestheticized.

We began this study with a particular, 1700s sense of aesthetics as the philosophy of sensuous response to the external stimuli that can be called beautiful or ugly. We have ended it, in the 1800s, with the modern sense of aesthetics as escape from moral responsibility into formalism. Hogarth, by way of the two Dulcineas and the "aesthetics of laughter," may have inaugurated this development with his anti-aesthetics (which began as an anti-Shaftesburian aesthetics) of the paragon corrected by the "living woman," of both taste and conventional moral judgment corrected by understanding. Both senses of aesthetics were implicit in *Don Quixote,* and by returning once again to that text Austen showed how it could serve as a foundation for the complex fictions of the English novel.

Preface

1. In Wilkins's play, *The Miseries of Enforced Marriage* (1606), act 3, a drunken character shouts, "Now am I armed to fight with a windmill." The first life of Cervantes was by the Spanish ambassador to England, Gregorio Mayans y Siscar (1738), and the first commentary was the *Annotaciones* of the Rev. John Bowle (1781). Beaumont's *Knight of the Burning Pestle* (1607) may have been the first adaptation.

2. [Pierre François Guyot Desfontaines], review of *Joseph Andrews*, in *Observations sur les écrits modernes* (1743), 31: 189–91; in Paulson and Thomas Lockwood, eds., *Henry Fielding: The Critical Heritage* (London, 1969), 128, 129.

3. Motteux, preface to his translation of *Don Quixote* (1700).

4. J. C. Weyerman, preface to a French translation of *Don Quixote* (The Hague, 1746), viii, cited in Hanns Hammelmann, *Book Illustrators in Eighteenth-Century England* (London, 1975), 82.

5. Cf. Miguel de Unamuno: "Spain remains one of the nations where the book is least read; moreover, it is without doubt the country where it is worst read. . . . I go so far as to believe that *Don Quixote* gains in translation, and that if it has been understood better outside of Spain, it is in good part because a preoccupation with the language has not veiled its beauty in foreign lands" (*The Life of Don Quixote and Sancho According to Miguel de Cervantes Saavedra*, trans. Homer P. Earle [New York, 1927], 445, 454). On its popularity in England, see Jerome Beasley: "whose fame exceeded that of any other single work, domestic or foreign" (*Novels of the 1740s* [Athens, Ga., 1982], 10).

6. Hobbes, *Leviathan*, ed. Michael Oakeshott (Oxford, 1960), 36.

7. In *The Amiable Humorist* (Chicago, 1960) Stuart Tave indicated the importance of *Don Quixote* in the transformation of satire into comedy and the

laughter of ridicule into the laughter of sympathy. See also Paulson, *Satire and the Novel* (New Haven, 1967).

8. Paulson, *The Beautiful, Novel, and Strange* (Baltimore, 1996). In one sense, the present book can be said to take off from p. 73 of that book.

9. McKeon, *The Origins of the English Novel, 1600–1740* (Baltimore, 1987), 280–82, 119–20. McKeon develops Georg Lukacs's pages on *Don Quixote* in *The Theory of the Novel* (1920), trans. Anna Bostock (Cambridge, Mass., 1971), 101–4. His formulation also seems to me to be a dialectical version of José Ortega y Gasset's brilliant image of Quixote's madness as a mirage vis-à-vis the hard, dry earth of La Mancha, which first gave me a purchase on *Don Quixote* forty years ago. I read it in Ortega y Gasset, "The Nature of the Novel," in the *Hudson Review* 10 (spring 1957): 27–28; this essay was included in the reprinting of the whole of Ortega's *Meditations on Quixote* (Madrid, 1914), trans. Evelyn Rugg and Diego Marin (New York, 1961).

10. Kundera, *Testaments Betrayed: An Essay in Nine Parts*, trans. Linda Asher (New York, 1995), 5–6.

11. Bergson, "Laughter" (1900), in *Comedy: "An Essay on Comedy" by George Meredith and "Laughter" by Henri Bergson*, ed. Wylie Sypher (New York, 1956), 84.

12. For a thorough account and stylistic analysis of Shelton's translation, see Sandra Forbes Gerhard, *"Don Quixote" and the Shelton Translation: A Stylistic Analysis* (Madrid, 1982). All references are to the 1725 edition.

13. For the judgment, see Samuel Putnam, trans., introduction to *Don Quixote* (New York, 1949), xii.

14. Bertram D. Wolfe, *New York Herald Tribune Weekly Book Review*, 17 Aug. 1947, 1–2; cited by Putnam, trans., *Don Quixote*, x.

15. Oldfield, in "Advertisement," Carteret edition of *Don Quixote* (1738), 1: xxviii.

16. Motteux divided part 1 into books and chapters, part 2 only into chapters. Jarvis followed Motteux in part 1 but in part 2 introduced an additional division into four books. Fielding, in the year of Jarvis's translation, published *Joseph Andrews*, which in imitation of Cervantes (as a reaction to the letter form of Richardson's *Pamela* [1740]) he divided into books and chapters.

CHAPTER 1. Imagination and Satire

1. *Don Quixote*, trans. Samuel Putnam (New York, 1949): all references are to this edition.

2. Erasmus, *Praise of Folly*, trans. Hoyt H. Hudson (Princeton, 1941), 9. As Walter L. Reed has noted, the *Praise of Folly* is more probably a source of the "autonomy of the speaker" in the *Lazarillo de Tormes* (1554) (*Reed, An*

Exemplary History of the Novel: The Quixotic versus the Picaresque [Chicago, 1981], 43–45).

3. Motteux, preface to his translation of *Don Quixote* (1700).

4. Steele, *Tatler* no. 178 (30 May 1710), in *The Tatler*, ed. Donald F. Bond (Oxford, 1987), 2: 469. All references are to this edition.

5. Fielding, *Don Quixote in England*, in *Complete Works of Henry Fielding, Esq.*, ed. W. E. Henley (London, 1903), 11: 69–70.

6. Johnson, *Rambler* no. 2 (24 Mar. 1750), in *The Rambler*, ed. W. J. Bate and Albrecht B. Strauss (New Haven, 1969), 1:11.

7. Walter L. Reed, however, argues that Quixote was first regarded as a satire of the social institutions of Spain and later of literary fashions. The turning point, he claims, came only with William Warburton's "Supplement" to the Jarvis translation of 1742: "For the ridicule of Cervantes," writes Warburton, "does not so much turn upon *that* [correcting Jarvis] as upon the *ideal* of chivalry, as it is to be found only in the old romances" ("A Supplement to the Translator's Preface," *Don Quixote*, trans. Jarvis [1742]; in Reed, *Exemplary History*, 124). Swift's practice, and indeed Molière's, would seem to suggest that the literary satire was under way long before Warburton wrote. Leo Spitzer argued that *Don Quixote* is about "*the problem of the book*, and its influence on life"; "the peril of wrong application of literature in life by individuals reading alone, severed from society"—precisely Swift's subject ("On the significance of *Don Quijote*," *Modern Language Notes* 77 [Baltimore, 1962]: 113–29).

8. For the *Lazarillo de Tormes* and the picaresque, see Paulson, *Fictions of Satire* (Baltimore, 1967), 58–73; Harry Sieber, *The Picaresque* (London, 1977), and *Language and Society in "La Vida de Lazarillo de Tormes"* (Baltimore, 1978).

9. Etymologically, *hidalgo* is the *fijo d'algo*, son of someone who matters.

10. The *Lazarillo*, placed on the *Index of Prohibited Books* in 1559, was reprinted with Lucas Gracian Dantisco's Spanish translation of Giovanni della Casa's *Galateo*. The episodes involving the friar and pardoner and other religious references were excised. See Harry Sieber, "Literary Continuity, Social Order, and the Invention of the Picaresque," in *Cultural Authority in Golden Age Spain*, ed. Marina S. Brownlee and Hans Ulrich Gumbrecht (Baltimore, 1995), 143–164, esp. 147–53. The translation of the *Lazarillo* is Sieber's (*Cultural Authority*, 152–53).

11. Hobbes, *Leviathan*, ed. Michael Oakeshott (Oxford, 1960), 10.

12. In his epistle to Davenant prefixed to Davenant's *Gondibert* (1651) (ed. David F. Gladish [Oxford, 1971]); see above, p. 67.

13. "On Enthusiasm," added to the fourth edition of *Leviathan*.

14. More, *Enthusiasmus Triumphatus* (1656; ed. 1662), 2, 4, 5–7, 8, 10. For an overview, see Susie I. Tucker, *Enthusiasm: A Study of Semantic Change* (Cambridge, 1972).

15. *A Tale of a Tub*, ed. A. C. Guthkelch and D. Nichol Smith (Oxford, 2d ed., 1958), 96.

16. Jonson, *Timber, or Discoveries, Works of Ben Jonson*, ed. C. H. Herford and Percy and Evelyn Simpson, vol. 8 (Oxford, 1947): 597. An early reference to Quixote's reading habit is in act 4 of Jonson's *Epicene, or The Silent Woman* (1610).

17. In Christian terms, as in Satan in *Paradise Lost*, evil is always secondary, merely a perversion of, and excrescence on, the good.

18. René Girard, *Deceit, Desire, and the Novel: Self and Other in Literary Structure*, trans. Yvonne Freccero (Baltimore, 1965), 2. Eve Kosofsky Sedgwick then gave this a feminist orientation: men are attracted to women only because they are imitating another man (*Between Men: English Literature and Male Homosocial Desire* [New York, 1985]).

19. Before the advent of the *Spectator*, Richard Steele seems to have had both Locke and Don Quixote, as well as Swift's "Digression concerning Madness," in mind when he wrote in *Tatler* no. 40 (12 July 1709): "[A] Fool is he that from right makes a wrong Conclusion; but a Madman is one who draws a just Inference from false Principles. . . . A Madman fancies himself a Prince; but upon his Mistake, he acts suitable to that Character; and tho' he is out in supposing he has Principalities, while he drinks his Gruel, and lies in Straw, yet you shall see him keep the Port of a distress'd Monarch in all his Words and Actions" (*Tatler* 1:290).

20. Shelton's translation is relevant for purposes of comparison: "and when he neither cares nor knows what may befall him, he finds himself in the midst of flourishing fields, with which the very *Elysian* plains can in no sort be compared; there it seems to him that the element is more transparent, and that the sun shines with a clearer light, than in our orb: There offers itself to his greedy and curious eye a most pleasing forest, replenish'd with so green and well-spread trees, as the verdure thereof both joys and quickens the sight; whilst the cares are entertain'd by the harmonious, tho' artless songs of infinite and enamell'd birds, which traverse the intricate boughs of that shady habitation: Here he discovers a small stream, whose fresh waters resembling liquid *chrystal*, slides over the small sands, and white little stones, which resemble sifted gold wherein oriental pears are enchafed" (book 2, chapter 23, 2:263).

21. *The Spectator*, ed. Donald F. Bond (Oxford, 1965), 3: 537. All references are to this edition.

22. Cf. James Engel, *The Creative Imagination: Enlightenment to Romanticism* (Cambridge, Mass., 1981). Justifying Addison's using "imagination" as a vehicle for "the appreciation of nature, literature, and art," Engel supposes the alternatives: "the pleasures of judgment," "of wit," or "of invention" (33–34). But Engel misses the point that these "pleasures" are in the "spectator" (after the

name of the journal), not in the creator or inventor, an aesthetics rather than a poetics; and they are a *recovery* of a discredited sense of "imagination" or "fancy."

23. Cf. Shelton: Quixote "perceiving that *Sancho* mocked him"; "*Sancho* seeing that he gained so ill earnest by his jests, fearing that his Master should go onward with it . . ."; and Sancho's reply: "[F]or by *Jove*, I did but jest. But why dost thou jest? I tell thee, I do not jest, quoth *Don Quixote*." And Sancho again: "But tell me, I pray you, now that we are in peace, as God shall deliver you out of all adventures that may befal you, as whole and sound . . . hath not the great fear we were in, been a good subject of laughter, and a Thing worthy the telling?" (1.167).

24. Shelton, 1:166.

25. The word Putnam translates as "as if to mock him" is literally "as in the mode of a joke or trick" (*fisga*). Sancho is said to be *gracioso* (droll; see Putnam, 1025, n. 16). Cf. Shelton: "Whereat *Don Quixote* was wonderfully enraged, but chiefly hearing him say in gibing manner" (1.166).

26. The modern *Oxford Spanish Dictionary* echoes the idea when it defines the phrase *no se puede cosificar a los niños* as "you can't treat children like objects." See, e.g., William H. Clamurro, "The Destabilizing Sign: Word and Form in Quevedo's *Buscón*," *Modern Language Notes* 95 (1980): 295–311.

27. Of Sancho there is initially no description (1.7.60); a few chapters later he is represented, in Cid Hamete Benengeli's Arabic manuscript, in an illustration of the battle between Quixote and the Biscayan (1.9.72).

28. Focusing on the theatrical side of *Don Quixote*, Alexander Welsh has treated what I have referred to as Quixote's "punishments" as "practical jokes." He reads these bloody encounters back from the vantage of the staged jokes played on Quixote and Sancho in the duke's court in part 2. Read from part 1, however, these episodes draw attention to the aspect of physical cruelty in the duke's jests. Welsh has a point in emphasizing the aspect of appearance-reality, of theatricality, in the delusion that is corrected by brutal violence in part 1, seen in the light of the theatrical fictions invented by the duke in part 2. See Welsh, *Reflections on the Hero as Quixote* (Princeton, 1981).

29. *Poetics* 5; I have conflated translations by S. H. Butcher (*Aristotle's Theory of Poetry and fine Art* [New York, 1951], 21) and W. Rhys Roberts and Ingram Bywater (*The Rhetoric and the Poetics of Aristotle* [New York, 1954], 229).

30. Scarron's *Roman comique* retains the theatrical context of *Don Quixote* part 2 in that it is about a troupe of actors. Among other French Quixotes, Sorel's "extravagant shepherd," Lysis (1627), is the young ward of a Parisian silk merchant. He refuses to be apprenticed and neglects his law studies but reads every romance he can get his hands on; his Dulcinea is an ugly waiting-maid named Charité. "For her sake" he leaves home and becomes a shepherd, wan-

dering through Quixotic adventures with a Sancho character named Carmelin, and at the end regains his sanity and marries the unprepossessing Charité. For these and others, see Paulson, *Satire and the Novel* (New Haven, 1967), 29–41.

31. See Paulson, *Satire and the Novel,* chapter 5.

32. Dennis, *Defence of Sir Fopling Flutter* (1722), in *Critical Works,* ed. E. N. Hooker (Baltimore, 1939), 2:245.

33. John Nichols argued that this *Tatler* was written by Addison; and it does fit into the argument Addison makes in the *Spectator* about satire and comedy. The formulation of Horatian versus Juvenalian satire made in this essay seems to me Addisonian; but the particular vocabulary of good nature is closer to Steele. Whatever the authorship, this is the seminal essay for the discussion of laughter that Addison develops in the *Spectator.*

34. On his Grand Tour the young Addison records that a Capuchin Father in Blois told him that "he did not question but laughter was the effect of Original Sin and that Adam was not Risible before the Fall" (cited, Peter Smithers, *The Life of Joseph Addison* [Oxford, 1954], 51).

35. See above, p. 39.

36. For an exception, see Defoe's story that it was a satire on the duke of Medina-Sidonia (see p. 34).

37. See, e.g., J. T. T. Greig, *Psychology of Laughter and Comedy* (London, 1923); A. M. Ludovici, *The Secret of Laughter* (London, 1932); Stephen Leacock, *Humor: Its Theory and Technique* (London, 1935); James Feibleman, *In Praise of Comedy* (New York, 1939); L. J. Potts, *Comedy* (Cambridge, 1949); Arthur Koestler, *Insight and Outlook* (New York, 1949); and D. H. Monro, *The Argument of Laughter* (Melbourne, 1951).

38. For a thorough account of the relations between Swift and Addison and Steele in this period, see Bertrand A. Goldgar, *The Curse of Party: Swift's Relations with Addison and Steele* (Lincoln, Nebraska, 1961), esp. chaps. 2 and 3.

39. *Prose Works,* ed. Herbert Davis, 3 (Oxford, 1957): 179.

40. The words are Goldgar's, *The Curse of Party,* 75. *The Spectator* was a journal that consistently praised Marlborough; each volume of the collected edition was dedicated to one of the Whig leaders.

41. On the *Spectator* and the theatrical metaphor, see below, p. 113.

42. *Spectator* no. 2, though signed by Steele, may well be a joint venture. One can see that no. 1 needed to be written by Addison, followed by no. 2 by Steele, but (despite the stories of Addison's dismay at Steele's assigning Sir Roger sex with the lower orders) it is difficult to imagine Addison not overseeing no. 2 and probably having a hand in it. The first lines about Sir Roger sound like Addison, the second part more like Steele. As the *Spectator* progresses, however, Addison develops an agenda of his own that has less and less to do with Steele.

43. *Miscellany Poems* (1694).

44. Cf. also *Spectator* no. 321 (3:169): "In its full beauty . . . there are

Multitudes of beauties in this great Author, especially in the descriptive Parts of his Poem"; also no. 303, 3:89.

45. Milton's politics continued to cause commentators such as Samuel Johnson to distinguish the poet from the poem; but the poem itself made its political argument unmistakable. Even before book 1, Milton's note on the verse form calls *Paradise Lost* the "first in English, of ancient liberty recovered"; that is, a true (spiritual) restoration as opposed to the false (political) "Restoration" of the Stuart monarchy (which Milton associates with the "bondage of Riming," the "lame Metre" of the court poets and dramatists; and this is followed by the verbs in the invocation to book 1: "till one greater Man / Restore us, and regain the blissful Seat," which apply on one level to the Son and on another to the Poet, both redeemers of the Fall (spiritual and political), one divine, the other human. Milton follows with descriptions of Belial's court rakes, the palladian architecture of Rome (associated with London), and Satan's monarchical splendor ("High on a Throne of Royal State" 2:1).

CHAPTER 2. Chivalry and Burlesque

1. Phillips, trans. *Don Quixote* (1687), sig. (A2v).

2. Temple, *An Essay upon the Ancient and Modern Learning* (1690), in *Critical Essays of the Seventeenth Century*, ed. J. E. Spingarn (Bloomington, 1957), 3: 71–72. See Spingarn's note, 3: 307.

3. Shaftesbury, "Miscellaneous Reflections," *Characteristics of Men, Manners, Opinions, Times, Etc.*, ed. John M. Robertson (New York, 1900), 2:313 (all citations are to this edition); Steele, *Tatler* no. 219, 3: 146, in *The Tatler*, ed. Donald F. Bond (Oxford, 1987) (all references are to this edition); Byron, *Don Juan*, XVIII, 11. Motteux (1700–1703) refers to "the Humour of Knight-Errantry": "The principal Design . . . is to ridicule by the finest Satyr in the World, the Humour of Knight-Erantry, and the Romantick Notions of Love and Honour" ("An Account of the Author," *Don Quixote* [3d ed., 1712], 1:iii); and Jarvis: "[T]he chief subject of the present satire is the false notion of zeal in the service of a mistress, the false honor of errantry and the false wit of romances" (*Don Quixote* [1742], 1:vii, xxii–xxiii). Carteret also refers to Cervantes' correction of chivalry and improvement of the Spanish nation (in his dedication to the 1738 Spanish-language edition published by Tonson).

4. Knowles, "Cervantes and English Literature," in *Cervantes across the Centuries*, ed. Angel Flores and M. J. Benardete (New York, 1969), 282, 284.

5. Ibid., 278, 283–84.

6. Ward, *The Life and Notable Adventures of that Renown'd Knight, Don Quixote de la Mancha, Merrily Translated into Hudibrastick Verse* (1711), A4–5.

7. Although Richard Braverman has shown that Butler's satire cuts in all directions, including the Cavaliers, it was widely regarded in its time as anti-

Puritan, and therefore, by the 1680s, as anti-Whig. See Braverman, *Plots & Counterplots: Sexual Politics & the Body Politic in English Literature, 1660–1730* (Cambridge, 1993), chapter 2.

8. Knowles, "Cervantes and English Literature": on Spain, 282; on France and *Hudibras*, 284. For an example of the distrust of the Spanish, see Robinson Crusoe's remark that he would rather be "delivered up to the savages and be devoured alive than fall into the merciless claws of the priests and be carried into the Inquisition" (*Robinson Crusoe* [New York, 1948], 270).

9. Defoe, *Serious Reflections during the Life and Strange Adventures of Robinson Crusoe*, in *Works*, ed. G. H. Maynadier (Boston, 1903), 2: x.

10. Temple, "Of Poetry," in Spingarn, ed., *Critical Essays*, 3: 101–3. Thomas Rymer's *Short View of Tragedy* (1692) ends with "And yet for modern Comedy, doubtless our English are the best in the World" (168).

11. "Humour [was] almost of English growth; at least, it does not seem to have found such Encrease on any other Soil." See Congreve, "Mr. Congreve to Mr. Dennis, Concerning Humour in Comedy" (1695), in Spingarn, ed., *Critical Essays*, 3: 252. See also (emphasizing the English climate) Sterne, *Tristram Shandy* (1759), ed. Melvyn and Joan New (Gainesville, Fla., 1978), 1: 71.

12. Motteux, trans., *Don Quixote* (1700), preface. Motteux himself was a Huguenot refugee and would seem to have been a Whig, but he was also a hack, and he collaborated on his translation with such known Tory-Jacobites as Ward.

13. For context, see Edward C. Riley, *Cervantes' Theory of the Novel* (Oxford, 1962); and Alban K. Forcione, *Cervantes, Aristotle, and the "Persiles"* (Princeton, 1970), chap. 3.

14. Shelton translation, bk. 4, chap. 21; 2:249–50.

15. In the Spanish translation of Elder Olson's *The Theory of Comedy* (*Teoría de la comedia*, Barcelona, 1978), Bruce W. Wardropper adds an essay on the Spanish use of the word in which he argues that it referred to all types of drama, including what is meant by the English "comedy" (190–91). A historical play could be referred to as a "comedia histórica," or a mythological play as a "comedia mitológica." He goes on to point out that "es mejor abstenerse de emplear las categorias tradicionales al escribir acerca de la comedia espanola" ("it is best to avoid using traditional categories when writing about the Spanish *comedia*" [194]).

16. López Pinciano, *Philosophia Antigua Poetica*, ed. Alfredo Carballo Picazo (Madrid, 1953), 2: 327.

17. Pinciano introduces the adjective *cómico* in his discussion of the plot (*fábula*), of which there are three kinds—epic, tragic, and comic (*fábula épica, trágica*, and *cómica*). He understands *fábula* as "plot," and points out that the primary plots are "épica, trágica y cómica" (2: 15). In a 1611 Spanish dictionary, *comedia* is given its Greek and Latin etymology and said to be a certain kind of *fábula*—in which it is a mirror of ordinary life and deals with the life of the city

and ordinary people (Cicero adapting Aristotle). As a play, it is defined as a structure that usually begins with fights, questions, and unfortunate happenings—and always ends in peace, concord, friendship, and contentment (Sebastián de Covarrubias, *Tesoro de la Lengua Castellana o Española* [Madrid, 1611], ed. Martín de Riquer [Barcelona, 1943], 341–42). In a modern Spanish dictionary, *comedia* means comedy; its historical sense is a play or drama.

18. Quixote stands "in his tight-fitting breeches and chamois-skin doublet, tall, lean, lanky, with cheeks that appeared to be kissing each other on the inside of his mouth. In short, he presented such an appearance that" it would cause spectators to "burst with laughing" (2.31.711).

19. "Your shoulders, at any rate . . . ought to be used to such squalls as that, but mine, accustomed to fine cambric and Dutch linen, naturally feel more acutely the pain that has befallen us" (1.15.111).

20. The one figure in classical comedy who may have inspired Quixote is the *miles gloriosus*, the braggart soldier, a mock-hero; in the Italian commedia dell'arte he is *el Capitano*, who speaks Spanish as a result of the Spanish occupation—as opposed to a supplementary, alternative character, the Bully, whose vocabulary is of the lower orders.

21. Shaftesbury, "Miscellaneous Reflections," *Characteristics*, 2:313–14. He refers to himself, the whetstone, as "a mere comic humorist in respect of those inferior subjects."

22. On burlesque, see, e.g., John D. Jump, *Burlesque: The Critical Idiom* (London, 1972).

23. Knox, *The Word Irony and its Context, 1500–1755* (Durham, N.C., 1961), 126.

24. Cambridge, *Scribleriad* (1752), iii–iv.

25. *Monthly Review*, 12 (1755):197; William Dodd, *A Day in Vacation* (1751), citing Cambridge's quotation from the *Scribleriad*; Joseph Warton, *Essay on Pope* 1 (1756): 242–43; all cited, Knox, *The Word Irony*, 171. In an essay in *The Adventurer*, no. 133 (1754), Thomas Warton preferred Cervantes to Lucian because of "his solemn and important air with which the most idle and ridiculous actions are related."

26. Jarvis, *Don Quixote* (1742), iv–v. Cf. also the *Monthly Review* 13 (Sept. 1955): 197, on Smollett's translation of 1755.

27. Attacking a pamphlet called *An Enquiry into the Reason of the Conduct of Great Britain* (arguing ironically that it is another *Gulliver's Travels*), Amhurst links *Gulliver* and *Don Quixote* as works that recount absurdities "in a grave and serious Manner, with the same solemn Grimace and repeated Professions of *Truth* and *Simplicity*"—"the same Manner that *Cervantes* exposes Books of *Chivalry*, or Captain *Gulliver* the Writings of *Travellers*" (*Craftsman* no. 14, 20 Jan. 1727; coll. ed. [1731], 1.79–80). Swift was customarily referred to as writing "with a seeming gravity, and true comic spirit," and as "the last to laugh at his

own jest" (*Monthly Review*, 12 [June, 1755], 510, and Joseph Spence, MS *Charliad*, both cited in Knox, *The Word Irony*, 172).

28. Addison, who saw Satan as an echo of Ulysses and his travels, misses the point: Satan is not in any sense going home; he is transferring his empire.

29. There are many other elements of parody in *Paradise Lost*; for example, the fallen angels building Pandemonium (besides building a seventeenth-century Rome centered on St. Peter's) recall the simile of bees Virgil attached to the Carthaginians, enemies of Rome, building their city. The conventions of pastoral in book 4 and of classical tragedy in book 9, especially if taken in the context of the denigration of classical reference (as in the case of Mulciber in book 1), also inject an element of parody, at least insofar as the reference in each is to Satan.

30. This is known variously as "The Scepter Lampoon," "A Satyr on Charles I," and "On King Charles"; see David Vieth, ed., *The Complete Poems of John Wilmot, Earl of Rochester* (New Haven, 1968), 60–61.

31. Charles-Antoine Coypel (1694–1752), of the well-known family of painters, executed a series of small paintings between 1714 and 1751 to serve as cartoons for the central medallions of Gobelin tapestries (Philip Conisbee, *Painting in Eighteenth-Century France* [Ithaca, 1981], 88). The engravings, by Nicolas Beauvais and others, published in Paris in 1724, were sold in London by Gerard Vandergucht. They were also copied, reduced, and reengraved by him for the 1725 edition of Shelton's translation of *Don Quixote* (advertised, *London Journal*, 27 Mar. 1725). Coypel's illustrations were used again for a 1731 edition for J. Walthoe and others (Hanns Hammelmann, *Book Illustrators in Eighteenth-Century England* [London, 1975], 82 n. 3). Johannes Hartau, *Don Quixote in der Kunst: Wandlungen einer Symbolfigur* (1987) has useful comments on Coypel's work (37–56).

32. The Watteau model becomes most evident in part 2 with the duke and duchess and their *fêtes*.

33. Jarvis (or Jervas), primarily a painter, was a close friend of Pope, whom he taught painting. He painted portraits of both Pope and Swift.

34. M. Cervantes Saavedra, *Vida y Hechos del Ingenioso Hidalgo Don Quixote de La Mancha*, 4 vols. 4to, printed "En Londres, por J. y R. Tonson," dated 1738; *The Life and Exploits o' the Ingenious Gentleman Don Quixote de La Mancha. Translated from the original Spanish . . . by Charles Jarvis*, 2 vols., 4to., "For J. and R. Tonson in the Strand, and R. Dodsley in Pall-Mall," dated 1742. There are sixty-seven illustrations, sixty-six by Vanderbank and engraved by Vandergucht (excluding no. 3, the subject of these pages). No. 15 was engraved by Bernard Baron and nos. 39, 43, and 49 by Claude du Bosc. A tailpiece was engraved by Paul Fourdrinier (1: 62). The frontispiece portrait of Don Quixote was engraved by George Vertue (as, too, was a frontispiece portrait of Cervantes, after William Kent). There are eighty-eight drawings by Vanderbank in

the British Museum (BM) Print Room (197*d14), dated between 1726 and 1730. An additional sixty-four drawings are in the Pierpont Morgan Library, New York, all dated 1729 (7½ by 11 in.). Many are duplicates; some are larger copies. Vanderbank also painted many copies in the following years.

35. See Paulson, *Hogarth's Graphic Works* (1965; 3d ed., London, 1989), nos. 94–99; "Don Quixote's Breastplate: The Seventh Hogarth Illustration," *Apollo*, forthcoming.

36. There is one sketch in the BM, of Quixote addressing the goatherds on the Age of Gold, in which he is wearing something that resembles Hogarth's breastplate (it is reproduced by Hartau, 72). However, in the engraving by Vandergucht and in the painting of this subject (Tate Gallery) this turns out to be a doublet. Apparently Vanderbank felt, reasonably enough, that Quixote, before taking his repast with the shepherds, would first remove his suit of armor. The Morgan drawings, which are more finished than those in the BM, do not include this scene or "The First Adventure." Hartau notes the discrepancy of the armor but concludes only that Vanderbank's drawing as well as the oil painting, both with full armor, "lassen keinen Zweifel, dass Vanderbank sich als Urheber dieser Komposition betrachtete" (69). For his section on Hogarth and Vanderbank, see 63–88.

37. We have to suppose that neither Vanderbank nor Tonson worried in this one instance about the discrepancy in Quixote's wearing apparel.

38. Following "The First Adventure," Vandergucht engraved the next five Vanderbank illustrations. These illustrate the innkeeper knighting Quixote, the destruction of Quixote's library, Quixote persuading Sancho to join him as his squire, another of Quixote and Sancho, and Quixote delivering his lecture on the "Golden Age" to the shepherds. Hogarth's second and third illustrations are the same as Vanderbank's sixth and seventh—"The Funeral of Chrysostom" and "The Innkeeper's Wife & Daughter taking Care of ye Don after being beaten & bruised." Vanderbank-Vandergucht followed with another scene inside the inn and two more before Hogarth joined them again, this time duplicating three scenes in a row: "Don Quixote seizes the Barber's Bason for Mambrino's Helmet," "Don Quixote releases the Galley Slaves," and "The Unfortunate Knight of the Rock meeting Don Quixote." Vanderbank proceeded with eleven more scenes. Hogarth's final illustration, "The Curate & Barber disguising themselves," was completely his own. It was omitted by Vanderbank.

39. The fact that this scene was engraved not by Vandergucht but by Baron may be evidence that Hogarth's engravings were intended to supplement Vandergucht's; that when he withdrew he was replaced by du Bosc, whom Baron assisted when du Bosc first arrived in England c. 1720. Baron's engraving is the reverse of Vanderbank's drawing.

40. The drawing is in the Royal Collection; for both drawings, see A. P.

Oppé, ed. *The Drawings of William Hogarth* (London, 1948), cat. no. 34 (plate 35) and cat. no. 35 (fig. 19). Both are the reverse of the engravings.

41. See Paulson, *Hogarth, Vol. 2: High Art and Low (1732–1750)* (New Brunswick, N.J., 1992), chap. 4.

42. Not that the attack on the windmills was unappreciated; the earliest reference in English (and in any language) was to the windmill, in George Wilkins in *The Miseries of Inforst Marriage* (1606), act III. Francis Hayman, in Smollett's translation of 1755, did illustrate the attack on the puppet show; earlier the scene was illustrated in the 1700 edition of Shelton's translation (revised by Stevens). But still Hayman omitted the windmills.

43. See Sir William Temple, *An Essay upon the Ancient and Modern Learning* (1690), in Spingarn, ed., *Critical Essays*, 3: 71–72; Anthony Ashley Cooper, third earl of Shaftesbury, "Miscellaneous Reflections," *Characteristics*, ed. Robertson, 2:313; Richard Steele, *Tatler* no. 219.

44. See, e.g., Thomas Burnet and George Duckett, *A Second Tale of a Tub* (1715), 157, 189–90, where Sacheverell is connected with chivalry, Quixote, and Hudibras. My thanks for this information to DeAnn DeLuna.

45. Carteret himself indicated that Oldfield "invented most" of the designs and gave Vanderbank instructions (whether also Hogarth is not clear, though given the similarity of their illustrations it is likely). See Carteret's letter to Sir Benjamin Keene (ambassador to Spain), accompanying a copy of Oldfield's "Advertisement" and a set of Vanderbank's illustrations, 24 Aug. 1737, in *Private Correspondence of Sir Benjamin Keene*, ed. Sir Richard Lodge (Cambridge, 1933), p. 7.

Carteret's "Dedication," dated 15 March 1738, is to the Contessa de Montijo, wife of the Spanish minister in London from 1732 to 1735; the latter contributed the life of Cervantes (the first—as also the "portrait" was the first), and his delay in completing it explains the delay in publication. Both Carteret's "Dedication" and Oldfield's "Advertisement" are in Spanish in the 1738 edition. Oldfield's is reprinted in English with the Vanderbank illustrations in the 1742 edition of Jarvis's translation. The Carteret quotation is on p. iv (my translation); I quote Oldfield from the English translation. For a general account, see Hammelmann, *Book Illustrators*, 81–82; Paulson, *Hogarth, vol. 1, The Modern Moral Subject (1697–1732)* (New Brunswick, 1990), 1:150–52.

46. Coypel, however, omits scenes that were crucial for the English illustrators: the curate and the barber masquerading (important for Hogarth), the freeing of the galley slaves, and the funeral of Grisóstomo.

47. The text of *Don Quixote* followed a series of illustrated classics published by Tonson (Racine and Tasso, 1723–24).

48. For Burlington's program in the arts and its relationship to Shaftesbury's aesthetics, see Rudolf Wittkower, *Palladio and Palladianism* (New York, 1974), esp. 178–81. Politically, though he was still serving within the Walpole govern-

ment, in 1726 as lord lieutenant of Ireland, Carteret's main influence was with the monarch and the court. There is a story connecting his undertaking of the edition of *Don Quixote* to the behest of Queen (or Princess) Caroline (H. S. Ashbee, in *Transactions of the Bibliographical Society,* 1 (1893): 123–24).

For Carteret, see Archibald Ballantyne, *Lord Carteret: A Political Biography, 1690–1763* (London, 1887), where the Cervantes project is not mentioned. For Carteret's culture and humanism, his admiration for Homer and Demosthenes, most notably for Swift, and (more curiously) for John Cleland (for whom he secured a pension), see pp. 401–10. The only significant detail is Carteret's admiration for Francis Hutcheson's *Inquiry into the Original of Our Ideas of Beauty and Virtue,* a Shaftesburian work of aesthetics (p. 406). Carteret began as a political associate of Lord Sunderland (who patronized Sir James Thornhill, Hogarth's father-in-law) and of Sir Luke Schaub, a collector of conventional old masters (he owned a painting by Furini that he was convinced was a Correggio).

All I know of Dr. Oldfield (1690–1748) is that he was an M.D. of Leyden and Cambridge and a physician at Guy's Hospital (Hammelmann, *Book Illustrators* p. 82 n. 2). He also published *Dissertatio de causis motum sanguinis circularem per vasa corporis animalis promoventibus ac obstantibus* (*Lugdoni Batavorum,* 1718).

49. For Murphy's distinction between the ridiculous and the burlesque see his essay in *Gray's Inn Journal* no. 50, 6 Sept. 1754. In the collected edition of 1756 the essay is renumbered 97 and redated 23 August 1754 (2:283–85). Murphy elaborated on these remarks in "An Essay on the Life and Genius of Henry Fielding, Esq.," in *The Works of Henry Fielding, Esq.: with the Life of the Author* (1762), 1:5–49.

50. For Shaftesbury's comment that the "burlesque work itself" was "despised," see "Miscellaneous Reflections," in *Characteristics,* ed. Robertson, 2:313–14.

51. William Dodd, *A Day in Vacation* (1751), p. 6 of the notes.

52. See Oliver Millar, *Pictures in the Royal Collection: Tudor, Stuart, and Early Georgian Pictures* (London, 1963), cat. no. 144, plate 64. The sons of Charles I were also painted in full armor. On the other hand, Prince Rupert had himself painted by Sir Peter Lely in breastplate only (reproduced by Millar). The truth is that generals on both sides probably wore breastplates only in combat but had themselves painted in full armor. The portraits of Cromwell, Fairfax, and Ireton show them in full armor.

53. For Vanderbank's illustration of this scene, see not only the drawing reproduced but a second drawing in the BM and an oil painting in Manchester, which follow the first drawing.

54. In the next chapter we are told that he was *armada de armas* (armed with arms) that "were as oddly matched as were his bridle, lance, buckler, and corselet" (*coselete*) (1.2.33).

55. The closest is a set by a German illustrator, Jacob Savery (1657). Quixote wears a corselet that does not cover his arms but extends down into bands that cover his hips. See Hartau, figs. 15–21.

56. Defoe, *Works*, ed. G.H. Maynadier, 3: 236.

57. "In the best-equipped infantry companies the men were provided with outer coats of thick, buff-coloured leather and steel back and breast plates" (Christopher Hibbert, *Cavaliers & Roundheads: The English Civil War, 1642–1649* [New York, 1993], p. 76).

58. This "Quixotism" took such forms as: "Instead of drinking, gaming, plundering, they pray and discourse"; they share "the sweetness, union and love that is amongst the saints"; Cromwell's "Ironsides" formed themselves into "gathered churches" or voluntary associations for worship. See Ian Gentles, *The New Model Army in England, Ireland and Scotland, 1645–1653* (Oxford, 1992), 103–4, 109; and Paulson, *Hogarth, vol. 1*, 322–23. For some of the implications of iconoclasm, see Paulson, *Breaking and Remaking* (New Brunswick, 1989), chap. 1.

59. Connisbee notes that Coypel "was one of a generation of painters almost obsessed with Le Brun's *Traité des passions*" and points out its applicability to history paintings such as *Ecce Homo*: "[T]he subject of Pilate presenting Christ to the people offered a whole range of conflicting emotions to be communicated by gesture and facial expression" (Conisbee, *Painting in Eighteenth-Century France*, 45). Of the *Don Quixote* paintings, he comments: "Coypel's pictorial space and overstressed characterization recall his obsession with the theatre and his not very successful aspirations as a dramatist" (88).

60. Aside from the direct imitation of Coypel's print in *The Mystery of Masonry* (1624; see above, 54), Hogarth executed direct theatrical satires (*Masquerades and Operas* and *A Just View of the British Stage* [1724]); illustrations framed by a stage structure (frontispieces for Charles Gildon's *New Metamorphosis* and *Royalty, Episcopacy, and Law* [1724]). His earliest paintings were of the stage: *Falstaff Examining his Recruits* (Guinness Collection) and the various versions of *The Beggar's Opera*, both 1728. The last, with a central dramatic action framed by distracted spectators on one side and by a very attentive one (the duke of Bolton eying Lavinia Fenton-Polly Peachum) on the other, carries over directly into the first plate of *A Harlot's Progress* (1732), where the two role-playing actors (the Harlot and Mother Needham) are framed by the self-interested clergyman on the left and the lecherous Charteris on the right.

61. Vanderbank illustrated both the ministering to Quixote and Quixote's confusion with Maritornes's bed.

62. In his illustrations for Smollett's translation (1755), Hayman copied the basic Vanderbank compositions, not even bothering in most cases to reverse the figures, only varying them. If his variations are usually improvements, it is

because he gives the figures livelier poses, particularizes their faces, emphasizes their expressions, and enlivens the contrasts. But Hayman—following Hogarth's works of the 1730s and 1740s (especially perhaps his "Four Groups of Heads")—also demonstrates the difference between comic theory in the 1720s and in the 1750s. The major changes he makes in Vanderbank's illustrations are to illustrate more of the comic scenes and to introduce the intervening concepts of "humorous character," if not "caricature."

For the story of Quixote, Sancho, and Maritornes, Vanderbank showed the maids seeing Quixote to bed; Hayman, perhaps instructed by the translator, illustrated the very Smollettian scene of the mistaken identities—the moment when Sancho fends off Maritornes, she responds in kind, and the innkeeper arrives with his lantern to illuminate the scene of mayhem. Maritornes with her prominently displayed breasts is the central feature.

63. Richardson, *Theory of Painting* (1715), in *Works* (1776), 6. Cf. Hogarth's words in his *Autobiographical Notes* (written in the early 1760s): "Subjects I consider'd as writers do / my Picture was my Stage and men and women my actors" (in Hogarth, *Analysis of Beauty*, ed. Joseph Burke [Oxford, 1955], 209; also 210, 212, 215). This, of course, follows from French academic theory and the theatricality of *l'expression des passions*.

64. He also includes the bearded duenna from "The Afflicted Matron complains to Don Quixote of her Inchanted Beard." He includes the bearded duenna (one of the duke and duchess's theatricals, in which a bearded man poses as woman) because he is playing in the print on rumors of cross-dressing and sodomy, which he wishes to attach to the Jacobite followers of the duke of Wharton, who led the splinter Freemasons.

65. See Paulson, *Hogarth's Graphic Works* (1989 ed.), nos. 82–93.

66. If the *Don Quixote* illustrations contrast Quixote's dignity and Sancho's commonplace, plebeian, and so comic commentary, in the *Hudibras* illustrations the roles and shapes are reversed. Quixote is now the roundish, indeed hunchbacked figure of Hudibras and Sancho is the tall, emaciated Ralpho. Cf. the similar figure Hogarth employed in his 1729 painting *The Denunciation* (see R. B. Beckett, *Hogarth's Paintings* [London, 1949], no. 15).

67. See *Annibale Carracci e i suoi incisori* (Rome, 1986), 112–13; I reproduce Nicolas Mignard's etching (see fig. 12).

68. Hogarth's frontispiece to *Hudibras* operates in the allegorical way, but in the subsequent plates the baroque forms are absorbed into the compositions themselves. Coypel's rather than Hogarth's use of these baroque and cloudy versions of Quixote's imagination may have been the source of Salvador Dali's similar effects in his illustrations for *Don Quixote*.

69. For the variations in the advertisements, see Paulson, *Hogarth's Graphic Works*, 58–59. A second, smaller set (book-sized) of seventeen illustrations for *Hudibras* followed in April. But they had presumably been executed earlier—

based on earlier book illustrations—and were brought out to exploit the popularity of the large plates.

70. *Gray's Inn Journal* (9 Feb. 1974), signed *X* but probably by Arthur Murphy.

71. I am grateful to William B. Warner for letting me read in manuscript his *Licensing Entertainment: The Elevation of the Novel in Britain (1684–1750)* (Los Angeles and Berkeley, forthcoming). My reference is to chapter 6.

72. See Paulson, *Hogarth's Graphic Works*, nos. 130, 131.

73. *Tatler* no. 27, 11 June 1709. Cf. David Dabydeen's theory that Hogarth intends to connect the Rake with Sir Robert Walpole, similarly a parvenu who attempts to raise his status (*Hogarth, Walpole and Commercial Britain* [London, 1987], 132–35).

74. Francis Coventry referred to Fielding as "our *English Cervantes*" in 1751; Arthur Murphy in 1762; and even Smollett, not always a friend to Fielding, wrote: "The genius of Cervantes was transfused into the novels of Fielding, who painted the characters, and ridiculed the follies of life with equal strength, humour and propriety." (See Coventry, *An Essay on the New Species of Writing founded by Mr. Fielding* [1751]; Murphy, "An Essay on the Life and Genius of Henry Fielding, Esq.," in *The Works of Henry Fielding, Esq.* [1762], in Paulson and Thomas Lockwood, *Henry Fielding: The Critical Heritage* [London, 1969]; Smollett, *Continuation of the Complete History of England* [1761, 4:127]).

75. Fielding, *Joseph Andrews*, ed. Martin C. Battestin (Oxford, 1967), 3–11. References are to this edition.

76. Fielding, "Essay on the Knowledge of the Characters of Men," *Miscellanies, Vol. 1*, ed. H. K. Miller (Middletown, Conn., 1972), 153–78. W. B. Coley phrases it neatly: to find "that high and low are not very different—perhaps even reversed" raises problems relating to both Jonathan Wild and Parson Abraham Adams. "If Wild is the exemplar of 'consummate imperfection,' the villain who parlays bad qualities perfectly, one has only to reverse the paradox, somewhat clumsily perhaps, to describe Adams as an imperfect consummator, the good man whose true qualities are either misapplied or misconstrued. Common to both characters is an ambiguousness, a paradoxical mixture of 'high' and 'low' elements. differing degrees, removed from the social norm" ("The Background of Fielding's Laughter," *ELH* 26 [1959]: 231–32, 44).

77. Aristotle, *Poetics*, 5; cf., e.g., Ben Jonson's version of the formulation: the purpose of comedy is to "sport with humane follies, not with crimes" (*Every Man in his Humour* [1598], in *Works of Ben Jonson*, ed. C. H. Herford and Percy and Evelyn Simpson, vol. 8 [Oxford, 1947], 3: 303).

78. Fielding cites Congreve's poem "Of Pleasing; an Epistle to Sir Richard Temple," which locates affectation in the theatrical context.

79. The supposed speaker is the old-fashioned Tory Sir Roger de Coverley, who comments that "any Man who thinks can easily see, that the Affectation of being gay and in fashion has very near eaten up our good Sense and our

Religion" (1:30). In *Tatter* no. 27, as we have seen, Steele applied "affectation" to would-be rakes (picked up by Hogarth in his *Rake* of 1735): a form of social role-playing. Affectation in the *Spectator*'s sense, goes back to Castiglione's *Il Cortegiano*, which contrasts "affectation" with "*sprezzatura*," which is "to conceal all art and make whatever is done or said appear to be without effort and almost without any thought of it." Affectation begins, therefore, as an aspect of politeness.

80. Act II, in *The Tender Husband*, ed. Calhoun Winton (Lincoln, Nebr., 1967), 38–39.

81. Warner, *Licensing Entertainment*. On reading, entertainment, and the market in this period, see esp. chapter 8. Warner uses the word *absorptive*, whereas I have tended to use Ortega y Gasset's word *immersive* as more descriptive. See Ortega, "Notes on the Novel" in *The Dehumanization of Art* (Princeton, 1948; reprinted New York, 1956), 57; and Paulson, *Satire and the Novel*, 7–8. As Stephen Gilman put it of Quixote and readers of the novel, citing Ortega, "immersion in fiction is a peril to identity" (Gilman, *The Novel according to Cervantes* [Berkeley and Los Angeles, 1989], 2.).

82. Mary Delariviere Manley, *The New Atlantis* (1709), 223–24, cited in Warner, *Licensing Entertainment*.

83. Ibid.

84. E.g., *Pamela*, ed. T. C. Duncan Eaves and Ben D. Kimpel (Boston, 1971), 45, 62, 160, 162.

85. As Fielding the playwright well knew, Molière had shown his *précieuse ridicules* learning their affectation from books; later in *The Beggar's Opera* John Gay had Polly Peachum succumb to Macheath by reading the romances with which he plies her.

CHAPTER 3. Wit and Humor

1. Motteux, preface, *Don Quixote* (1700), 1: iii.

2. Sarah Fielding, *The Cry* (1754), 3: 124. Pope also refers to Quixote's foible in *Essay on Criticism* (1711), ll. 267–84.

3. See Alvin Kernan, *The Cankered Muse* (New Haven, 1960); Paulson, *Satire and the Novel* (New Haven, 1967), chap. 5, about Smollett's novels, which, from *Roderick Random* to *Humphry Clinker*, show a joining of the Quixotic and the Jonsonian use of the dehumoring plot and denouement.

4. *The Repository: A Select Collection of Fugitive Pieces in Prose and Verse* (1741; 1783 ed.), 20.

5. Davenant, *Sir William Davenant's "Gondibert,"* ed. David F. Gladish (Oxford, 1971), 22.

6. Davenant, *Gondibert*, 18; for Hobbes's "Answer . . . to Sir Will. D'Avenant's Preface," see *Gondibert*, 48–49.

7. Milton, *Paradise Lost* (1667; 1674 ed.), 9.91–94. For a useful discussion of the political dimension of inspiration and wit, see Steven N. Zwicker, *Lines of Authority: Politics and English Literary Culture, 1649–1689* (Ithaca, 1993), 17–36.

8. See Locke, *Essay concerning Human Understanding* (1690), 2.11, ed. Alexander Campbell Fraser (London, 1959), 2.11.2; 3.10.34.

9. John Tillotson, "The Folly of Scoffing at Religion," *Works* (1696), 41, cited in Stuart Tave, *The Amiable Humorist* (Chicago, 1960), 23.

10. Morris, *Essay towards Fixing the True Standards of Wit, Humour, Raillery, Satire, and Ridicule* (1744), 1.

11. Morris is less direct about this quality of his third literary humorist, Sir John Falstaff, but he does conclude: "And it is impossible to be tired or unhappy in his Company" (29).

12. Although he changed sides in 1741.

13. Morris, *Essay*, xxiv.

14. On Walpole's retirement, see ibid., xxxi.

15. For the emasculating of oral jokes in the printed examples of "wit" in Morris's *Essay*, see Paulson, *Popular and Polite Art in the Age of Hogarth and Fielding* (Notre Dame, 1979), 73–74.

16. *Spectator* no. 106, 1: 440.

17. Murphy, *Gray's Inn Journal*, no. 50, 6 Sept. 1754. In the collected edition of 1756 the essay is renumbered 97 and redated 23 August 1754 (2:283–85). Murphy elaborated on these remarks in "An Essay on the Life and Genius of Henry Fielding, Esq.," in *The Works of Henry Fielding, Esq.: with the Life of the Author* (1762), 1:5–49; my page references are to Paulson and Lockwood, eds. *Henry Fielding: The Critical Heritage*.

18. He elaborates the earlier account with Adams's "travelling to London to sell a set of sermons, and actually *snapping his fingers and taking two or three turns round the room in exstacy*, when introduced to a bookseller in order to make an immediate bargain; and then immediately after, not being able to find those same sermons, when he exclaims, 'I profess, I believe I left them behind me.'"

19. Murphy's contrast of the ridiculous and the burlesque is also instructive: impatient to "discover a real Incongruity," as in the ridiculous, writers of burlesque "by the Force of their own Imaginations . . . create it for themselves, and by obtruding Circumstances which perhaps do not belong to the Object, they are frequently very successful in rendering Things apparently ridiculous, which to an attentive Eye may not wear the motly Livery, however it may serve the Purposes of Mirth to invest it with it" (377). In short, they employ wit rather than judgment.

In practice, however, Murphy means that they employ simply the mock-heroic or travesty mode: "if any Object which comes before the *Burlesque*

Writer, be low in its own Nature, he immediately bethinks himself of conferring on it a mock Dignity, in which it begins to look big, like the Champion at a Coronation, who boldly challenges all Mankind when he knows no Body will fight him. . . . In this case the great Disproportion between the two Objects strikes our Imagination, and our Laughter bursts out at that which is, without Foundation, set in Competition" (378).

20. In *An Apology for the Life of Mr. Colley Cibber . . . Written by Himself* of 1740, Cibber makes the connection between himself and his master Walpole (who presumably appointed him poet laureate). Defending Walpole, he argues that since there are more qualified ministers than places, *all* first ministers are satirized: "Tho' I can hardly forbear thinking, that they who have been *longest* rail'd at, must, from that Circumstance, shew, in some sort, a Proof of Capacity" (referring to the longevity of Walpole's ministry). Fielding makes the obvious connection between Cibber and Walpole in the *Champion* (22 Apr. 1740): Cibber's book has "much greater Matters in View" than the merely theatrical, "and may as properly be stiled an Apology for the Life of **one** who hath played a very comical Part, which, tho' Theatrical, hath been Acted on a much larger Stage than *Drury Lane*."

21. The "white-rob'd Maids" have been interpreted as either the Graces or the Virtues; though Virtues were white-rob'd, as Lonsdale points out, Collins was probably recalling Parnell's "To Mr. Pope" (ll. 27–28). Given Collins's poetic agenda, based on the replacement of the moral, the Graces, givers of beauty, seem the more likely. See Roger Lonsdale, ed., *The Poems of Thomas Gray, William Collins, Oliver Goldsmith* (London, 1969), 470.

22. Parnell, "To Mr. Pope," ll. 27–28, cited Lonsdale, *Poems*, 473 n.

23. He could also have understood Milesian tales as the Abbé Huet used the term, which included Apuleius's *Golden Ass* (Pierre-Daniel Huet, *Letter on the Origin of the Romances* [trans. English, 1672], xxix).

24. For the relationship between Collins's *Odes* and the Forty-Five (and the battle of Fontenoy on the Continent), see Howard Weinbrot, "William Collins and the Mid-Century Ode: Poetry, Patriotism, and the Influence of Context," in Weinbrot and Martin Price, *Context, Influence, and Mid-Eighteenth-Century Poetry* (Los Angeles, 1990), 3–39.

25. Warton, *Odes on Various Subjects* (1746), A2.

26. Warton's "Subjects for a Picture" in his "Gathering Book" (1739), among the Warton papers at Trinity College, Oxford, cited in Richard Wendorf, *William Collins and Eighteenth-Century English Poetry* (Minneapolis, 1981), 29.

27. Warton, *An Essay on the Writings and Genius of Pope* (London, 1756), xi.

28. As Lonsdale says, "He does not mean that Humour expresses, or is the product of, powerful emotions, but that Humour (still combining something of the older sense of a person's temperament with the later comic sense)

involves an understanding of individual human 'passions' or 'humours' "
(*Poems of . . . William Collins*, 474 n.).

CHAPTER 4. Aesthetics

1. Hume, *Essays Moral, Political, and Literary* (1757), 234–35.

2. Characteristically, Thomas D'Urfey's Sancho makes no case for the "beauty" of the "Country Wench"; all that he plays upon is the contrast of "Dulcinea" and the woman that Sancho tries to convince Quixote is she (part II, 1.i).

3. In a note in the margin of Cid Hamete Benengeli's MS, she is said to be best at salting pigs (1.9.72).

4. But cf. the story Quixote tells of the woman who settles for body, which he relates to the function of his own "imagination" (1.25.205–6). As in many other ways, in this too, Quixote and Sancho tend to join and become indistinguishable. The point of the episode may be that Quixote's and Sancho's aesthetic senses are only compatible in the presence of the peasant maid who is *supposed* to be Dulcinea.

5. For a good account of the problems in Hume's discussion of the wine tasting, see David Marshall, "Arguing by Analogy: Hume's Standard of Taste," *Eighteenth-Century Studies* 28 (1995): 323–43. Marshall points out that Hume also alters Cervantes' two senses, taste and smell, to taste, in conformity with the title and subject of his essay (341, n. 22). See also Ralph Cohen, "David Hume's Experimental Method and the Theory of Taste," *ELH* 25 (1958): 288; Redding S. Sugg Jr., "Hume's Search for the Key with the Leathern Thong," *Journal of Aesthetics and Art Criticism* 16 (1957): 96–102; and Steven Sverdlik, "Hume's Key and Aesthetic Rationality," *Journal of Aesthetics and Art Criticism*, 45 (1986): 72–73.

6. One wonders why Hume did not use the second wine-tasting episode: when Sancho is governor of Barataria, he *legislates* the issue he had earlier discussed as a matter of taste, declaring that "wine might be imported from any region whatever *so long as its place of origin was declared* in order *that a price might be put upon it* according to *its reputation* for quality and that *esteem* in which it was held, while anyone who watered wine or *put a false name on it* was to pay for it with his life" (2.51.848, emphasis added).

7. Sancho's wide experience with wine is indicated from time to time: in 1.11, while Quixote holds forth on the Golden Age, Sancho "kept quiet and went on munching acorns [which had set Quixote off on his harangue], taking occasion very frequently to pay a visit to the second wine bag, which they had suspended from a cork tree to keep it cool" (82–83).

8. I quote from Hume, *An Enquiry concerning the Principles of Morals* (1751;

1777 ed.), App. 1.242, ed. P. H. Nidditch (Oxford, 1975), 291–92. For "The Skeptic," see *Essays, Moral, Political, and Literary* (1742), ed. Eugene F. Miller (Indianapolis, 1985), 165.

9. V. K. Krishna Menon, *A Theory of Laughter* (London, 1931), 13–14.

10. Hogarth, *The Analysis of Beauty*, ed. Ronald Paulson, (New Haven and London, 1997), 39, 59. All references are to this edition.

11. *The Enraged Musician* was published in 1741; *The Shrimp Girl* was probably painted in the 1740s.

12. Quixote describes the knight-errant's devotion to his lady in comparison with a monk's to God. While "the state of knight-errant" is not "as holy as that of the cloistered monk," Quixote does affirm, "from what I myself endure, that ours is beyond a doubt the more laborious and arduous calling, more beset by hunger and thirst, more wretched, ragged, and ridden with lice. It is an absolute certainty that the knights-errant of old experienced much misfortune in the course of their lives" (1.13.94).

13. Near the end of part 2 (58.883–84) this scene is echoed by the one in which Quixote encounters the "images carved in relief to be used in an altarpiece" of Saint George on horseback, "a protector of damsels"; Saint Martin and the beggar, representing "charity," the sublimation of eros; San Diego Matamoros, patron saint of Spain, the Moor-slayer; and the conversion of Saint Paul—"the greatest enemy that the Church of Our Lord God had to combat, and he became the greatest champion it will ever have, a knight-errant in life." The last, representing Paul falling from his horse at Damascus, is by this time an image that automatically summons up the paradigmatic Quixotic fall from Rocinante.

14. Alban K. Forcione, *Cervantes, Aristotle, and the "Persiles"* (Princeton, 1970), 109.

15. See Lewis, *The Allegory of Love* (Oxford, 1936); also, Denis de Rougement, *Love in the Western World*, trans. Montgomery Belgion (New York, 1957).

16. El Saffar, *Beyond Fiction: The Recovery of the Feminine in the Novels of Cervantes* (Berkeley, 1984), 96.

17. Putnam, trans. *Don Quixote*, 1.569–70; Shelton, 3.66.

18. Ovid's *Remedia Amoris* 191–92 is usually cited: but Ovid's lover, who slips into his lady's dressing room, is put off by her cosmetics, not her bodily functions, and his advice is to keep plain desire uncontaminated by passion (by which he means love): "As for the act of love—keep passion away altogether." Juvenal's aim was to demystify women, whose control over men lay in their apparent beauty; "but, look behind, / And then she dwindles to the pigmy kind" (Satire 6, ll. 647–48). Again, at the turn of the eighteenth century Ned Ward, in *Female Policy Detected* (1695), urged men "to surprize her in a Morning undrest, and it is Ten to One but you will find your Goddess hath shifted off her

Divinity, and the Angel you so much admir'd turn'd into a Magmallion" ("magma," the dregs of cosmetics). This is Ward's prescription for freeing man of the imaginings that trap him into marriage. As Felicity Nussbaum writes of such poetry, "the dressing room scenes are warnings to men to penetrate the disguises of women in order to protect themselves. Since the boudoir is the site of woman's preparation for attacking and destroying men, to penetrate it is to disarm the women." Swift, Nussbaum writes, "exposes the madness of loving a Corinna, and allows us to see the vain imaginings passion brings. Both women and men commit the sins of the imagination—men in seeking a phantom ideal, women in seeking to fulfill that ideal in the idolatrous ritual of the dressing table" (Nussbaum, *The Brink of All We Hate: English Satires on Women, 1660–1750* [Lexington, 1984], 106–7).

19. My text is Pat Rogers, ed., *Jonathan Swift: The Complete Poems* (New Haven, 1983).

20. Strephon's first stage of response, in "The Lady's Dressing Room," overlaps with Gulliver's similar response to the Yahoos; but in the poem it is beauty to which he responds, and in Houyhnhnmland it is virtue.

21. *Poetics* 5; see chap. 1, n. 29.

22. For a recent discussion, see N. F. Lowe, "Hogarth, Beauty Spots, and Sexually Transmitted Diseases," *British Journal of Eighteenth-Century Studies* 15 (1991): 69–79.

23. The blemish was focused in the popular consciousness on the most notorious words of the Old Testament, on which Shaftesbury focused his scorn and his aesthetics: "And if a man cause a blemish in his neighbor; as he hath done, so shall it be done to him; breach for breach, eye for eye, tooth for tooth: as he hath caused a blemish in a man, so shall it be done to him again" (Lev. 24.19–20).

24. Putnam, 1.16.115; Shelton, 1652 ed., 29.

25. *Matthew Henry's Commentary on the Whole Bible* (1706; Peabody, Mass., 1991), 1: 416–17.

26. It seems to me evidence for Hogarth's use of Shelton's translation of *Don Quixote* that only Shelton up to that time introduces the peasant maid (Sancho's "Dulcinea") as "a country wench, and not very well-favoured, for she was blub-fac'd, and flat-nos'd" (3:66). The detail is omitted by Motteux, though recovered by Jarvis's translation of 1742 (2.48).

27. Cf. Richardson's use of the sacrificial lamb: Mrs. Jervis refers to Pamela, under attack by Mr. B., as a "Lamb" (*Pamela*, ed. T. C. Duncan Eaves and Ben D. Kimpel [Boston, 1971]), esp. p. 67, where she says he could prey upon the "wicked ones in the World" [the harlots] but not "such a Lamb as this!"). The term becomes ironic when Mr. B. calls her an "innocent Lamb" and Mrs. Jewkes adds "poor innocent Lamb" (162, 169).

28. Addison, "Essay on the Georgics," *Works of John Dryden*, 5: 151.

29. The passage concerning Socrates' dialogue with Aristippus and Parrhasius on "fitness" was translated for Hogarth by Thomas Morell (BL, Add. MS 27992, ff.[33–35]; *Memorabilia*, trans. O. J. Todd [Cambridge, Mass., Loeb Library, 1923], 3.8).

30. The form the blemish takes for Swift is excrement, which he associates with the moral and theological evils released into the world from Pandora's box. In "The Lady's Dressing Room" when Strephon reaches to the bottom of Celia's close-stool, all the Pandorian evils have flown out (the odors), and only hope, the excrement itself, remains. The opening of the close-stool's lid is compared with Sin opening the gate of hell. She opens it *for* Satan; she and Satan are the viewers of chaos "dark and deep" and she and Death then build a pathway from which they can make their way to earth. In effect, Strephon is compared with Satan persuading Sin to open the gate of hell; this gate opens onto chaos, and the evils come along with Satan, Sin, and Death, who transport them from hell to the created world. Strephon and Celia are the actual villains. Strephon has in common with Satan his spiteful quest ("for you to exercise your spite"), and Celia (Sin) opens the gate of hell but is not strong enough to close it again. It is thus the realization that women are not goddesses that releases Satan, Sin, and Death into the world—a more pessimistic interpretation of the results of the Fall than Pope's upbeat description of Belinda applying makeup to her only slightly "fallen" face, the sign of a *felix culpa*.

31. These examples are discussed in Paulson, *The Beautiful, Novel, and Strange: Aesthetics and Heterodoxy* (Baltimore, 1996), chap. 6.

32. *Matthew Henry's Commentary*, 1:636.

33. *A Tale of a Tub*, ed. A. C. Guthkelch and D. Nichol Smith (Oxford, 2d ed., 1958), 81–82.

34. *Tom Jones*, 10.1.527; Horace, *Ars Poetica*, H. R. Fairclough trans., cited in Battestin's note (for Battestin, see chap. 2, n. 69).

35. The passage cited, however, is followed by a contrasting example—a parody of this sort of hero in chapter 3 with Mr. Fitzpatrick.

CHAPTER 5. Religion

1. See, e.g., *Spectator* no. 48; 1: 207. The earliest Quixote in English was the apprentice Rafe in Beaumont's *Knight of the Burning Pestle* (1607), performed just two years after the publication of part 1 of *Don Quixote* and the same year as the first French translation, but long before the publication of part 2 with the episode of the puppet show. While taking hints from part 1, Beaumont is drawing on the tradition of the play within a play (Shakespeare's *Taming of the Shrew*, *Midsummer Night's Dream*, and, even, *Hamlet*). From *Quixote* he may take the figure who challenges the boundaries between art and life, play and reality, actors and audience. See The Revels edition, ed. Sheldon P. Zitner

(Manchester, 1984), 40; and Jackson I. Cope, *The Theater and the Dream: From Metaphor to Form in Renaissance Drama* (Baltimore, 1973), 196–200.

2. It is reported at Quixote's death that he retracted the story of Montesinos's cave and confessed that he had invented the incident (2.24.666).

3. Duffield, *Don Quixote, His Critics and Commentators* (London, 1881), 66n. Vladimir Nabokov, who doubts Duffield, also notes the parody and, while he discredits Duffield, he draws his own parallels—often tacitly, and perhaps for effect in a classroom lecture—between Quixote and Christ. One parallel he draws surely goes too far: he construes Quixote hanging by one arm from the gate, with his hand through the hole into which Maritornes has persuaded him to insert it, and his feet precariously on Rocinante's back, as Christ on the cross (1.43.391–96; Nabokov, *Lectures on Don Quixote*, ed. Fredson Bowers [New York, 1983], 63, 73).

In fact, Nabokov is drawing parallels between Quixote's story and the stories of knights-errant such as Lancelot in order to conclude that Quixote "cannot be considered a distortion of those romances but rather a logical continuation, with the elements of madness and shame and mystification increased" (47; see 44–47). And so Nabokov's parallel is actually between the knights and their model, Christ. It is fascinating to think of Nabokov writing his Harvard lectures on Quixote and his obsession with Dulcinea in 1952 as he was also writing the story of Humbert and Lolita.

4. The statements about Quixote's Catholic Christianity are often double-edged. We are told of the crows and jackdaws that fly out of the Cave of Montesinos: "had he been as much of a believer in augury as he was a good Catholic Christian, he would have taken this as an ill omen and would have declined to bury himself in such a place as that" (2.22.654). On the one occasion (noted by Ruth El Saffar as evidence of his growing piety pointing toward his deathbed conversion) when he makes a conventional Christian speech, it is merely apropos of the occasion and is followed by another beating (2.27.691–92). See El Saffar, *Beyond Fiction: The Recovery of the Feminine in the Novels of Cervantes* (Berkeley, 1984), 121.

5. Skepticism, evident in Cervantes' attitude toward the truth of his text and the authorial role, extends to all texts and so might explain the phenomenon of demystification. Sextus Empiricus, after all, was the authority for classical skepticism as well as the namesake of empiricism. See Maureen Ihrie, "Classical Skepticism and Narrative Authority in *Don Quijote de la Mancha*," in *Studies on "Don Quixote,"* ed. Donald W. Bleznick (York, S.C., 1984), 31–37.

6. Cf., for example, Georg Lukacs of *Don Quixote* in *The Theory of the Novel* (1919): "the first great novel of world literature stands at the beginning of the time when the Christian God began to forsake the world" (trans. Anna Bostock [Cambridge, 1971], 103–4).

7. René Girard, *Deceit, Desire, and the Novel: Self and Other in Literary Structure*, trans. Yvonne Freccero (Baltimore, 1965), 1–4.

8. See Richard Braverman, *Plots & Counterplots: Sexual Politics & the Body Politic in English Literature, 1660–1730* (Cambridge, 1993), chap. 2.

9. For a discussion of Addison and the metaphor of life-as-theater, especially in its theological context, see Paulson, *The Beautiful, Novel, and Strange* (Baltimore, 1996), 55–61.

10. Addison, "Notes on Ovid," in *Miscellaneous Works of Joseph Addison*, ed. A. C. Guthkelch (London, 1914) 1:135.

11. And, by Hume's time, there was also Francis Hutcheson's version of Shaftesbury, *An Inquiry into the Original of our Ideas of Beauty and Virtue* (1725).

12. Shaftesbury, *Characteristics of Men, Manners, Opinions, Times, Etc.*, ed. John M. Robertson (New York, 1900), 1: 96, 279.

13. This quotation, cited by Nabokov (16), is apparently the conflation of two quotations, neither of which I am able to locate. Nabokov writes: "As his squire correctly remarks, his attitude toward Dulcinea is *religious*." But, Nabokov adds, "Don Quixote's thoughts never go beyond rendering her homage *for her own sake*, with no expectance of *any reward* other than being accepted as her champion" (16). Quixote's thoughts about her do, we have seen, center on rewards and punishments in defense of her honor. I question Nabokov's twentieth-century horror at the cruelty of the pain in *Don Quixote*, and ask whether punishment is not another term, like satire and imagination, that is being problematized by Cervantes.

14. Shaftesbury, "Miscellaneous Reflections," *Characteristics*, 2:313–14.

15. Shaftesbury tends to use humor and ridicule as synonyms for the risible, the merely laughable; but he invokes Horace's contrast of *ridiculum* with *acri* (or lampoon, a sharp, *acrimonious* personal satire): "There is a great difference between seeking how to raise a laugh from everything, and seeking in everything what justly may be laughed at"—that is, the aspect, humor, or foible that is risible (*Characteristics*, 1:11, 85; Horace, Satire 1.x, 14–15).

16. The "Hippocratic novel," an addendum to "Hippocrates' Aphorisms," comments on the "madness" of Democritus as expressed in his laughter— "directed at the life of man and at all the vain fears and hopes related to the gods and to life after death" (cited, Mikhail Bakhtin, *Rabelais and his World*, trans. Helene Iswolsky [Cambridge, Mass., 1968], 67). Bakhtin adds the demarcated area of laughter—freedom from ordinary restraint, as in the Roman Saturnalia; the triumphs in which emperors and generals were derided ("Home we bring the bald whore-monger, Romans lock your wives away")—as "its positive, regenerating, creative meaning" (71).

17. *De Anima*, bk. 3, chap. 10; see Bakhtin, *Rabelais and his World*, 167.

18. Shelton, 1.166; Putnam, 1.20.154.

19. Isaac Barrow had argued that religion is not "altogether sullen and sour, requiring a dull, lumpish, morose kind of life, barring all delight, all mirth, all good humour: whereas on the contrary it alone is the never-failing source of true, pure, steady joy . . . . our Religion doth not onely allow us, but even doth oblige us to be joyfull . . . charging us in all times, upon all occasions, to be chearfull." Cheerfulness Barrow contrasted to "ludicrous divertisements and amusements of fancy," "frothy conceits, bitter scoffs, or profane railleries." This is decidedly not the pleasure of laughter, "for *Even* (as *Solomon* observed) *in laughter, the heart is sorrowfull, and the end of that mirth is heaviness*"; nor is it the "wild impertinent mirth, . . . '*I said of laughter, It is mad; and of mirth, What doth it?*'" Rather it is a "grave, sober . . . and steady joy" (Isaac Barrow, "Rejoice Evermore," *Works*, 3 [1686]: 124–26, cited in Stuart Tave, *The Amiable Humorist* [Chicago, 1960], 4).

20. See Tave, *Amiable Humorist*, 8. It is quite in line with Addison's position to invoke Jesus—"the Sacred Person who was the great Pattern of Perfection was never seen to Laugh," but was apparently "affable and obliging," a source of "good Humour in those" who came into contact with him. Jesus was invoked in similar ways by contemporary deists. Addison proceeds: "An inward Chearfulness is an implicit Praise and Thanksgiving to Providence under all its Dispensations" (430).

21. *Spectator* no. 502, 4:280; *The Conscious Lovers*, ed. Shirley Strum Kenny (Lincoln, Nebr., 1968), 5.

22. See, e.g., Hippocrates, *Humours*, 6, in *Hippocrates*, trans. W. H. S. Jones, 4 (Cambridge, Mass., 1931), 74–77. Cf. Congreve's remark, cited on p. 35; and Hobbes, *Leviathan*, 3.34, 264–65.

23. Bulkeley, *A Vindication of My Lord Shaftesbury, On the Subject of Ridicule* (1751), 19–20, cited in Tave, *Amiable Humorist*, 36.

24. For Shaftesbury on Hobbes, see *Characteristics*, 1:61 ff.

25. Pocock, "The Varieties of Whiggism from Exclusion to Reform," in *Virtue, Commerce, and History: Essays on Political Thought and History, Chiefly in the Eighteenth Century* (Cambridge, 1985), 219.

26. For Shaftesbury's political positions, see Lawrence E. Klein, *Shaftesbury and the Culture of Politeness: Moral Discourse and Cultural Politics in early Eighteenth-Century England* (Cambridge, 1994), chap. 7.

27. *Correspondence of Jonathan Swift*, ed. Harold Williams, 1 (Oxford, 1963): 100.

28. Shaftesbury to John Somers, Mar. 1708; P.R.O. 30/24/22/4, ff.67–70, cited in Klein, 157n.

29. In *An Inquiry Concerning Virtue or Merit* Shaftesbury refers to "the men of wit and raillery, whose pleasantest entertainment is in the exposing the weak sides of religion"—which echoes Swift's "Preface": "The Wits of the present Age . . . pick Holes in the weak sides of Religion and Government" (1: 39).

30. Shaftesbury, *Characteristics*, 1: 6.

31. *Soliloquy; or, Advice to an Author* (1710), *Characteristics*, 222.

32. In *Sensus Communis* Shaftesbury makes the same case against Hobbes, as the spokesman of realism: "Of what advantage is it to you to deliver us from the cheat? The more are taken in it the better. 'Tis directly against your interest to undeceive us and let us know that only private interest governs you, and that nothing nobler, or of a larger kind, should govern us whom you converse with. Leave us to ourselves, and to that notable art by which we are happily tamed, and rendered thus mild and sheepish" (1:63).

33. While defending ridicule as the test of truth in his two polemical works, in his private writings Shaftesbury drew a line between this and "free-talking about matters of Religion & of Establishd Rites of Worship . . . especially if it be done after a certain manner: that is to say, if it be not still with a certain Economy & Reserve: if it be vehemently . . . acutely . . . as shewing Witt . . . ridiculingly & with Contempt" (P.R.O. 30/24/27/10, pp. 120–21 [ff.61v–624], cited in Klein, 157n).

34. Tillotson, "The Folly of Scoffing at Religion," *Works* (1696), 40–41.

35. *Tale*, 49.

36. It is interesting to note that Cervantes gives to Marcela an image that substitutes a sword for the razor and beauty for wit: "Beauty in a modest woman is like a distant fire or a sharp-edged sword: the one does not burn, the other does not cut, those who do not come near it" (1.14.104).

37. Swift, in *propria persona* in the "Author's Apology," writes: "[A]s Wit is the noblest and most useful Gift of humane Nature, so Humor is the most agreeable, and where these two enter far into the Composition of any Work, they will render it always acceptable to the World" (18).

38. Tillotson, "The Folly of Scoffing at Religion," ibid. Cf. in the 1740s Fielding's sister Sarah holding forth on wit as practiced by atheists and especially what she calls butterflies. The latter (a butterfly), "as he could not think deep enough to consult on which side Truth lay, he never considered farther than what would give him the best Opportunity of *displaying his Wit.* He openly professed himself a great *Lover of Ridicule*, and thought no Subject so fit to exercise it on, as religion and the Clergy." He therefore ridicules "the *Pride* of priests, their being greedy after their Tythes, &c." (*David Simple* [1744], book 3, chapter 4; 178).

39. Wotton, *A Defense of the reflections upon Ancient and Modern Learning* (1705), 52, 48.

40. See Wotton, 49–50.

41. Swift, sermon "On the Trinity," in *Prose Works*, ed. Davis, 9: *Irish Tracts and Sermons* (Oxford, 1963), 167.

42. See Pocock, "Introduction," *The Political Works of James Harrington* (Cambridge, 1977), 77–81. "Attacks on 'priestcraft' were," one historian writes,

"a well-established part of the language of opposition Whiggery," and another historian notes that English Whiggery "was born as much in anticlericalism as in constitutionalism, and church history was as natural a stamping ground for Whig polemicists as was parliamentary history." Christine Gerrard, *The Patriot Opposition to Walpole: Politics, Poetry, and National Myth, 1725–1742* (Oxford: Clarendon Press, 1994), 24; Mark Goldie, "Priestcraft and the Birth of Whiggism," in Nicholas Phillipson and Quentin Skinner, eds., *Political Discourse in Early Modern Britain* (Cambridge, 1993), 214 (209–31). For a valuable overview, see Richard Ashcraft, "Anticlericalism and Authority in Lockean Political Thought," in *The Margins of Orthodoxy,* ed. Lund, 73–96.

43. John Toland, for example, was a strong Whig as well as a deist, and the editor of Harrington's works and the author of a *Life of Milton*. See Pocock, "The Varieties of Whiggism," *Political Works of Harrington,* 232.

44. *An account of the Trial of Thomas Woolston, B.D.* (1729), A2. See also the anonymous *Life of Mr. Woolston, with an Impartial Account of his Writings* (1733), 15–25.

45. See Joseph Levine, *The Battle of the Books: History and Literature in the Augustan Age* (Ithaca, 1991).

46. Hogarth calls Sancho's response "astonishment," while in the text he is "terrified" (2.684). Cervantes' Sancho's response, the blunted one of the "dull and languid" bystanders to the wine tasting by "men of taste," is the same to both experiences: terror; but in fact in the first case the figures of Death and the rest "struck fear in Sancho's heart" (575); whereas, in the second it is Quixote's attack on the Moorish puppets that "terrified" him, for "he had never seen his master in such a towering passion" (684).

47. Hogarth uses an engraving by Carlo Maratta. See *Annibale Carracci e i suoi incisori,* 88–89 (no. 1).

48. Hawkesworth, *Adventurer* no. 82, 18 Aug. 1753. The review, probably by Hawkesworth, is in *Gentleman's Magazine* 23 (Dec. 1753): 593; 24 (Jan. 1754): 11–15.

49. In fact, Hogarth adapts Coypel's design in the same way Hayman adapts Vanderbank's: he works variations on the figures (using, of course, his own version of Sancho's face, found in his other illustrations, rather than Coypel's). He makes his a daylight scene, instead of Coypel's candlelit scene. (For a reproduction of the painting in the Louvre, see Philip Conisbee, *Painting in Eighteenth-Century France* [Ithaca, 1981], 88, fig. 70.)

50. Hayman's illustrations show no influence of Hogarth's *Quixote* plates. But he does seem to have seen Hogarth's *Sancho's Feast* (though a friend of Hogarth's in the 1730s, he may not have seen Hogarth's *Quixote* plates) and he could, of course, have seen it, for it was published. In this one instance he turns from Vanderbank's illustration and works variations on Hogarth's, and/or Hogarth's source, Coypel's. He has moved the serving boy to the right and brought

forward the royal physician with wand in a more dramatic gesture—but at the expense of shifting emphasis from Sancho to the physician.

51. The publication date has to be before 1734 since it carries the publication line of Overton and J. Hoole, who separated in that year. See Paulson, *Hogarth's Graphic Works* (1965; 3d ed., London, 1989) no. 100.

52. See Paulson, *Hogarth, Vol. 1 (1697–1732)* (New Brunswick, 1990), 153. Hogarth's drawing for *Sancho's Feast* was sold in London, at Christie's, on 8 April 1997 (lot no. 4). Hogarth replaced his first thought for Sancho's face with the one that appears in the engraving by pasting a piece of paper over it. The revision resembles Hogarth's face even more than the face in the engraving; it is a pudgier version of Roubiliac's bust made in the 1740s (London, National Portrait Gallery).

53. See, e.g., Hogarth's *Masquerades and Operas* of 1724, in which the works of Shakespeare, Jonson, and Congreve are being carted away from a London street now dominated by masquerades and operas (Paulson, *Hogarth's Graphic Works*, no. 44).

54. The following pages are a radical condensation of Paulson, "Putting out the Fire in Her Imperial Majesty's Apartment: Opposition Politics, Anticlericalism, and Aesthetics," *ELH* 63 (1996): 79–108. Detailed accounts of *The Punishment of Lemuel Gulliver* and *Cunicularii* are to be found there.

55. *Cunicularii* was announced as published in the *Post-Boy* of 22–24 December, just two days before *The Punishment of Lemuel Gulliver*. See *Hogarth's Graphic Works*, no. 106.

56. Collins, *Discourse of the Grounds and Reasons of the Christian Religion* (1724), 41–42, 53.

57. *First Discourse* (5th ed., 1728). 55–56.

58. The *Harlot* was followed directly in both title and focus on Bishop Gibson and a corrupt clergy by Richard Savage's *Progress of a Divine* (1735). And at this time the *Old Whig*, another antiministerial journal, was still equating "C–d–x" with monks, popes, and popish bishops (8 May 1735).

59. If Amhurst is the author of *The Twickenham Hotch-Potch*, signed by Caleb D'Anvers, a spinoff of *The Beggar's Opera* that spells out its anti-Walpole satire, he is certainly not friendly toward the Scriblerians, whom he calls "an impertinent *Scotch*-Quack, a Profligate *Irish*-Dean, the Lacquey of a Superannuated Dutchess, and a little virulent Papist" (vi).

60. On the diversity of opposition writing and outlook, see Gerard, 16–17.

61. Cf. the pudgy body and round, unprepossessing face of Toft in John Laguerre's portrait, engraved in mezzotint by John Faber, *Mary Tofts of Godelman the pretended Rabbit Breeder* (announced 21 Jan. 1726/27, *Mist's Weekly Journal*, BM sat. 1783).

62. See Addison, "Notes on Ovid," *Miscellaneous Works* 1:143.

63. Charity was itself, of course, a secularization of institutionalized religious

worship based on the teachings of Jesus; a phenomenon that, in the eighteenth century, can be taken either as an aspect of deism or middling respectability, reinstitutionalized in the Foundling Hospital and other charitable foundations.

64. *Ridiculous* was a word whose root was *rideo, risi, risum,* either to laugh at or laugh with, though it was usually used as the former; *ludicrous,* whose root was *ludus,* referred to the jocular or playful (as in *Spectator* no. 191); and, as we have seen, *comedy* usually applied to plays with a happy ending.

65. I include Stuart Tave, in *The Amiable Humorist,* and myself in *Satire and the Novel.*

66. The same problem follows when Tom and Partridge attend a performance of *Hamlet* (16.5). If the puppet-master derided the low and was proved wrong, and Tom laughs at the low, in the *Hamlet* scene he laughs at the naïvete of Partridge. But, like the puppet-master, he is hoist by his own petard: when he leaves the theater he cannot tell play from reality and is caught up in the play just as Partridge (or, earlier, Grace) was. He finds himself playing Hamlet in a London of actors playing Laertes, Old Hamlet, Gertrude, and Claudius. Within the theater the laughter, arising from the discrepancy between the tragedy onstage and the (burlesque) Quixotic misunderstandings of Partridge, presumably kept Tom from immersion in the tragedy of Hamlet. Among other things, what he (and we) learn is that he is (like Joseph Andrews) a character who transcends theatrical roles.

We might also note that in both performances—of *The Provok'd Husband* and of *Hamlet*—there is an allusion to a religious alternative, as in *Don Quixote* the puppet show was preceded by the Corpus Christi play, *The Parliament of Death.* The performance of *The Provok'd Husband* is supplemented with the landlady's preference for *Jeptha's Rash Vow* and plays in which the devil appears; and *Hamlet* reminds Partridge, who confuses the Ghost with the devil, of the deliverance service for Guy Fawkes Day. As Sheridan Baker has noted, the inn's sign of a crown and coffin could "appropriately advertise the puppet show, a crown for King Jephthah, a coffin for his daughter." Partridge mistakes the sign for the standard of the Young Pretender, Bonnie Prince Charlie, alluding to the rebellion that goes on behind the theatrical and nontheatrical main action of the novel (Tom is confused with the Prince and Sophia with his mistress, Jennie Cameron). See Sheridan Baker, ed., *Tom Jones* (New York, 1973), notes, 487, 491.

67. *Shamela,* in *"Joseph Andrews" with "Shamela" and Related Writings,* ed. Homer Goldberg (New York, 1987), 283.

68. *Tom Jones,* 12.11.623; citing L'Estrange's *Fables of Aesop* (1692), fable 61. See Paulson, *Popular and Polite Art in the Age of Hogarth and Fielding* (Notre Dame, 1979), 2.5, "The Iatrohydraulic System."

69. Shaftesbury, *Sensus Communis,* 1.5; *Characteristics of Men, Manners, Opinions, Times, Etc.,* ed. John M. Robertson (New York, 1900), 1:52.

70. Of Adams riding in a coach we are told, Aeschylus "entertained him

for three hours together, without suffering him once to reflect on his fellow-traveller" (2.2). This is different from his response to the story of Leonora the Jilt, when his "insatiable curiosity" and "hunger" for the "news" is strongly contrasted with the physical hunger of the rest of the party (92); his response in this case is moral as well as human—he "fetched a deep groan" at Leonora's behavior. He treats this oral story differently from the written one of a play by Aeschylus. In the first he is an interested listener and responder, whereas when he reads Aeschylus he forgets all that goes on around him and is immersed in Aeschylus's text. The justice's interested response to the "Aeschylus" is to interpret it as legal evidence. The Greek characters become a dangerous cypher, according to the clerk and justice, who take "Aeschylus" to be Adams's code name—"an outlandish name," "a fictitious name," "a false name"; in other words, a lie, another of the equivalents of Quixote's romances.

71. See Eric J. Ziolkowski, *The Sanctification of Don Quixote* (University Park, Pa., 1991).

72. The "comical and diverting humors of Somebody and Nobody" appear in Luckless's puppet play in *The Author's Farce*, Fielding's first great stage success of the next year. For Somebody-Nobody, see Paulson, *Hogarth, Vol. I*, 323–24. As to Fielding's use of Sanchoesque proverbs (especially evident in *Don Quixote in England*), see Sheridan Baker, "Henry Fielding and the Cliché," *Criticism* I (1959): 354–56.

73. *Covent-Garden Journal*, no. 24, ed. Bertrand Goldgar, 160.

74. [Richard Allestree], *The Whole Duty of Man* (1673), 389, referring to Romans 13.19. Duties to our neighbors, primarily on charity, are dealt with from page 213 to the end (400).

75. Sterne, *Tristram Shandy*, ed. Melvyn and Joan New (Gainesville, Fla., 1978), 12. All citations are from this text.

76. Referring in a letter to his description of Dr. Slop's arrival at Shandy Hall, he writes: "I will reconsider Slops fall & my too Minute account of it—but in general I am perswaded that the happiness of the Cervantic humour arises from this very thing—of describing silly and trifling Events, with the Circumstantial Pomp of Great Ones" (*Letters*, 77; also 120–21). Robert Alter sees Sterne's sense of "Cervantick" embodied not in the hobby-horses but, more generally, in soaring fantasy versus earthbound, coarse-grained actuality: Quixote and Sancho as Walter and Toby, Walter and Mrs. Shandy, Toby and Trim, Tristram and Jenny, Dr. Slop and Obadiah, all the Shandys and the bull. Sexuality is every person's Sancho Panza, and Tristram's puns reveal the rock-bottom sexuality under all Quixotic gestures (Robert Alter, *Partial Magic: The Novel as a Self-Conscious Genre* [Berkeley and Los Angeles, 1975], 39–40; on *Don Quixote* in general, see pp. 3–29).

77. Arthur Cash, *Laurence Sterne: The Later Years* (New York, 1986), 71.

78. Alter refers to Sterne's "use of laughter as the defense-action of an embat-

tled psyche, its chief means of confronting the terrors of loneliness, frustration, pain, of its own inevitable extinction," but does not relate this to the "Cervantick" (*Partial Magic*, 42). As Michael McKeon has noted, Quixote's way of dealing with (living in) the world is his "theory of enchantments," the notion that every contingency was imposed just on him by an enemy enchanter. This is his explanation when he sees not Dulcinea but a peasant maid and, again, when he explains to Ginés de Pasamonte how he mistook his puppets for real Moors. McKeon sees this as a method that "permits its user to believe without really believing"—McKeon, *The Origins of the English Novel, 1600–1740* (Baltimore, 1987), 280. True, Quixote presumably does believe by way of this useful "belief" (a belief that only Sancho regards, as we do, as a fiction). But in McKeon's argument, the Quixote "theory of enchantments" is an "aestheticizing" of belief in Dulcinea; in the terms of my argument, it parodies the belief in an immanent God and his intervention in everyday life, but only to replace this belief with the belief in a beautiful princess and Moorish puppets. If the "theory of enchantments" is one way of replacing belief, another (McKeon also notes) is the humoring of Quixote by the duke and duchess, which replaces recalcitrant nature with a theatrical simulacrum of Quixote's delusion—but to the knowledgeable practical jokers a semblance only; and a semblance that nevertheless retains, on at least some occasions, the painful consequences of the real world for Quixote.

79. Cf. Paulson, *Beautiful, Novel, and Strange*, 167.

80. *Serious Reflections of Robinson Crusoe*, in *Works of Defoe*, ed. Maynardier, 2:x.

81. Bunyan, *The Pilgrim's Progress*, ed. James Blanton Wharey (Oxford, 2d ed., 1975), 8–9, 11.

CHAPTER 6. The Female Subject

1. The most palpable interpolation in *Don Quixote* is the MS of "The Foolish Curiosity," read to the group by the curate (1.33–35). In *Joseph Andrews* the story of Leonora the Jilt is told by one of the women in the coach, but from the perspective of Leonora, with the themes of love and honor, the pathetic emotions.

2. See Harry Sieber, "Society and the Pastoral Vision in the Marcela-Grisóstomo Episode of *Don Quixote*," *Extudios literearios de Hispanistas Norteamericanos dedicados a Helmut Hatzfeld con motivo de su 80 aniversario* (Barcelona, 1974), 187–94.

3. The Cardenio and Dorotea stories also balance the subjectivity of the man and the woman. Cardenio loves Luscinda but is cheated of her by his "friend" Don Fernando. Dorotea, the peasant beauty (beauty presumably on a par with Marcela's), has been seduced by Fernando; this event, before his

turning to Luscinda, ties together the two stories. Abandoned, both Cardenio and Dorotea retire to the wastes of the Siera Morena—he to do penance and she, a typical romance heroine, to fend off potential rapists and then, joining the "plot" of the curate and barber, to pose as a persecuted princess for Quixote.

4. I quote the whole passage in Shelton's version:

> Heaven, as you say, hath made me beautiful, and that so much, that my features move you to love, almost whether you will or no. And for the affection you shew unto me, you say, I and you affirm that I ought to love you again. I know by the natural instinct that *Jove* hath bestow'd on me, that each fair thing is amiable; but I cannot conceive, why for the reason of being beloved, the Party that is so beloved for her beauty, should be bound to love her lover, although he be foul. And seeing that foul things are worthy of hate, it is a bad argument to say, I love thee because fair; therefore thou must affect me, although uncomely. But set the Case that the beauties occur equal on both sides, it follows not therefore that their Desires should run one way. For all beauties do not enamour, for some do only delight the sight, and subject the will; for if all beauties did enamour and subject together, mens wills would ever run confused and straying, without being able to make any election; for the beautiful Subject being infinite, the desires must also perforce be infinite. (1:102)

5. Shelton: "[F]or Beauty in an honest woman, is like fire afar off, or a sharp-edged sword; for neither that burns, nor this cuts any but such as come near them" (1:103).

6. D'Urfrey, *Don Quixote*, 23. Earlier D'Urfey had conflated the stories of Grisóstomo and Marcela, Fernando and Dorotea, by introducing Dorotea at Grisóstomo's funeral, and so when Ambrosio curses women she can respond with her reference to Fernando: "To me I'm sure a Man has been a greater [plague], and bred more desolation" than women (18). Marcela appears in part 1, act 2; Dorotea's actual story unfolds in act 3.

7. See Catherine Gallagher, *Nobody's Story: The Vanishing Acts of Women Writers in the Marketplace, 1670–1820* (Berkeley and Los Angeles, 1994), 152, 154. See also Laurie Langbauer, *Women and Romance: The Consolations of Gender in the English Novel* (Ithaca, 1990), chap. 2 ("Diverting Romance: Charlotte Lennox's *The Female Quixote*").

8. *Covent-Garden Journal* no. 24, in *The Covent-Garden Journal,* ed. Goldgar, 158–61. On *The Female Quixote*, cf. Paulson, *Satire and the Novel* (New Haven, 1967), 275–79; and Susan Staves, "Don Quixote in Eighteenth-Century England," *Comparative Literature* 24 (1972): 197.

9. Lennox is herself familiar with the convention, remarking that Sir George's subjects of conversation "would afford *Arabella* an Occasion of shew-

ing her Foible" (Lennox, *The Female Quixote: or The Adventures of Arabella,* ed. Margaret Dalziel [London, 1970], 86; all references are to this edition).

10. William B. Warner, *Licensing Entertainment: The Elevation of the Novel in Britain (1684–1750)* (Los Angeles and Berkeley, forthcoming), conclusion.

11. The only significant female Quixote prior to Lennox's was Marivaux's in *Pharsamond* (1712), who (in fact, a Dulcinea) operates vis-à-vis a male Quixote. She is ostensibly a Quixote's dream come true, and since there are two of them, they can retain their original relationship of subject and object.

12. See Susan Kubica Howard, introduction to her edition of Charlotte Lennox, *The Life of Harriot Stuart, as Written by Herself* (Madison, 1995).

13. Both of these details were pointed out to me by Robert Folkenflik. For Fielding's use of "Jacobite," see *Jacobite's Journal,* W. B. Coley, introduction to *The Jacobite's Journal and Related Writings* (Middletown, 1974).

14. Thus at the end of book 4 she is sufficiently carried away to cry to Lucy,

> Do you think I have any Cause to accuse myself, tho' Five thousand Men were to die for me! 'Tis very certain, my Beauty has produced very deplorable Effects: The unhappy *Harvey* has expiated, by his Death, the Violence his too desperate Passion forced him to meditate against me: The no less guilty, the noble Unknown, *Edward,* is wandering about the World, in a tormenting Despair; and stands exposed to the Vengeance of my Cousin, who has vowed his Death. My Charms have made another Person, whose Character ought to be sacred to me, forget all the Ties of Consanguinity; and become the Rival of his Son, whose Interest he once endeavoured to support: And, lastly, the unfortunate *Bellmour* consumes away in an hopeless Passion. (175)

We can imagine Swift's reading of this passage.

15. Lennox's Arabella leads us to suspect that, as Ruth El Saffar has noted, "Alonso Quijano's entire obsession with reading may be an aspect of his fear of the body"—El Saffar, *Beyond Fiction: The Recovery of the Feminine in the Novels of Cervantes* (Berkeley, 1984), 54. In his homage to the lost Golden Age, Quixote emphasizes that it is the knight's duty to protect young women "in this detestable age of ours, [where] no maiden is safe" (1.11.82). In his encounter with, for example, the procession of priests carrying an image of the Virgin, he is defending a princess from abduction and rape (a theme Fielding reiterates in *Joseph Andrews*). But—the basis of the Quixotic aesthetics—these are women Quixote wants to defend from vulgar eyes and hands rather than to have sex with them himself. This is a position that is turned around in *Pamela* and *The Female Quixote* and used by the woman herself as a guard against commitment to a man.

16. Sarah Fielding, *The Adventures of David Simple* (1744), ed. Malcolm Kelsall (Oxford, 1969), 26–27. Fielding supports the Cervantean allusion in his preface to the *Familiar Letters between the Principal Characters in David Simple* (1747): This "little Book" (as he twice calls it—5, 8) fits into the comic work

with not one action but "a Series, as Butler in Verse, and Cervantes in Prose have done"; that is, "a Series of separate Adventures detached from, and independent on each other, yet all tending to one great End," a form that can be traced back to the *Odyssey* (6).

17. *Northanger Abbey*, ed. R. W. Chapman, in *Novels of Jane Austen* (Oxford, 1923), 5: 162. All references are to this edition.

18. Austen expressed her appreciation of Lennox's *Female Quixote* in a letter to her sister Cassandra, 7 January 1807: It "now makes our evening amusement; to me a very high one, as I find the work quite equal to what I remembered it" (*Jane Austen's Letters*, ed. Deirdre le Faye [Oxford, 1995], 116).

19. Addison, *Miscellaneous Works of Joseph Addison*, ed. A. C. Guthkelch (London, 1914), 1:146.

20. If the wit in *Northanger Abbey*, established on the first page, is the author's, within the novel Tilney's wit, always conveyed with "solemnity . . . of voice" (160), serves as a naturalized version of the authorial. In the third chapter Catherine meets Tilney, who "suddenly" addresses her with provocative assertions, affects "astonishment" and "surprise" at her replies, and gives a "smirk" in order to step back out of the role he has assumed; at which point "Catherine turned away her head, not knowing whether she might venture to laugh," as Sancho had done with his master after the episode of the fulling hammers. A bit later, in a larger group that includes Mrs. Allen, she fears "that he indulged himself a little too much with the foibles of others." His own explanation of his behavior is that it is "to tease" her, "and nothing in the world advances intimacy so much" (28–29). In short, there is a conflict or contrast in *Northanger Abbey* between the wit of the author and the naïveté of the heroine; and within the plot other versions of wit are offered in the social "quizzing" of Tilney, who assumes ironic poses, takes burlesque roles, and knowingly parodies the fashionable tattle of Bath society, and in the cruder "lies" of John Thorpe. ("Quizzing," a favorite word of the characters, signifies a jest or *burla*.)

21. *Pride and Prejudice*, in Chapman, ed. *Novels of Jane Austen*, 2:158.

22. The discussion is extended to chapter 7 where John Thorpe, representative of young Oxford "quizzing" his female friends, gives his opinion that novels do *some* good. He cites *Tom Jones* and *The Monk*—presumably men's novels—but regards all the others, women's novels (including *Udolpho*), as "the stupidest things in creation" (48). Again, somewhat later, Henry Tilney praises the Gothic only to dismiss it as a "good read," a page-turner.

23. Austen's "polyvalent irony" is Claudia L. Johnson's phrase: "Austen's Irony typically functions like a Möbius strip, first setting up two clear and discrete planes, and later showing them on the contrary to be coextensive" (Johnson, *Jane Austen: Women, Politics, and the Novel* [Chicago, 1988], 30–31).

24. Swift's "author" claims that "We whom the World is pleased to honor with the Title of *Modern Authors*, should never have been able to compass our

great Design of an everlasting Remembrance, and never-dying Fame, if our Endeavours had not been so highly serviceable to the general Good of Mankind" (*A Tale of a Tub*, ed. A. C. Guthkelch and D. Nichol Smith [Oxford, 2d ed., 1958], 123).

25. Cf. Clara Reeve's simple distinction between romance and novel: romance, "an heroic fable, which treats of fabulous persons and things"; whereas the novel "gives a familiar relation of such things as pass every day before our eyes" (*The Progress of Romance*, 1785, 1:111). Tony Tanner remarks that "*Northanger Abbey* has often been seen as a novel ironising romance. But looking at it in another way it could be seen as a *kind* of romance slyly ironising a *kind* of novel. We cannot ever be *quite* sure how to read Jane Austen—or how to read her reading of other novels and romances" (Tanner, *Jane Austen* [Cambridge, Mass., 1986], 57).

26. It is telling that Catherine and Isabella "shut themselves up, to read novels together" (37); not each alone in her chamber as we were led to believe (by Fielding at least) was the practice of the female readers of *Pamela* but as the socializing readers of the *Spectator* did in coffeehouses. On Austen and Addison, cf. George Saintsbury, who believed that Austen's "humour seems to possess a greater affinity, on the whole, to that of Addison than to any other of the numerous species of this great British genius"; Frank Bradbrook, who ignores the irony in the passage on the novel, infers that Austen thinks the *Spectator* is condescending to women (Saintsbury, preface, *Pride and Prejudice* [London, 1894], xiii; Frank Bradbrook, *Jane Austen and her Predecessors* [Cambridge, 1966], 4–10); picked up by Park Honan, *Jane Austen: Her Life* (New York, 1987), 59.

27. For earlier versions of this particular Quixotic reading of *Northanger Abbey*, see John K. Mathison, "*Northanger Abbey* and Jane Austen's Conception of the value of Fiction," *Journal of English Literary History* 24 (1957): 138–52; and Paulson, *Satire and the Novel*, 292–93.

28. See Paulson, *Representations of Revolution* (New Haven, 1983), 216.

29. *Spectator* no. 412; quoted on pp. 14–15.

30. See Paulson, *Hogarth's Graphic Works* (1965; 3d ed., London, 1989), nos. 183, 184.

31. For Smollett there were separate scenes of sentiment alternating with scenes of satire, romantic high and comic low life, until in *Sir Launcelot Greaves* he not only supplied a romantic Quixote and a comic Sancho but a second, comic Quixote in Captain Crowe. Finally in *Humphry Clinker* (1771) he combined the romantic and comic Quixotes in the same person, Matthew Bramble, who is a sentimental satirist. The result of Smollett's division of his characters into the satiric and sentimental aspects of *Don Quixote* was less to shift emphasis from satire to sentiment than to show how they could coexist (as they did successfully in *Tristram Shandy*).

32. Richard Hurd, *Letters on Chivalry and Romance* (1762), ed. Hoyt Trowbridge (Los Angeles, 1963), 22, 57.

33. See Paulson, *Popular and Polite Art in the Age of Hogarth and Fielding* (Notre Dame, 1979), 195–201.

34. Hurd's *Letters* gives the historical (we might say euhemerist) explanation (20, 22–23).

35. Burke, *Reflections on the Revolution in France and on the proceedings in Certain Societies in London Relative to that Event* (1790), ed. William B. Todd (New York, 1959), 6–7. Following from Burke's Quixote were such anti-Jacobin novels as Charles Lucas's *The Infernal Quixote: A Tale of the Day* (1801).

36. Wollstonecraft, *A Vindication of the Rights of Men* (1790), 111–14, 11, 157; cf. my account in *Representations of Revolution*, 79–87. In *A Vindication of the Rights of Woman with Strictures on Political and Moral Subjects* (1792), Wollstonecraft writes: "To endeavour to reason love out of the world would be to out Quixote Cervantes, and equally offend against common sense"; she intends instead "to prove that it should not be allowed [as Burke allows it] to dethrone superior powers, or to usurp the sceptre which the understanding should ever coolly wield" (ed. Gina Luria [New York, 1974], 53).

37. Johnson, *Jane Austen*, 34. Johnson convincingly shows how Austen "appropriated the gothic, in a distinctively progressive way"; that is, at a time of conservative and counterrevolutionary attitudes, she focused on the tyrannical father and the patriarchal family, and the "moral and physical coercion of powerless females," which she sees as throughout the contemporary equivalent of the Gothic (35, 37, 47).

38. See Alastair M. Duckworth, *The Improvement of the Estate: A Study of Jane Austen's Novels* (Baltimore, 1971).

39. An addendum, which reaches beyond the scope of this book, would be the Picturesque Quixote, the last of the great comic Quixotes of the eighteenth century. William Combe's Dr. Syntax, setting out on a quest after the Picturesque (he has read William Gilpin's books on the Picturesque), ignores the beautiful women, the young lovers, and the beautiful scenery for Gilpin's shaggy animals and unkempt landscapes. Thomas Rowlandson, who illustrated Combe's text with drawings that are much better known than the poem, returns the Picturesque, the landscape-oriented aesthetics, to Hogarth's Novel and human-oriented aesthetics.

40. Artist unknown, *The Combat* (1762); see Paulson, *Hogarth, Vol. 3: Art and Politics* (New Brunswick, 1993), fig. 86.

41. Hogarth, in fact, distinguishes between the country dance and the minuet: the former is comic and the latter beautiful, the one entertaining rustics and the other nobles; but the dancers of the minuet are implicated in adulteries and presided over by Henry VIII, while the country dance, presided over by Queen Elizabeth, is without vice.

Steele, Richard, 22, 31, 32, 40, 44, 47, 182, 198n. 19, 200n. 42; and affectation, 60; *The Conscious Lovers*, 33, 118; and insanity, 4; and laughter, 118; "Mimicks and Imitators," 57, 58; and satire, 23, 27; *The Tender Husband*, 60
Sterne, Laurence, 17; *Tristram Shandy*, 150–58, 192, 193
Stevens, Capt. John, translation of *Don Quixote*, xvii, xix, 33, 206n. 42
Strange, the, xiii, xv, 15, 20, 25, 36, 182, 183, 185, 186, 191
Sublime, the, ix, 182, 186, 190, 191; in aesthetics, 120
Sunderland, Robert Spencer, earl of, 207n. 48
Swift, Jonathan, xiv, xix, 11, 15, 55, 63, 206–7n. 48; antipapist satire, 128; *Battle of the Books*, 49, 106; and beauty, 96; and blemish, 99; and burlesque, 39, 42; and Carteret, 49; "Digression concerning Madness," 9, 12, 14, 30, 123, 126, 198n. 19; and *Don Quixote*, 29; and empiricism, 130; and enthusiasm, 42, 123; as freethinker, 128; and grave irony, 42; *Gulliver's Travels*, 42, 136, 138; and imagination, 12–13, 42; and inspiration, 42; "Lady's Dressing Room," 95–97, 102, 165, 216n. 20, 217n. 30; and laughter, 26; and madhouse, 97; obituary of (Fielding), 128; as Old Whig, 138; opposition to Walpole, 138; and philosophy, 13; and political satire, 26, 27, 31, 72; and Quixote, 22–23; and religion, 13, 124–25, 127–28; and ridicule, 125; and satire, xii, 14, 17, 31, 35, 61, 90–91, 172; satire on Marlborough, 72; "Sermons on the Trinity," 128; "Strephon and Chloe," 95, 96, 97, 98, 99, 164, 165; *A Tale of a Tub*, xii, 9, 10, 12, 42, 60, 105–6, 121, 122, 123, 124, 126, 127, 128, 129, 152, 181; and wit, 68, 125, 126

Tanner, Tony, 230n. 25
Taste, 29, 86, 89, 97, 108, 115, 176, 189,

214n. 4; and Addison, 83–84; and Hume, 87–88, 92; in romance, 110; and Sancho, 133–34; in wine and beauty, 110
Tave, Stuart, 118, 195n. 7
Temple, Sir William, 32, 34, 35, 36, 47, 67
Test Act, 121
Tillotson, Archbishop John, 69, 125, 126
Tindal, Matthew, 122
Toft, Mary, 136–37, 139
Toland, John, 122, 222n. 43; *Christianity Not Mysterious*, 127
Tonson, Jacob, 45, 46, 201n. 3, 206n. 47
Tory / Tories, xiv, xvi, 22, 27, 28, 29, 30, 33, 35, 41, 55–56, 102, 124, 129; Bolingbroke, 121; Jacobites, 41, 120, 202n. 12; nostalgia, 138; Quixote as, 50; satire, 24, 27
Treaty of Utrecht, 157
Trinity, the, 43, 132, 139; doctrine of, 127

Ugly, the, 20, 26, 72, 90, 95, 98, 100, 101, 102; aesthetics of, 165; Ugliness, 104
Unamuno, Miguel de, 195n. 5
Uncommon, the. *See* Novel, New, or Uncommon, the

Van Dyck, Sir Anthony, *Charles I on Horseback*, 49
Vanderbank, John, illustrations by, x–xi, 45–47, 49–50, 52, 53, 54, 73, 167, 185, 206n. 45, 222n. 49
Vandergucht, Gerard, 46, 204n. 31, 205nn. 36, 38
Vega, Lope de, 38
Vertue, George, 45, 46, 48, 204n. 34
Virgil, 44, 102, 139, 159, 168, 204n. 29; *Aeneid*, ix, 11, 42, 106; *Georgics*, ix, 11

Waller, Edmund, "The Countess of Carlisle in Mourning," 25
Walpole, Sir Robert, xiv, xv, 61, 73, 79, 81, 210n. 73; and Carteret, 48, 49; fall of, 184; as humorous character, 74–75; opposition to, 51, 136, 138; satire of, 136
Walthoe, J., 204n. 31